Bus
Handbook

May 1995

British Bus Publishing

The Yorkshire Bus Handbook

The Yorkshire Bus Handbook is part of the Bus Handbook series that details the fleets of stage carriage and express coach operators. Where space allows other significant operators in the areas covered are also included. These handbooks are published by *British Bus Publishing* and cover Scotland, Wales and England north of London. The current list is shown at the end of the book. Together with similar books for southern England published by Capital Transport, they provide comprehensive coverage of all the principal operators' fleets in the British Isles.

Quality photographs for inclusion in the series are welcome, for which a fee is payable. The publishers unfortunately cannot accept responsibility for any loss and request you show your name on each picture or slide. Details of changes to fleet information are also welcome.

More information on the Bus Handbook series is available from:

British Bus Publishing,
The Vyne,
16 St Margaret's Drive
Wellington
Telford,
Shropshire TF1 3PH

Series Editor: Bill Potter

Principal Editors for *The Yorkshire Bus Handbook*: David Donati and Bill Potter

Acknowledgements:
We are grateful to Keith Grimes, Mark Jameson, Andrew Jarosz
Colin Lloyd, Steve Sanderson, the PSV Circle and the operating
companies for their assistance in the compilation of this book.
To keep the fleets up to date we recommend Buses, published monthly by Ian Allan and the news-sheets of the PSV Circle.
The cover photographs are by Tony Wilson
Contents correct to April 1995

ISBN 1 897990 10 3
Published by *British Bus Publishing*
The Vyne, 16 St Margarets Drive, Wellington,
Telford, Shropshire, TF1 3PH
© British Bus Publishing, April 1995

CONTENTS

Overleaf, top: **A general view of Sheffield taken from Park Hill with a South Yorkshire Supertram in the foreground and Sheffield's bus station behind.** *Lee Whitehead*

Overleaf, bottom: **The latest take-over in the Yorkshire area is that of Sheffield Omnibus which is now part of the Yorkshire Traction group. The latest Olympians in the fleet were part of a Volvo stock order placed with Alexander, a combination which has been used to supply midi and full-sized single-deck buses also. First of the batch is 1601, L601NOS.** *Lee Whitehead*

ABBOTTS

DC & CG Abbott, Aumans House, Leeming, North Yorkshire DL7 9RZ
Blueline Express Ltd, Aumans House, Leeming, North Yorkshire DL7 9RZ

Depots: Sussex Street, Bedale; Claro Road, Harrogate & The Garage, Leeming.

352BWB	Bedford SB8	Plaxton	C41F	1962	Ex Kirkby, Harthill, 1969
DPY660L	Bedford YRT	Duple Dominant	C53F	1973	Ex Dobson, Bedale, 1984
LBZ5108	Leyland Leopard PSU3B/4R	Plaxton Elite III Express	C53F	1973	Ex Mayne, Manchester, 1994
NED351M	Daimler Fleetline CRG6LX	East Lancashire	H43/29F	1973	Ex Warrington, 1992
NED355M	Daimler Fleetline CRG6LX	East Lancashire	H43/29F	1973	Ex Warrington, 1992
NED356M	Daimler Fleetline CRG6LX	East Lancashire	H43/29F	1973	Ex Warrington, 1992
NAT343M	Leyland Atlantean AN68/1R	Roe	H43/29F	1973	Ex K-Line, Huddersfield, 1994
NAT351M	Leyland Atlantean AN68/1R	Roe	H43/29F	1973	Ex K-Line, Huddersfield, 1994
PPY650M	Bedford YRT	Duple Dominant	C53F	1974	
RPY660M	Bedford YRT	Duple Dominant	C53F	1974	Ex Dobson, Bedale, 1984
LBZ5107	Leyland Leopard PSU3E/4R	Plaxton Elite Express III	C53F	1974	Ex Mayne, Manchester, 1994
LBZ5109	Leyland Leopard PSU3E/4R	Plaxton Elite Express III	C53F	1974	Ex Mayne, Manchester, 1994
GVN914N	Bedford YRT	Duple Dominant	C53F	1975	
GNG716N	Bristol VRT/SL2/6LX	Eastern Coach Works	H43/31F	1975	Ex K-Line, Huddersfield, 1994
GAT202N	Leyland Atlantean AN68/1R	Roe	H43/29F	1975	Ex K-Line, Huddersfield, 1994
KHN85P	Bedford YRT	Plaxton Supreme III	C53F	1975	Ex Dobson, Bedale, 1984
MUA869P	Leyland Atlantean AN68/1R	Park Royal	H43/30F	1976	Ex Farmer, Ashford, 1994
JOV741P	Ailsa B55-10	Alexander AV	H44/35F	1976	Ex K-Line, Huddersfield, 1994
JOV742P	Ailsa B55-10	Alexander AV	H44/35F	1976	Ex K-Line, Huddersfield, 1994
JOV764P	Ailsa B55-10	Alexander AV	H44/35F	1976	Ex K-Line, Huddersfield, 1994
MNU629P	Leyland Atlantean AN68A/1R	East Lancashire	H47/31D	1976	Ex K-Line, Huddersfield, 1994
OWW906P	Bristol VRT/SL3/6LXB	Eastern Coach Works	H43/31F	1976	Ex K-Line, Huddersfield, 1994
MRB804R	Bristol VRT/SL3/6LX	Eastern Coach Works	H43/34F	1976	Ex K-Line, Huddersfield, 1994
PVO815R	Bristol VRT/SL3/501	Eastern Coach Works	H43/31F	1976	Ex K-Line, Huddersfield, 1994
ONR90R	Bedford YMT	Duple Dominant	C53F	1976	Ex Dobson, Bedale, 1984
OFP88R	Bedford YMT	Plaxton Supreme III Express	C53F	1976	Ex Gibson, Barlestone, 1981
REF141R	Bedford YMT	Plaxton Supreme III	C53F	1977	
ACA188S	Bedford YMT	Duple Dominant II	C53F	1977	Ex Hanmer, Southsea, 1978
TUT660S	Bedford YMT	Duple Dominant II	C53F	1977	Ex Dobson, Bedale, 1984
YUM517S	Bristol VRT/SL3/6LXB	Eastern Coach Works	H43/31F	1977	Ex K-Line, Huddersfield, 1994
UET677S	Leyland Atlantean AN68A/1R	Alexander AL	H45/29D	1978	Ex K-Line, Huddersfield, 1994
UDT180S	Leyland Atlantean AN68A/1R	East Lancashire	H45/31F	1978	Ex Border, Burnley, 1994
UFT917T	Bedford YMT	Plaxton Supreme IV	C53F	1978	Ex Moor Dale, Newcastle, 1981
BDC881T	Bedford YMT	Plaxton Supreme IV	C53F	1979	
DAY660T	Bedford YMT	Duple Dominant II	C53F	1979	Ex Dobson, Bedale, 1984

When Plaxton introduced the Premiére model for single-deck coaches they continued with the Paramount 4000 as the double-deck option although this has now been replaced. The last example of the model delivered is J684THN, seen here on a Blueline service. This example is built on a rear-engine and tri-axle SBR3000 model.
Andrew Jarosz

5

FHN773V	Bedford YMT	Plaxton Supreme IV	C53F	1980	
LHN433W	Bedford YNT	Plaxton Supreme IV	C53F	1981	
KTY426X	Bedford YNT	Duple Dominant IV Express	C53F	1981	Ex Dobson, Bedale, 1983
TPY801X	Bedford YNT	Plaxton Supreme V	C53F	1982	
TPY802X	Bedford YNT	Plaxton Supreme V	C53F	1982	
AWK516Y	Bedford YNT	Duple Dominant IV	C53F	1982	Ex Ardenvale, Knowle, 1984
ANH660Y	Bedford YNT	Duple Dominant IV	C53F	1983	Ex Dobson, Bedale, 1984
BVN371Y	Bedford YNT	Plaxton Paramount 3200	C53F	1983	
CAJ168Y	Bedford YNT	Plaxton Paramount 3200	C53F	1983	
774FUO	Volvo B10M-61	Plaxton Paramount 3500	C53FT	1984	
D902NUS	Freight Rover Sherpa	Scott	C16F	1986	
D320NWG	Aüwaerter Neoplan N122/3	Aüwaerter Skyliner	CH57/20CT	1986	Ex Zebra, Trimdon Grange, 1988
D321NWG	Aüwaerter Neoplan N122/3	Aüwaerter Skyliner	CH57/20CT	1986	Ex Zebra, Trimdon Grange, 1988
D322NWG	Aüwaerter Neoplan N122/3	Aüwaerter Skyliner	CH57/20CT	1986	Ex Zebra, Trimdon Grange, 1988
D323NWG	Aüwaerter Neoplan N122/3	Aüwaerter Skyliner	CH57/20CT	1986	Ex Zebra, Trimdon Grange, 1988
D324NWG	Aüwaerter Neoplan N122/3	Aüwaerter Skyliner	CH57/20CT	1986	Ex Zebra, Trimdon Grange, 1988
D38GAJ	Scania K112CRB	Van Hool Alizée	C53F	1987	
D39GAJ	Scania K112CRB	Van Hool Alizée	C53F	1987	
D40GAJ	Scania K112CRB	Van Hool Alizée	C53F	1987	
D41GAJ	Scania K112CRB	Van Hool Alizée	C53F	1987	
D904FHN	Leyland Royal Tiger RTC	Leyland Doyen	C49FT	1987	
D905FHN	Leyland Royal Tiger RTC	Leyland Doyen	C49FT	1987	
E532LAJ	Scania K112CRB	Van Hool Alizée	C49FT	1987	
E268NAJ	Scania K112CRB	Van Hool Alizée	C49FT	1988	
E905NVN	Scania K112CRB	Van Hool Alizée	C49FT	1988	
E906NVN	Scania K112CRB	Van Hool Alizée	C49FT	1988	
E97LWP	DAF SB2305DHTD585	Duple 340	C57F	1988	Ex Hackett, Stretton, 1993
F655KNL	Iveco Daily 49.10	Carlyle Dailybus 2	B23F	1988	Ex Busways, 1993
F26ARN	DAF SB2305DHTD585	Duple 340	C59F	1989	Ex Jackson, Blackpool, 1994
F432VUY	DAF SB2305DHTD585	Duple 340	C53FT	1989	Ex Hardings, Redditch, 1994
G997HKW	Scania K93CRB	Duple 320	C55F	1990	Ex K-Line, Kirkburton, 1993
G851NUP	Scania K113TRB	Van Hool Astrobel	CH53/14CT	1990	Ex Busways, 1994
G155NJX	MCW MetroRider MF154/1	MCW	C26F	1990	Ex Pride of the Road, Huddersfield, 1995
J684THN	DAF SBR3000DKZ570	Plaxton Paramount 4000 III	CH55/19CT	1991	
J685THN	DAF SB2305DHS585	Duple 340	C57F	1991	
J686THN	DAF SB2305DHS585	Duple 340	C57F	1991	
J238VVN	Scania K113TRB	Van Hool Alizée	C52FT	1992	
J239VVN	Scania K113TRB	Van Hool Alizée	C52FT	1992	
J240VVN	Scania K113TRB	Van Hool Alizée	C51FT	1992	

Previous Registrations:

365BWB	From new	LBZ5107	PNN767M	LBZ5109	ONN282M
774FUO	A717JDC	LBZ5108	RVO671L		

Van Hool supply various models of the Alizée. Occasionally the H, DH and SH markings are shown. However, the most noticeable difference between models is the depth of the window over the door. Seen in Eastbourne is E532LAJ, an example of the SH version. *Keith Grimes*

AJC COACHES

AJC Fallas of Leeds Ltd, 245 Elland Road, Leeds, West Yorkshire, LS11 8TU

Reg	Chassis	Body	Seating	Year	Notes
NPD161L	Leyland National 1151/1R/0402		B49F	1973	Ex Yorkshire Terrier, 1994
NAO361M	Leyland National 1151/1R/0401		B52F	1973	Ex Yorkshire Terrier, 1994
JWG194P	Leyland National 10351/1R		B40D	1975	Ex White Rose, Castleford, 1995
THX113S	Leyland National 10351A/2R		B36D	1977	Ex Pride of the Road, 1995
THX164S	Leyland National 10351A/2R		B36D	1978	Ex Pride of the Road, 1995
XEU858T	Leyland National 10351B/1R		B44F	1979	Ex Parfitt's, Rhymney Bridge, 1994
XEU859T	Leyland National 10351B/1R		B44F	1979	Ex Parfitt's, Rhymney Bridge, 1994
AAK108T	Leyland National 10351B/1R		B44F	1979	Ex Pride of the Road, 1995
AKU164T	Leyland National 10351B/1R		B44F	1979	Ex Mainline, 1995
FAO927V	Leyland National 106L11/2R		B43F	1979	Ex Vale of Manchester, 1995
OPS742X	Leyland Leopard PSU3F/5R	Duple Dominant IV	C53F	1981	Ex Leask, Lerwick, 1992
C932EWW	DAF MB200DKFL600	Plaxton Paramount 3500 II	C53F	1986	Ex J&S Fallas, Collingham, 1991
MIW4890	Scania K112CRS	Van Hool Alizée	C53FT	1985	Ex Ivy, Huddersfield, 1992
D326VVV	Scania K112CRB	Jonckheere Jubilee P50	C51FT	1987	Ex Ivy, Huddersfield, 1992
D241LNW	DAF MB200DKFL600	Duple Caribbean 2	C53F	1987	Ex J&S Fallas, Collingham, 1991
E108WUA	Mercedes-Benz L307D	Reeve Burgess	M12	1988	
G314CKB	Mercedes-Benz 609D	North West Coach Sales	C24F	1989	
H114UYG	Volvo B10M-60	Plaxton Expressliner	C46FT	1991	
H741WWU	Volvo B10M-60	Plaxton Expressliner	C46FT	1991	
K524RJX	DAF SB3000DKVF601	Van Hool Alizée	C51FT	1993	Ex Hallmark, Luton, 1995
K526RJX	DAF SB3000DKVF601	Van Hool Alizée	C51FT	1993	Ex Hallmark, Luton, 1995
K531RJX	DAF SB3000DKVF601	Van Hool Alizée	C51FT	1993	Ex Cronin, Cork, 1994

Previous Registrations:

AIJ9843	YMJ560S		
		JWG194P	JWG194P, 2444MN
MIW4890	C408HVH		

Livery: Dark blue; National Express D241LNW, H114UYG, H741WWU,K531RJX; Yorkshire Express K524/6RJX.

AJC coaches also uses the trading name of Anglo Blue. Competitive services within the Leeds area have recently expanded and NPD161L is one of three Leyland Nationals obtained second-hand from Yorkshire Terrier. In April 1995 the former Yorkshire Travel express services which ran in competition with National Express were taken over by the latter and immediately sub-contracted to AJC who now operated two DAF coaches in that livery. *Phillip Stephenson*

ANDREWS

Andrews (Sheffield) Ltd, Upper Sheffield Road, Barnsley,
South Yorkshire, S70 4PP

Depots : 20 Acres Hill Road, Darnhill, Sheffield

Part of the Yorkshire Traction Group

102	OKW515R	Leyland Fleetline FE30AGR	MCW	H46/25D	1977	Ex Mott, Stoke Mandeville, 1989
106	GWA822N	Daimler Fleetline CRG6LXB	Eastern Coach Works	H43/29F	1975	Ex Ball, Windle, 1990
108	SDA516S	Leyland Fleetline FE30AGR	MCW	H43/33F	1977	Ex West Midlands Travel, 1991
109	TVP868S	Leyland Fleetline FE30AGR	MCW	H43/33F	1978	Ex West Midlands Travel, 1990
110	NOC482R	Leyland Fleetline FE30AGR	MCW	H43/33F	1977	Ex West Midlands Travel, 1991
111	SDA501S	Leyland Fleetline FE30AGR	MCW	H43/33F	1977	Ex West Midlands Travel, 1990
112	SDA647S	Leyland Fleetline FE30AGR	Park Royal	H43/33F	1978	Ex West Midlands Travel, 1990
113	CWE797N	Daimler Fleetline CRG6LXB	Eastern Coach Works	H43/27D	1974	Ex Skill, Nottingham, 1988
115	NOC476R	Leyland Fleetline FE30AGR	MCW	H43/33F	1977	Ex West Midlands Travel, 1990
117	TVP893S	Leyland Fleetline FE30AGR	MCW	H43/33F	1978	Ex West Midlands Travel, 1990
120	SDA570S	Leyland Fleetline FE30AGR	MCW	H43/33F	1978	Ex West Midlands Travel, 1990
121	LDC81P	Daimler Fleetline CRL6	Northern Counties	H43/31F	1976	Ex Cleveland Transit, 1989
123	SDA691S	Leyland Fleetline FE30AGR	MCW	H43/33F	1978	Ex West Midlands Travel, 1991
126	NOC496R	Leyland Fleetline FE30AGR	MCW	H43/33F	1977	Ex West Midlands Travel, 1990
127	PWE535R	Leyland Fleetline FE30AGR	Alexander AL	H45/29D	1977	Ex South Yorkshire, 1990
128	LDC79P	Daimler Fleetline CRL6	Northern Counties	H45/31F	1976	Ex Eagles & Crawford, Mold, 1990
130	NOC483R	Leyland Fleetline FE30AGR	MCW	H43/33F	1977	Ex West Midlands Travel, 1990
131	SDA797S	Leyland Fleetline FE30AGR	MCW	H43/33F	1978	Ex West Midlands Travel, 1991
132	SDA762S	Leyland Fleetline FE30AGR	MCW	H43/33F	1978	Ex West Midlands Travel, 1991
134	SDA697S	Leyland Fleetline FE30AGR	MCW	H43/33F	1978	Ex West Midlands Travel, 1991
135	DWH684W	Leyland Fleetline FE30AGR	Northern Counties	H43/32F	1980	Ex GM Buses, 1991
136	NOC426R	Leyland Fleetline FE30AGR	MCW	H43/33F	1976	Ex West Midlands Travel, 1991
138	NOC594R	Leyland Fleetline FE30AGR	Park Royal	H43/33F	1976	Ex West Midlands Travel, 1992
139	NOC461R	Leyland Fleetline FE30AGR	MCW	H43/33F	1977	Ex Advent Travel, Upholland, 1992
140	SDA749S	Leyland Fleetline FE30AGR	East Lancashire	H43/33F	1977	Ex Kettle Products, Kinglassie, 1992

The Yorkshire Traction subsidiary, Andrews of Sheffield, has continued many of the previous owners' practices including the naming of vehicles. DWH684W, a Northern Counties-bodied Leyland Fleetline, whilst given fleet number 135 also proudly displays its name in honour of of Sergeant A. **Loosemore** VC DCM.
Keith Grimes

The Andrews double-deck fleet has now been augmented with Leyland National Mark 1 vehicles from parent Yorkshire Traction. No150, YWG463T, displays the version of this operators livery carried on this model which is blue and yellow without the additional white. *Lee Whitehead*

141	NOC437R	Leyland Fleetline FE30AGR	MCW	H43/33F	1977	Ex West Midlands Travel, 1990
142	PRJ497R	Daimler Fleetline CRG6LXB	Northern Counties	H43/32F	1977	Ex Rossendale, 1992
144	NOC389R	Leyland Fleetline FE30ALR	MCW	H43/33F	1976	Ex Boro'line, 1992
145	NOC480R	Leyland Fleetline FE30AGR	MCW	H43/33F	1977	Ex West Midlands Travel, 1992
147	DET474V	Leyland National 11351A/1R		B52F	1979	Ex Yorkshire Traction, 1993
148	DET476V	Leyland National 11351A/1R		B52F	1979	Ex Yorkshire Traction, 1993
149	NWG418R	Leyland National 11351A/1R		B52F	1976	Ex Yorkshire Traction, 1993
150	YWG467T	Leyland National 11351A/1R		B52F	1978	Ex Yorkshire Traction, 1993
151	SGR563R	Leyland National 11351A/1R		B49F	1976	Ex Yorkshire Traction, 1994
152	DET475V	Leyland National 11351A/1R		B52F	1979	Ex Yorkshire Traction, 1994
153	YWG463T	Leyland National 11351A/1R		B52F	1978	Ex Yorkshire Traction, 1994
154	CPT636S	Leyland National 11351A/1R		B49F	1978	Ex Yorkshire Traction, 1994

Livery: Blue, yellow and white

Named vehicles:

102 *Benjamin Huntsman*
106 *Elizabeth Anne*
108 *Genevieve*
109 *Gladstone Guest*
110 *Lady Hamilton*
111 *John Brown*
112 *Jimmy Mack*
113 *Jumbo*
115 *Little John*
117 *Mandy*
120 *Lord Nelson*
121 *Nick Broughton*
123 *Oliver Cromwell*

126 *Robin Hood*
127 *Sherriff of Nottingham*
128 *Capt P J Sillitoe*
130 *Steel Peech Tozer*
131 *Sheffield Wednesday*
132 *Sheffield United*
133 *Walter Ardron*
134 *Yasoob*
136 *Humpty Dumpty*
138 *Murphy Gang*
139 *Accrington Stanley*
140 *Dennis the Menace*
141 *Sgt Ian McKay VC*

142 *Desperate Dan*
144 *Rotherham United*
145 *Berkeley Castle*
147 *Captain Hook*
148 *Tinkerbell*
149 *Wendy*
150 *Peter Pan*
151 *Reg Peake*
152 *Maid Marion*
153 *Helen Sharman*
154 *PC Sam Radford GM*

ASTON EXPRESS

M W Hydes, Bailey Drive, Killamarsh, Sheffield,
South Yorkshire, S31 8JF

Depot: Bailey Drive, Killamarsh

TIB9288	Leyland Leopard PSU5A/4R	Plaxton Supreme III	C53F	1976	Ex Border Bus, Trawden, 1995
UPK132S	Leyland Atlantean AN68A/1R	Park Royal	H43/30F	1978	Ex Frontrunner SE, Dagenham, 1992
EPM125V	AEC Reliance 6U2R	Duple Dominant II Express	C53F	1979	Ex Yeomans, Hereford, 1993
VRY609X	DAF SB2005DHU605	Plaxton Supreme IV	C53F	1982	Ex Elsey, Gosberton, 1994
D896DSF	Renault-Dodge S56	Alexander AM	B25F	1987	Ex Fife Scottish, 1994
E235NFX	Freight Rover Sherpa	Carlyle Citybus 2	B20F	1987	Ex Midland Red North, 1993
E575ANE	Renault-Dodge S56	Northern Counties	DP27F	1988	Ex Heatons Travel, Leigh, 1994
E95WKY	MCW MetroRider MF150/29	MCW	B25F	1988	Ex Dunn-Line, Nottingham, 1994
F138HNC	Renault-Dodge S56	Northern Counties	B25F	1988	Ex HAD Coaches, Shotts, 1994

Livery: Blue and white

Previous Registrations:
TIB9288   LVS437P

The majority of the Aston Express fleet comprises minibuses but there are four larger vehicles one of which was obtained from Yeomans of Hereford in 1993. Seen at Halfway, Sheffield is EPM125V immediately recognizable as a former London Country RB Class vehicle. *Daniel Hill*

BARNSLEY & DISTRICT

The Barnsley & District Traction Co Ltd, Upper Sheffield Road, Barnsley,
South Yorkshire, S70 4PP

Part of the Yorkshire Traction Group
Depot: Wakefield Road, Barnsley

100w	GOG591N	Daimler Fleetline CRG6LXB	Park Royal	H43/33F	1975	Ex Andrews, Sheffield, 1992
101	NOC420R	Leyland Fleetline FE30ALR	MCW	H43/33F	1976	Ex Andrews, Sheffield, 1992
102	MOM577P	Leyland Fleetline FE30AGR	Park Royal	H43/33F	1975	Ex Andrews, Sheffield, 1992
103	NOC495R	Leyland Fleetline FE30AGR	MCW	H43/33F	1977	Ex Andrews, Sheffield, 1993
104	SDA773S	Leyland Fleetline FE30AGR	MCW	H43/33F	1978	Ex Andrews, Sheffield, 1994
105	NFN78M	Leyland National 1151/1R/2402		B52F	1974	Ex Jowitt, Tankersley, 1990
106w	BRH181T	Leyland National 10351B/1R		B37DL	1979	Ex Yorkshire Traction, 1991
107	NWG417R	Leyland National 11351A/1R		B52F	1977	Ex Yorkshire Traction, 1991
108	OWF420R	Leyland National 11351A/1R		B52F	1977	Ex Yorkshire Traction, 1991
109	SWE437S	Leyland National 11351A/1R		B52F	1977	Ex Yorkshire Traction, 1991
110	SWE438S	Leyland National 11351A/1R		B52F	1977	Ex Yorkshire Traction, 1991
111	SWE440S	Leyland National 11351A/1R		B52F	1977	Ex Yorkshire Traction, 1991
112	SWE445S	Leyland National 11351A/1R		B52F	1977	Ex Yorkshire Traction, 1991
113	YWG460T	Leyland National 11351A/1R		B52F	1978	Ex Yorkshire Traction, 1991
114	YWG461T	Leyland National 11351A/1R		B52F	1978	Ex Yorkshire Traction, 1991
115	YWG464T	Leyland National 11351A/1R		B52F	1978	Ex Yorkshire Traction, 1991
116	DET471V	Leyland National 11351A/1R		B52F	1979	Ex Yorkshire Traction, 1991
117	XAK458T	Leyland National 11351A/1R		B52F	1978	Ex Yorkshire Traction, 1994
118	SGR551R	Leyland National 11351A/1R		B49F	1976	Ex Go-Ahead Northern, 1992
119	GOL405N	Leyland National 11351/1R		B49F	1975	Ex South Riding, 1995
120w	KSO69P	Leyland National 10351/2R		B25DL	1976	Ex Suffolk CC, Ipswich, 1992
123	VPT949R	Leyland National 11351A/1R		B49F	1977	Ex Miramare, Morley, 1993
124	DET473V	Leyland National 11351A/1R		B52F	1979	Ex Yorkshire Traction, 1993
125	VPT599R	Leyland National 11351A/1R		B49F	1977	Ex Yorkshire Traction, 1994
126	XAK455T	Leyland National 11351A/1R		B52F	1978	Ex Yorkshire Traction, 1994
127	VPT598R	Leyland National 11351A/1R		B49F	1977	Ex Yorkshire Traction, 1994

Barnsley & District, South Riding and Andrews fleets now share the same management, all now part of the Yorkshire Traction group. Photographed in Barnsley bus station is 118, SGR551R, a Leyland National new to Northern General in 1976. *Phillip Stephenson*

The majority of vehicles in the Barnsley & District fleet have arrived from other members of the Yorkshire Traction group. All the double-deck fleet were previously with Andrews and originated with West Midlands Travel. Seen in Sheffield is 103, NOC495R.
Paul Wigan

The Meadowhall Interchange sees vehicles from many of the operators in the Sheffield area as core-time shopping moves from the centre of the city to this shopping complex, arguably with major consequences for the city centre. Leyland National 123, VPT949R is seen here.
Lee Whitehead

132	RKY773R	Leyland Leopard PSU3E/4R(DAF)	Duple Dominant	C49F	1977	Ex Yorkshire Traction, 1994
133	GHE696V	Leyland Leopard PSU3E/4R	Plaxton Supreme IV Express	C49F	1978	Ex Yorkshire Traction, 1992
140	G681KNW	Mercedes-Benz 811D	Optare StarRider	B33FL	1989	Ex Jowitt, Tankersley, 1990
141	G682KNW	Mercedes-Benz 811D	Optare StarRider	DP29FL	1989	Ex Jowitt, Tankersley, 1990
142	E286OMG	Mercedes-Benz 709D	Reeve Burgess Beaver	B25F	1988	Ex Jowitt, Tankersley, 1990
143	D522SKY	MCW MetroRider MF150/22	MCW	B23F	1987	Ex Yorkshire Traction, 1992
144	D524SKY	MCW MetroRider MF150/22	MCW	B23F	1987	Ex Yorkshire Traction, 1992
145	D525SKY	MCW MetroRider MF150/22	MCW	B23F	1987	Ex Yorkshire Traction, 1993
146	D526SKY	MCW MetroRider MF150/22	MCW	B23F	1987	Ex Yorkshire Traction, 1994
202	EDT202V	Leyland National 2 NL116L11/1R		B52F	1980	Ex Yorkshire Traction, 1994
203	EDT203V	Leyland National 2 NL116L11/1R		B52F	1980	Ex Yorkshire Traction, 1994
205	EDT205V	Leyland National 2 NL116L11/1R		B52F	1980	Ex Yorkshire Traction, 1994
206	EDT206V	Leyland National 2 NL116L11/1R		B52F	1980	Ex Yorkshire Traction, 1994

Previous Registrations:

GHE696V	DAK257V, 1737HE	RKY773R	PWB252R, HE8054

Livery: Blue, white and red

BIBBY'S OF INGLETON

Bibby's of Ingleton Ltd, New Road, Ingleton, North Yorkshire, LA6 3NU

Reg	Chassis	Body	Seating	Year	Notes
ACC629	Bedford OB	Duple Vista	C29F	1950	Ex Turner, Lockerbie, 1976
LCP524W	Ford R1014	Plaxton Supreme IV	C45F	1981	Ex Cropper, Pudsey, 1992
BIB5428	DAF MB200DKTL600	Plaxton Supreme V	C51F	1982	Ex Braithwaite & Inliff, Tebay, 1992
FFV807Y	Leyland Leopard PSU5/2L	Plaxton Paramount 3200	C53F	1983	
BIB7670	Volvo B10M-56	Plaxton Paramount 3200	C53F	1983	Ex Silver Badge, Bowness, 1989
BIB3994	Leyland Tiger TRCTL11/3R	Plaxton Paramount 3500	C53F	1984	
BIB728	Leyland Tiger TRCTL11/3R	Plaxton Paramount 3200 II	C53F	1985	
C28BPR	Ford Transit	Carlyle	B16F	1986	Ex SUT, 1989
BIB5740	Leyland Tiger TRCTL11/3R	Plaxton Paramount 3200 III	C55F	1987	
BIB4843	DAF SB3000DKV601	Plaxton Paramount 3500 III	C53F	1988	
BIB7667	Freight Rover Sherpa	Made-to-Measure	C16F	1989	
VWU529	DAF SB3000DKV601	Plaxton Paramount 3500 III	C53F	1989	
BIB9842	Leyland-DAF 400	Made-to-Measure	C16F	1990	Ex Independent, Burnley, 1994
BIB5491	DAF SB2305SDHS585	Plaxton Paramount 3200 III	C53F	1991	
K522RJX	DAF SB3000DKV601	Van Hool Alizée	C53FT	1993	Ex Hallmark, Luton, 1994
L525EHD	DAF SB2700HS585	Van Hool Alizée	C49FT	1993	

Previous Registrations:

ACC629	ACC629, J3617, ACC629, TRN618A	BIB5740	D105MEC
BIB728	B891OEC	BIB7667	F294GNB
BIB3994	A281GEC	BIB7670	A64BEC, ABM351A
BIB4843	E52WEC	BIB9842	G53VVM
BIB5428	TND426X	FFV807Y	VWU529
BIB5491	H550YCX	VWU529	F656OHD

Named vehicles:

ACC629 *Old Faithful*; LCP524W *Dales Bandit*; BIB5428 *Dales Conquest*; FFV807Y *Dales Endeavour*; BIB3994 *Dales Cruiser*; BIB5740 *Dales Drifter*; BIB4843 *Dales Monarch*; VWU529 *Dales Princess*; BIB5491 *Dales Viking*; L525EHD *Dales Diplomat*.

BIB5491, in common with other members of the Bibby's of Ingleton fleet, carries an index mark originating in Northern Ireland whose letters have an affinity with the operators name. This coach is a Plaxton Paramount 3200-bodied DAF and features the name 'Dales Viking' on its grey, white and red livery. *Steve Sanderson*

BLACK PRINCE

B Crowther, York Cottage, Texas Street, Morley,
West Yorkshire LS27 0HG

Depot: Fountain Street, Morley

u	EHL335	Leyland Tiger PS2/13A	Roe	C35F	1952	Ex Gra'Cars, Featherstone, 1992
u	RTC822	Leyland Titan PD2/12	Leyland	H31/25R	1953	Ex Rossendale, 1992
RM441	LDS341A	AEC Routemaster 52RH	Park Royal	H36/28R	1960	Ex Western Scottish, 1990
	FTF702F	Leyland Titan PD3/4	East Lancashire	H41/32F	1967	Ex Alpha, Bootle, 1984
610	KHD921K	Leyland Leopard PSU3B/4R	Marshall	B53F	1972	Ex Ivy, Huddersfield, 1991
610	LUF549	Leyland 1151/1R/0401(Volvo)	East Lancs Greenway(1993)	B49F	1973	Ex Ribble, 1993
	LUG101P	Leyland Atlantean AN68/1R	Roe	H43/33F	1975	Ex Yorkshire Rider, 1994
	LKP385P	Ailsa B55-10	Alexander AV	H44/35F	1975	Ex Powell, Wickersley, 1993
	MGE183P	Ailsa B55-10	Alexander AV	H44/35F	1975	Ex Bell, Newtonards, 1994
388	LWB377P	Ailsa B55-10	Van Hool McArdle	H44/31D	1976	Ex Powell, Wickersley, 1993
	641UTO	Volvo B58-56	East Lancs EL2000(1991)	DP49F	1976	Ex Dunn-Line, Nottingham, 1990
	PWR256P	Ailsa B55-10	Alexander AV	H43/35F	1976	Ex Maidstone & District, 1992
	JOV745P	Ailsa B55-10	Alexander AV	H44/35F	1976	Ex Wombwell Deisels, 1994
	JOV746P	Ailsa B55-10	Alexander AV	H44/35F	1976	Ex Metrowest, Coseley, 1993
	JOV748P	Ailsa B55-10	Alexander AV	H44/35F	1976	Ex London Buses, 1990
	JOV749P	Ailsa B55-10	Alexander AV	H44/35F	1976	Ex A1 (Meney), Ardrossan, 1995
	JOV757P	Ailsa B55-10	Alexander AV	H44/35F	1976	Ex London Buses, 1989
	JOV772P	Ailsa B55-10	Alexander AV	H44/35F	1976	Ex Four Seasons, Glasshoughton, 1993
	JOV783P	Ailsa B55-10	Alexander AV	H44/35F	1976	Ex A1 (Meney), Ardrossan, 1995
	MUA870P	Leyland Atlantean AN68/1R	Park Royal	H43/30F	1976	Ex Goldthorp, Batley, 1991
	NSP315R	Ailsa B55-10	Alexander AV	H44/35F	1976	Ex Maidstone & District, 1992
	NSP316R	Ailsa B55-10	Alexander AV	H44/35F	1976	Ex Maidstone & District, 1992
	NSP318R	Ailsa B55-10	Alexander AV	H44/35F	1976	Ex Maidstone & District, 1992
	NSP321R	Ailsa B55-10	Alexander AV	H43/34F	1976	Ex LB Travel, Kettering, 1994
	NSP322R	Ailsa B55-10	Alexander AV	H43/35F	1976	Ex Maidstone & District, 1992
	UCS186S	Ailsa B55-10	Alexander AV	H44/31D	1978	Ex A1 (Steele), Ardrossan, 1995
	SSN249S	Ailsa B55-10	Alexander AV	H44/31D	1977	Ex Tayside, 1994
	SSN250S	Ailsa B55-10	Alexander AV	H44/31D	1977	Ex Tayside, 1994
	SSN254S	Ailsa B55-10	Alexander AV	H44/31D	1978	Ex Tayside, 1994
	213ONU	Leyland National 11351A/1R(V)	East Lancs Greenway(1993)	B49F	1978	Ex National Welsh, 1993
	CUP667S	Leyland National 11351A/1R		B49F	1978	Ex Edinburgh Transport, 1994
	EMB642S	Leyland National 10351B/1R		B44F	1978	Ex Midland, 1994

Far left, top: **The latest delivery to Black Prince are four MAN11.190s with Optare Vecta bodywork.
M73WYG was seen at the Optare works just prior to delivery. The operator strives to ensure that
each vehicle in the fleet has suttle variations in livery and this equally applies to the new deliveries.**
Andrew Jarosz

Far left: **1994 was the silver jubilee of Black Prince and to mark this event LWB377P was painted into a special livery, seen here in Leeds.**
Lee Whitehead

FTF702F started life with Ramsbottom UDC and this East Lancashire-bodied Leyland Titan PD3/4 was one of the last of this model built and now carries the red and yellow livery of Black Prince.
Phillip Stephenson

	TWN797S	Leyland National 11351A/1R		B52F	1978	Ex Brewers, 1995
	TWN799S	Leyland National 11351A/1R		B52F	1978	Ex Brewers, 1995
	GMB662T	Leyland National 10351B/1R		B44F	1978	Ex Midland, 1994
	JTU580T	Leyland National 10351B/1R		B44F	1979	Ex Midland, 1994
	JTU595T	Leyland National 10351B/1R		B44F	1979	Ex Midland, 1994
	WWN808T	Leyland National 11351A/1R		B52F	1979	Ex Brewers, 1995
	WTS262T	Ailsa B55-10	Alexander AV	H44/31D	1979	Ex Tayside, 1994
	LHS736V	Ailsa B55-10 MkII	Alexander AV	H44/35F	1979	Ex Kelvin Central, 1991
	LHS752V	Ailsa B55-10 MkII	Alexander AV	H44/35F	1979	Ex Reliance, Sutton-on-the-Forest, 1993
	ODM679V	Leyland National 10351B/1R		B44F	1979	Ex Midland, 1994
	NGD19V	Volvo B58-56	Duple Dominant	B53F	1980	Ex Irvine, Law, 1994
	KSD94W	Ailsa B55-10 MkII	Alexander AV	H44/35F	1980	Ex Clydeside 2000, 1993
	KSD95W	Ailsa B55-10 MkII	Alexander AV	H44/35F	1980	Ex Clydeside 2000, 1993
	KSD101W	Ailsa B55-10 MkII	Alexander AV	H44/35F	1980	Ex Clydeside 2000, 1993
	KSD108W	Ailsa B55-10 MkII	Alexander AV	H44/35F	1980	Ex Clydeside 2000, 1993
	KSD109W	Ailsa B55-10 MkII	Alexander AV	H44/35F	1980	Ex Clydeside 2000, 1993
V113	KSD113W	Ailsa B55-10 MkII	Alexander AV	H44/35F	1980	Ex Clydeside 2000, 1993
	LTN753X	Volvo B58-56	Duple Dominant III Express	C49F	1991	Ex Ashall, Gorton, 1994
u	A103SUU	Volvo-Ailsa B55-10 MkIII	Alexander RV	H36/30F	1984	Ex London Buses, 1992
	C101CUL	Volvo Citybus B10M-50	Alexander RV	H43/37F	1985	Ex A1 (McMenemy), Ardrossan, 1989
	E641LNV	LAG Panoramic G355Z	LAG	C49FT	1988	Ex Gray, Datchet, 1992
	E130SNY	MCW MetroRider MF150/52	MCW	B23F	1988	Ex Victoria Travel, 1995
	E208EPB	Hestair Duple SDA1510	Duple 425	C57F	1987	Ex Swanbrook, Cheltenham, 1994
S113	F113OMJ	Scania N113CRB	Alexander PS	B51F	1989	Ex London Buses, 1991
	G842LWR	Optare MetroRider	Optare	B23F	1990	Ex Optare demonstrator, 1991
	K167FYG	Optare MetroRider MR01	Optare	B31F	1992	Ex Heatons Travel, Leigh, 1995
	K168FYG	Optare MetroRider MR01	Optare	B31F	1992	Ex Heatons Travel, Leigh, 1995
	M71WYG	MAN 11.190	Optare Vecta	B41F	1995	
	M73WYG	MAN 11.190	Optare Vecta	B41F	1995	
	M74WYG	MAN 11.190	Optare Vecta	B41F	1995	
	M75WYG	MAN 11.190	Optare Vecta	B41F	1995	
	M270WWW	EOS E180Z	EOS 90	C49FT	1995	

Previous Registrations:

213ONU	SKG924S	LUF549	PTF743L
641UTO	LUB512P	PWR256P	LES48P
LDS341A	WLT441	SIB6728	A562YCS, 9708KM, A969WUS

Livery: Red and yellow (buses); green and white (coaches); blue (Amberley Services) 249/50/4/62, 385, 752/83.

AEC Routemaster LDS341A was obtained by Black Prince from Western Scottish in 1990. This vehicle had left London Buses as part of a mass move of the type into Scotland at the time of deregulation. Still maintaining its links with London, the vehicle carries on the bonnet its original London fleet number, RM441.
David Cole

The East Lancashire Greenway project completely restyled the appearance of the Leyland National. LUF549 was built some 22 years ago as Ribble PTF743L. The vehicle was transformed in 1993 and looks set to give many more years of service. *Phillip Stephenson*

New to London Transport as the Cumulo experimental bus, C101CUL entered the Black Prince fleet after a spell on the Ayrshire coast in A1 livery. Seen here in Leeds, it is based on the Volvo Citybus B10M chassis and it carries an Alexander RV-style body style. *Tony Wilson*

CITY TRAVELLER

P W Dalton, 33 Ferensway, Hull, North Humberside, HU2 8LZ

VSM783V	Leyland Leopard PSU3E/4R	Duple Dominant II	C53F	1980	OK Travel, 1994
RNG824W	Leyland Leopard PSU3F/4R	Duple Dominant IV	C53F	1981	OK Travel, 1994
E283RKH	Mercedes-Benz L207D	?	M12	1988	
F407BWF	Mercedes-Benz 407D	Whittaker	M16	1988	
F415GAG	Toyota Hiace	Toyota	M11	1989	
H41BRH	Citroen C25D	Citroen	M15	1991	
H521SWE	Mercedes-Benz 814D	Whittaker	DP33F	1990	
J751HAT	Mercedes-Benz 410D	Autobus Classique	M13	1992	

Livery: Silver with blue, red and orange stripes.

Previous Registrations:
VSM783V   XPT566V

City Traveller of Hull operates a service to the north of the city via the University. A regular performer on this route was H522SWE a Whittaker-bodied Mercedes-Benz 814D. It is seen leaving the main bus station in the centre of Hull. Although no longer in the fleet, its twin H521SWE remains.
Keith Grimes

CLARKSONS

Ken Clarkson Ltd, 52 Doncaster Road, South Elmsall, West Yorkshire, WF9 2JN

NEL123P	Leyland National 11351A/1R		B49F	1976	Ex Blandford Bus Company, 1994
UHG726R	Leyland National 11351A/1R(Volvo)		B49F	1976	Ex Ribble, 1994
ACW920R	Leyland National 11351A/2R(Volvo)		B52F	1977	Ex Halton, 1994
ABR860S	Leyland National 11351A/1R		B49F	1977	Ex Northumbria, 1993
D950VCN	Freight Rover Sherpa	Dormobile	B16F	1986	Ex Northumbria, 1994
F164SMT	Leyland Swift LBM6T/2RS	Reeve Burgess Harrier	C37F	1989	Ex Palmer, Normanton, 1993
H624FUT	Bova FHD12.290	Bova Futura	C51FT	1991	
H965VWF	Mercedes-Benz 609D	Crystals	C26F	1991	
J360LAY	Bova FHD12.290	Bova Futura	C55F	1991	
J92YKU	Mercedes-Benz 609D	Whittaker Europa	C21F	1992	
K588VBC	Volvo B10M-60	Caetano Algarve II	C51FT	1993	
L974OWY	Volvo B10M-62	Plaxton Excalibur	C49FT	1994	
L975OWY	Volvo B10M-62	Plaxton Excalibur	C49FT	1994	
L533XUT	Volvo B10M-60	Plaxton Premiére 350	C49FT	1994	
M605RCP	DAF SB220LT550	Ikarus CitiBus	B49F	1995	
M606RCP	DAF SB220LT550	Ikarus CitiBus	B49F	1995	

Livery: White and blue

Previous Registrations:
MIW2422   VHB679S

Named vehicles: H624FUT *Benjamin John*; H965VWF *Marie*; J360LAY *Matthew Paul*

A number of coach operators in industrial Yorkshire have sought new opportunities following the loss of British Coal contracts as the mining industry has contracted. Clarksons of South Elmsall have expanded into local bus operation and ABR860S is one of a number of Leyland Nationals bought for this work although some have been replaced recently with new DAFs. It is seen in Pontefract bus station. *David Longbottom*

DON VALLEY BUSES

Don Valley Buses Ltd, 323 Petre Street, Sheffield, South Yorkshire, S4 8LU

A subsidiary of Mainline Group Ltd.

29	D129OWG	Renault-Dodge S56	Reeve Burgess	DP25F	1987	Ex Mainline, 1992
30	D303MHS	Renault-Dodge S56	Alexander AM	B21F	1986	Ex Kelvin Central, 1992
31	D314MHS	Renault-Dodge S56	Alexander AM	B21F	1986	Ex Kelvin Central, 1992
39	D139OWG	Renault-Dodge S56	Reeve Burgess	DP25F	1987	Ex Mainline, 1992
53	D153RAK	Renault-Dodge S56	Reeve Burgess	B25F	1987	Ex Mainline, 1992
59	D159RAK	Renault-Dodge S56	Reeve Burgess	B25F	1987	Ex Mainline, 1992
60	G590PKL	Mercedes-Benz 811D	Dormobile Routemaker	B24F	1989	Ex Skills, Nottingham, 1991
66	G566SNN	Mercedes-Benz 709D	Carlyle	B33F	1990	Ex Skills, Nottingham, 1991
68	F68LNU	Mercedes-Benz 709D	Robin Hood	B29F	1989	Ex Skills, Nottingham, 1991
69	F69LNU	Mercedes-Benz 709D	Robin Hood	B29F	1989	Ex Skills, Nottingham, 1991
70	F70LAL	Mercedes-Benz 811D	Alexander AM	DP33F	1989	Ex Skills, Nottingham, 1991
72	F725USF	Mercedes-Benz 811D	Alexander AM	DP33F	1989	Ex Skills, Nottingham, 1991
75	G75ONN	Mercedes-Benz 609D	Alexander AM	DP24F	1989	Ex Skills, Nottingham, 1991
163	D163RAK	Renault-Dodge S56	Reeve Burgess	B25F	1987	Ex Mainline, 1994
166	D166RAK	Renault-Dodge S56	Reeve Burgess	B25F	1987	Ex Mainline, 1994
168	D168RAK	Renault-Dodge S56	Reeve Burgess	B25F	1987	Ex Mainline, 1994
182	E182UWF	Renault-Dodge S56	Reeve Burgess	B25F	1987	Ex Mainline, 1994

Livery: Green and white

The Don Valley Buses operation of Mainline has its roots in the Skills of Nottingham services in Sheffield which were purchased by Mainline in 1991. One of the vehicles obtained from Skills at this time was 68, F68LNU, a Robin Hood-bodied Mercedes-Benz 709D. *Phillip Stephenson*

EAST YORKSHIRE

East Yorkshire Motor Services Ltd & East Yorkshire Travel Ltd,
252 Anlaby Road, Hull, North Humberside, HU3 2RS

Depots: Springfield Way, Anlaby; Mill Lane, Beverley; St John Street, Bridlington; Middle Street, Driffield; Back Street, Easington; Stockbridge Road, Elloughton; Primrose Valley Road, Filey; Cliff Road, Hornsea; Anlaby Road, Hull; Hedon Road, Hull; Outgang Road, Pickering; Railway Street, Pocklington; Dunslow Road, Scarborough; Bannister Street, Withernsea.

1	NBD101Y	Leyland Tiger TRCTL11/3R	Plaxton Paramount 3200 E	C48F	1983	Ex Luton & District, 1991
4	GRH4Y	Leyland Tiger TRCTL11/3R	Plaxton Paramount 3200 E	C48FT	1983	
5	A573SRH	Leyland Tiger TRCTL11/3R	Plaxton Paramount 3200 E	C53F	1983	
6	165DKH	Leyland Tiger TRCTL11/3R	Plaxton Paramount 3200 E	C53F	1983	
7	3277KH	Leyland Royal Tiger B50	Roe Doyen	C50F	1984	
8	508DKH	Leyland Royal Tiger B54	Roe Doyen	C50F	1984	
9	46EYB	Leyland Royal Tiger B54	Roe Doyen	C50F	1984	
11	794EYD	Leyland Tiger TRCTL11/3RH	Plaxton Paramount 3200 II	C50F	1985	
15	C310JAT	Leyland Royal Tiger RTC	Leyland Doyen	C47FT	1985	
18	665EYL	MCW Metroliner DR130/24	MCW	CH57/22FT	1986	
19	926BWV	Leyland Tiger TRCTL11/3RZ	Duple 340	C46FT	1986	
20	787EYC	Leyland Tiger TRCTL11/3RZ	Duple 340	C46FT	1986	
21	421CKH	Leyland Tiger TRCTL11/2R	Plaxton Paramount 3200 E	C49F	1983	Ex United, 1986
22	A520EVN	Leyland Tiger TRCTL11/2R	Plaxton Paramount 3200 E	C49F	1983	Ex United, 1986
23	NDC239W	Leyland Leopard PSU3E/4RT	Plaxton Supreme IV Express	C49F	1981	Ex United, 1986
26	A10EYD	Leyland Tiger TRCTL11/3R	Plaxton Paramount 3500	C46FT	1984	Ex United, 1986
27	CRH182X	Leyland Tiger TRCTL11/3R	Duple Dominant IV	C49F	1982	Ex Vanguard, Bedworth, 1991
28	YPD123Y	Leyland Tiger TRCTL11/2R	Duple Dominant IV	C49F	1983	Ex Kinch, Barrow-on-Soar, 1991
29	YPD141Y	Leyland Tiger TRCTL11/2R	Duple Dominant IV	C49F	1983	Ex Kinch, Barrow-on-Soar, 1991
30	YPD143Y	Leyland Tiger TRCTL11/2R	Duple Dominant IV	C49F	1983	Ex Kinch, Barrow-on-Soar, 1991
31	571XKN	Leyland Tiger TRCTL11/3RZ	Duple 320	C55F	1987	
32	EYD1T	Volvo B10M-61	Duple 340	C55F	1987	
33	EYD2T	Volvo B10M-61	Duple 340	C46FT	1987	
34	NJI1255	Leyland Leopard PSU5B/4R	Plaxton Supreme III	C51F	1978	Ex United, 1986
42	D42OKH	Iveco Daily 49-10	Robin Hood City Nippy	DP19F	1987	
43	D43OKH	Iveco Daily 49-10	Robin Hood City Nippy	DP19F	1987	
44	D44OKH	Iveco Daily 49-10	Robin Hood City Nippy	DP19F	1987	
46	271CLT	Leyland Tiger TRCTL11/3RZ	Plaxton Paramount 3200 II	C53F	1986	Ex Hornsby, Ashby, 1994
47	95EYM	Volvo B10M-61	Plaxton Paramount 3200 II	C53F	1985	Ex Excelsior, Bournemouth, 1987
48	YUU556	Volvo B10M-61	Plaxton Paramount 3200 II	C53F	1985	Ex Capital, West Drayton, 1988
49	834EYD	Volvo B10M-61	Plaxton Paramount 3200 II	C53F	1985	Ex Capital, West Drayton, 1988
50	80EYC	Volvo B10M-61	Plaxton Paramount 3200 II	C53F	1985	Ex Capital, West Drayton, 1988

The East Yorkshire Diplomat and Cherrys of Beverley identities have now been combined under the East Yorkshire Travel banner. Displaying the latter is 32, EYD1T, a Duple 340 bodied Volvo B10M. The index number on this vehicle reflects the former East Yorkshire Diplomat fleetnames that were carried by this vehicle.
Phillip Stephenson

51	E51URH	Leyland Tiger TRCTL11/3RZ	Duple 340	C48FT	1988	
53	E53URH	Leyland Tiger TRCTL11/3RZ	Duple 340	C51FT	1988	
54	H54VRH	Volvo B10M-60	Plaxton Expressliner	C46FT	1990	
55	H155VRH	Volvo B10M-60	Plaxton Expressliner	C46FT	1990	
56	H56VRH	Volvo B10M-60	Plaxton Expressliner	C46FT	1990	
57	H157AKH	Volvo B10M-60	Plaxton Expressliner	C46FT	1991	
58	J58ERH	Volvo B10M-60	Plaxton Expressliner	C46FT	1991	
59	J159HAT	Volvo B10M-60	Plaxton Expressliner	C46FT	1992	
60	J160HAT	Volvo B10M-60	Plaxton Expressliner	C46FT	1992	
61	K161TKH	Volvo B10M-60	Plaxton Expressliner II	C46FT	1993	
62	L62VAG	Volvo B10M-60	Plaxton Expressliner II	C46FT	1993	
63	G391PNV	Volvo B10M-60	Plaxton Expressliner	C46FT	1990	Ex Premier Travel, 1993
64	L64CKH	Volvo B10M-60	Plaxton Expressliner II	C46FT	1994	
65	E365NEG	Volvo B10M-61	Plaxton Paramount 3200 III	C53F	1988	Ex Cambridge Coach Services, 1994
66	E366NEG	Volvo B10M-61	Plaxton Paramount 3200 III	C53F	1988	Ex Cambridge Coach Services, 1994
67	M67LAG	Scania K113CRB	Van Hool Alizée	C49FT	1995	
68	M68LAG	Scania K113CRB	Van Hool Alizée	C49FT	1995	
76	GGD671T	Volvo B58-61	Duple Dominant II	C57F	1979	Ex Connor & Graham, 1994
80	ECU770W	Ford Transit	Dormobile	B16F	1981	Ex Connor & Graham, 1994
81	FAZ2781	Leyland Tiger TRCTL11/3R	Plaxton Paramount 3500	C49FT	1983	Ex Connor & Graham, 1994
87	741DYE	Volvo B10M-61	Van Hool Alizée	C49FT	1984	Ex Connor & Graham, 1994
90	TND123X	Volvo B58-61	Duple Dominant II	C53F	1982	Ex Connor & Graham, 1994
96	OJI7078	Volkswagen LT55	Optare City Pacer	B25F	1987	Ex Connor & Graham, 1994
99	DV7890	Leyland Lion LT2	Burlingham (1947)	C31F	1931	Ex preservation, 1989
100	KSU381	Bedford OB	Duple Vista	C29F	1949	Ex Tours, Isle of Man, 1990
101	1918KH	Leyland National 1151/1R/0402		DP21DL	1973	Ex London Country NE, 1988
169	RAG169R	Leyland National 11351A/1R		DP49F	1976	
188	OBT693M	Leyland Leopard PSU3B/4R	Plaxton Elite III	C53F	1973	Ex Connor & Graham, 1994
189	CPT822S	Leyland Leopard PSU3E/4R	Plaxton Supreme III Express	C53F	1978	Ex Connor & Graham, 1994
190	8225KH	Leyland Leopard PSU3E/4R	Plaxton Supreme IV Express	C49F	1979	
192	JKH192V	Leyland Leopard PSU3E/4R	Plaxton Supreme IV Express	C49F	1979	
193	JKH193V	Leyland Leopard PSU3E/4R	Plaxton Supreme IV Express	C49F	1979	
194	VOD626S	Leyland Leopard PSU3E/4RT	Plaxton Supreme III Express	C49F	1978	Ex Metro, Hull, 1992
195	BUR443T	Leyland Leopard PSU5C/4R	Plaxton Supreme IV	C53F	1978	Ex Metro, Hull, 1992
196	YOI7898	Leyland Leopard PSU3C/4R	Plaxton Supreme IV Express	C53F	1977	Ex Thornton Dale, Pickering, 1992
197	EGR571S	Leyland Leopard PSU3E/4R	Plaxton Supreme IV Express	C49F	1978	Ex Thornton Dale, Pickering, 1992
198	GWV935V	Leyland Leopard PSU3E/4R	Plaxton Supreme IV Express	C48F	1980	Ex Thornton Dale, Pickering, 1992
199	EGV367Y	Leyland Leopard PSU5E/4R	Plaxton Supreme V	C50F	1982	Ex Thornton Dale, Pickering, 1992
200	NAT200V	Leyland National 2 NL116L11/1R		B49F	1980	
207	XAG207X	Leyland Leopard PSU3F/4R	Willowbrook 003	C49F	1981	

Two interesting single-deck buses are featured in our colour plate, top is 600, PHN178L, a Bristol RELL now converted to open-top, still an uncommon modification. It is seen in Scarborough where it can normally be found on sea-front services. *Tony Wilson*

Opposite, bottom: **East Yorkshire's 261, L261AKH, is a Volvo B6 that has a Northern Counties Paladin style body and was added to the fleet in 1994 as the only totally new single-deck bus since the Leyland National 2s of 1980. It was photographed in Hull.** *Tony Wilson*

The business of Thornton Dale Coaches of Pickering was acquired by East Yorkshire in 1992. One of the vehicles from that fleet was 198, GWV935V, a Leyland Leopard new to Southdown and now wearing the Primrose Valley livery.
David Longbottom

Many operators fleets include vintage vehicles which are used for promotional work, proclaiming not only the quality of engineering but also an interest in local transport heritage. East Yorkshire have a Bedford OB with 1949 Duple Vista bodywork, a very popular design in the early 1950s. Now numbered 100, with index mark KSU381, this splendid example is seen at Sheffield Meadowhall. *Tony Wilson*

Few of the Ford Transit minibuses remain in East Yorkshire's fleet and those that do feature the silver, blue and red Skipper livery on Carlyle bodywork. Photographed in Hull is 316, C316DRH, an example from 1985 and one of those ordered in quantity by the National Bus Company. *Keith Grimes*

Skipper livery is worn by the vehicles which provide town service in Scarborough. One of the Greenway re-built Leyland Nationals in that livery is 259, IIL2159 seen in the town. The low sunlight can be seen reflecting from the DiPTAC handrails. *Malc McDonald*

208	XAG208X	Leyland Leopard PSU3G/4R	Duple Dominant IV Express	C49F	1981	
209	PNW309W	Leyland Leopard PSU3F/4R	Plaxton Supreme IV	C49F	1981	Ex Hardwicks, 1988
211	PNW311W	Leyland Leopard PSU3F/4R	Plaxton Supreme IV	DP53F	1981	Ex Hardwicks, 1988
212	PNW312W	Leyland Leopard PSU3F/4R	Plaxton Supreme IV	DP53F	1981	Ex Hardwicks, 1988
214	G214RKH	Mercedes-Benz 811D	Whittaker	C19F	1990	
231	39EYD	Leyland Leopard PSU3F/4R	Plaxton Supreme IV	C49F	1981	Ex Hardwicks, 1988
232	PNW332W	Leyland Leopard PSU3F/4R	Plaxton Supreme IV	C49F	1981	Ex Hardwicks, 1988
234	SIB6614	Leyland Leopard PSU3F/4R	East Lancs EL2000 (1992)	DP49F	1981	
235	SIB6615	Leyland Leopard PSU5B/4R	East Lancs EL2000 (1992)	DP51F	1977	Ex United, 1986
236	DDZ236	Leyland Leopard PSU5D/4R	East Lancs EL2000 (1991)	DP47F	1981	Ex Hardwicks, 1988
240	NGR120T	Leyland Leopard PSU5C/4R	Plaxton Supreme IV	C53F	1979	Ex United, 1986
255	IIL2155	Leyland National 10351B/1R	East Lancs Greenway(1992)	B41F	1978	
256	IIL2156	Leyland National 10351B/1R	East Lancs Greenway(1992)	B41F	1978	
257	IIL2157	Leyland National 10351A/2R	East Lancs Greenway(1992)	B41F	1979	Ex Lucky Bus, Watford, 1991
258	IIL2158	Leyland National 10351B/1R	East Lancs Greenway(1992)	B41F	1979	
259	IIL2159	Leyland National 10351B/1R	East Lancs Greenway(1992)	B41F	1979	
260	IIL2160	Leyland National 10351B/1R	East Lancs Greenway(1992)	B41F	1979	
261	L261AKH	Volvo B6-9.9M	Northern Counties Paladin	B40F	1994	
282	32CHY	Leyland Tiger TRCTL11/3R	Plaxton Paramount 3500	C49FT	1983	Ex Cherry, Beverley, 1987
283	FKX283T	Leyland Leopard PSU3E/4R	Plaxton Supreme IV	C53F	1979	Ex Cherry, Beverley, 1987

312-319

| | | Ford Transit 190D | Carlyle | B18F* | 1985-86 | *312/3 are B16F; 319 is B20F |

| 312 | C312DRH | **314** | C314DRH | **316** | C316DRH | **318** | C318DRH | **319** | C319DRH |
| 313 | C313DRH | **315** | C315DRH | **317** | C317DRH | | | | |

320	D535HNW	Ford Transit 190D	Carlyle	B16F	1986	Ex West Yorkshire, 1988
321	D542HNW	Ford Transit 190D	Carlyle	B16F	1986	Ex West Yorkshire, 1989
324	PHE814M	Bristol VRT/SL2/6G	Eastern Coach Works	H43/34F	1974	Ex Yorkshire Traction, 1990
327	HWE827N	Bristol VRT/SL2/6G	Eastern Coach Works	H43/34F	1975	Ex Yorkshire Traction, 1990
329	HWE829N	Bristol VRT/SL2/6G	Eastern Coach Works	H43/34F	1975	Ex Yorkshire Traction, 1991
341	E101XVM	Mercedes-Benz 609D	PMT	DP21F	1988	Ex Finglands, 1992
342	E102XVM	Mercedes-Benz 609D	PMT	DP24F	1988	Ex Finglands, 1992
345	D905RVM	Mercedes-Benz 609D	Reeve Burgess	DP19F	1987	Ex Finglands, 1992

Passing through Westbrough, Scarborough is Mercedes-Benz 811 448, K448RRH, new to the East Yorkshire fleet in 1993 as a replacement for 432. Fitted with a Plaxton Beaver locally-built body it is seen in Skipper livery while working service 6 to Briercliffe. *Keith Grimes*

353	WLT694	Leyland Tiger TRCTL11/3R	Plaxton Paramount 3200	C53F	1984	Ex Finglands, 1993
363	EWU963T	Ford R1114	Plaxton Supreme IV	C53F	1979	Ex Primrose Valley, 1990
371	DDC711T	Bedford YMT	Plaxton Supreme IV	C53F	1979	Ex Four Oaks, 1990
389	MIJ999	Leyland Leopard PSU5D/5R	Duple Dominant III	C57F	1981	Ex Primrose Valley, 1990
399	YUE599S	Bedford YMT	Plaxton Supreme III	C53F	1978	Ex Primrose Valley, 1990

406-419

Mercedes-Benz L608D — Reeve Burgess — B20F — 1986 — Ex United, 1986 — *406/7 are DP19F

406	C406VVN	409	C409VVN	412	C412VVN	415	C415VVN	418	C418VVN
407	C407VVN	410	C410VVN	413	C413VVN	416	C416VVN	419	C419VVN
408	C408VVN	411	C411VVN	414	C414VVN	417	C417VVN		

420-437

Mercedes-Benz 811D — Reeve Burgess Beaver — B31F* — 1989 — *435-7 are DP31F

420	F420GAT	424	F424GAT	428	F428GAT	431	F431GAT	435	F435GAT
421	F421GAT	425	F425GAT	429	F429GAT	433	F433GAT	436	F436GAT
422	F422GAT	426	F426GAT	430	F430GAT	434	F434GAT	437	F437GAT
423	F423GAT	427	F427GAT						

438-445

Mercedes-Benz 709D — Reeve Burgess Beaver — B25F* — 1989 — *438/9 are DP25F; 443-5 are B23F

| 438 | F438GAT | 440 | F440GAT | 442 | F442GAT | 444 | F444GAT | 445 | F445GAT |
| 439 | F439GAT | 441 | F441GAT | 443 | F443GAT | | | | |

446	H446YKH	Iveco Daily 49-10	Reeve Burgess Beaver	B25F	1990	
447	H447YKH	Iveco Daily 49-10	Reeve Burgess Beaver	B25F	1990	
448	K448RRH	Mercedes-Benz 811D	Plaxton Beaver	B31F	1993	

501-510

Bristol VRT/SL3/501 — Eastern Coach Works — H43/31F — 1979 — 508 fitted with a Gardner engine.

| 501 | JKH501V | 503 | JKH503V | 505 | JKH505V | 507 | JKH507V | 509 | JKH509V |
| 502 | JKH502V | 504 | JKH504V | 506 | JKH506V | 508 | JKH508V | 510 | JKH510V |

To meet the National Bus Company need for double-deck coaches, Eastern Coach Works developed a coach-styled body to match the lengthened version of the Leyland Olympian. Supplied to NBC for commuting work, four examples can now be found in the East Yorkshire fleet, following a period on Green Line duties. Seen while working service 181 in Hull is 544, 334EYL. *Tony Wilson*

511-527

| | | | | | | Bristol VRT/SL3/6LXB | | Eastern Coach Works | | H43/31F | 1980-81 |

511	PAG511W	514	PAG514W	518	PAG518W	522	WKH522X	525	WKH525X
512	PAG512W	515	PAG515W	519	PAG519W	523	WKH523X	526	WKH526X
513	PAG513W	517	PAG517W	520	WKH520X	524	WKH524X	527	WKH527X

| 528 | GRH2Y | Leyland Olympian ONLXB/1R | Eastern Coach Works | H45/32F | 1983 |
| 529 | GRH3Y | Leyland Olympian ONLXB/1R | Eastern Coach Works | DPH41/29F | 1983 |

530-535

| | | Leyland Olympian ONLXB/1R | Eastern Coach Works | DPH42/28F* 1984-85 *533-5 are DPH42/30F |

| 530 | A530OKH | 532 | A532OKH | 533 | B533WAT | 534 | B534WAT | 535 | B535WAT |
| 531 | A531OKH | | | | | | | | |

536	C536DAT	Leyland Olympian ONLXB/1RH	Eastern Coach Works	DPH42/29F	1986	
537	C537DAT	Leyland Olympian ONLXB/1RH	Eastern Coach Works	DPH42/29F	1986	
539	A239GHN	Leyland Olympian ONLXB/1R	Eastern Coach Works	DPH41/29F	1984	Ex United, 1986
540	B249NVN	Leyland Olympian ONLXB/1R	Eastern Coach Works	H45/32F	1985	Ex United, 1986
541	B250NVN	Leyland Olympian ONLXB/1R	Eastern Coach Works	H45/32F	1985	Ex United, 1986
542	B254RAJ	Leyland Olympian ONLXB/1R	Eastern Coach Works	DPH42/30F	1985	Ex United, 1986
543	B111WAT	Leyland Olympian ONTL11/2Rsp	Eastern Coach Works	CH45/24F	1985	Ex London Country NE, 1988
544	334EYL	Leyland Olympian ONTL11/2Rsp	Eastern Coach Works	CH45/24F	1985	Ex London Country NE, 1988
545	B109LPH	Leyland Olympian ONTL11/2Rsp	Eastern Coach Works	CH45/24F	1985	Ex London Country NE, 1988
546	546EYB	Leyland Olympian ONTL11/2Rsp	Eastern Coach Works	CH45/24F	1985	Ex London Country NE, 1988

547-552

| | | Leyland Olympian ON2R56C13Z4 | Northern Counties Palatine | H51/34F | 1990 |

| 547 | H547VAT | 549 | H549VAT | 550 | H550VAT | 551 | H551VAT | 552 | H552VAT |
| 548 | H548VAT | | | | | | | | |

| 553 | F261RHJ | Leyland Olympian ONCL10/1RZ | Alexander RL | H45/30F | 1989 | Ex Southend, 1991 |

554-570

Leyland Olympian ON2R50G13Z4 Northern Counties Palatine H47/29F 1991-92

554	H154BKH	558	H158BKH	562	J562HAT	565	J565HAT	568	J568HAT
555	H155BKH	559	H159BKH	563	J563HAT	566	J566HAT	569	J569HAT
556	H156BKH	560	H160BKH	564	J564HAT	567	J567HAT	570	J570HAT
557	H157BKH	561	J561HAT						

571	A1EYD	DAF DB250WB505	Optare Spectra	H44/27F	1992

572-583

Leyland Olympian ON2R50G13Z4 Northern Counties Palatine H47/29F* 1993 *572/3 are DPH43/25F

572	K572RRH	575	K575RRH	578	K578RRH	580	K580RRH	582	K582RRH
573	K573RRH	576	K576RRH	579	K579RRH	581	K581RRH	583	K583RRH
574	K574RRH	577	K577RRH						

584-589

Volvo Olympian YN2RV18Z4 Northern Counties Palatine II H../..F 1995 On order

584	M	586	M	587	M	588	M	589	M
585	M							

590-603

Volvo Olympian YN2RV18Z4 Alexander Royale H../..F 1995 On order

590	593	596	599	602
591	594	597	600	603
592	595	598	601	

600	PHN178L	Bristol RELL6G	Eastern Coach Works	OB50F	1972	Ex United, 1986
602	202YTE	Leyland Titan PD2/37	East Lancashire	O37/28F	1962	Ex Sykes, Barnsley, 1989
608	CYC658A	Leyland Atlantean AN68/1R	Park Royal	O43/32F	1972	Ex Hardwicks, 1988
610	NCN110L	Leyland Atlantean PDR1A/1	Eastern Coach Works	O45/27F	1972	Ex Northern, 1986
619	WBN959L	Leyland Atlantean AN68/1R	Park Royal	O43/32F	1972	Ex Hardwicks, 1988
628	HWE828N	Bristol VRT/SL2/6G	Eastern Coach Works	O43/34F	1975	Ex Yorkshire Traction, 1990
636	VDV136S	Bristol VRT/SL3/6LXB	Eastern Coach Works	CO43/31F	1977	Ex Devon General, 1992
637	DRB307H	Bristol VRT/SL6G	Eastern Coach Works	O39/31F	1969	Ex Trent, 1991
638	VDV138S	Bristol VRT/SL3/6LXB	Eastern Coach Works	CO43/31F	1978	Ex Devon General, 1992
639	VDV139S	Bristol VRT/SL3/6LXB	Eastern Coach Works	CO43/31F	1977	Ex Devon General, 1992
640	VDV140S	Bristol VRT/SL3/6LXB	Eastern Coach Works	CO43/31F	1978	Ex Devon General, 1992
644	VKH44	AEC Regent V MD3RV	Willowbrook	H30/26RD	1956	Ex preservation, 1990
660	BHN760N	Bristol VRT/SL2/6G	Eastern Coach Works	O43/31F	1974	Ex United, 1986
704	KKY834P	Bristol VRT/SL3/501	Eastern Coach Works	H43/34F	1976	Ex Yorkshire Traction, 1993
708	PUF584R	Bristol VRT/SL3/6LXB	Eastern Coach Works	H43/31F	1977	Ex United, 1992
710	PUF591R	Bristol VRT/SL3/6LXB	Eastern Coach Works	H43/31F	1977	Ex United, 1986
711	PUF592R	Bristol VRT/SL3/6LXB	Eastern Coach Works	H43/31F	1977	Ex United, 1986
712	PUF593R	Bristol VRT/SL3/6LXB	Eastern Coach Works	H43/31F	1977	Ex United, 1986
714	XAK914T	Bristol VRT/SL3/501(6LXB)	Eastern Coach Works	H43/31F	1979	Ex Yorkshire Traction, 1993
716	AUP716S	Bristol VRT/SL3/6LXB	Eastern Coach Works	H43/31F	1978	Ex United, 1986
717	PKM117R	Bristol VRT/SL3/6LX	Eastern Coach Works	H43/31F	1977	Ex Stagecoach South, 1993
718w	BPT918S	Bristol VRT/SL3/6LX	Eastern Coach Works	H43/31F	1978	Ex United, 1986
721	BPT921S	Bristol VRT/SL3/6LX	Eastern Coach Works	H43/31F	1978	Ex United, 1986
725	BPT925S	Bristol VRT/SL3/6LX	Eastern Coach Works	H43/31F	1978	Ex United, 1986
729	CPT729S	Bristol VRT/SL3/6LX	Eastern Coach Works	H43/31F	1978	Ex United, 1986
730	WRC830S	Bristol VRT/SL3/501(6LXB)	Eastern Coach Works	H43/31F	1978	Ex Trent, 1993

732-764

Bristol VRT/SL3/6LXB Eastern Coach Works H43/31F 1978 Ex United, 1986

732	CPT732S	741	DUP741S	750	DUP750S	754	DUP754S	764	HUP764T
733	CPT733S	748	DUP748S						

765	PPH461R	Bristol VRT/SL3/501(6LXB)	Eastern Coach Works	H43/31F	1977	Ex Western National, 1993
766	PPH466R	Bristol VRT/SL3/501	Eastern Coach Works	H43/31F	1977	Ex Western National, 1993
767	PPH467R	Bristol VRT/SL3/501(6LXB)	Eastern Coach Works	H43/31F	1977	Ex Western National, 1993
771	CBV7S	Bristol VRT/SL3/501	Eastern Coach Works	H43/31F	1977	Ex RoadCar, 1993
772	CBV12S	Bristol VRT/SL3/501	Eastern Coach Works	H43/31F	1977	Ex RoadCar, 1993
773	CBV13S	Bristol VRT/SL3/501	Eastern Coach Works	H43/31F	1977	Ex RoadCar, 1993
774	CBV14S	Bristol VRT/SL3/501	Eastern Coach Works	H43/31F	1977	Ex RoadCar, 1993
775	XAK903T	Bristol VRT/SL3/501(6LXB)	Eastern Coach Works	H43/31F	1978	Ex RoadCar, 1994
776	XAK907T	Bristol VRT/SL3/501(6LXB)	Eastern Coach Works	H43/31F	1978	Ex RoadCar, 1994
777	XAK910T	Bristol VRT/SL3/501(6LXB)	Eastern Coach Works	H43/31F	1979	Ex RoadCar, 1994
778	KTL28V	Bristol VRT/SL3/6LXB	Eastern Coach Works	H43/31F	1979	Ex RoadCar, 1994
779	KTL29V	Bristol VRT/SL3/6LXB	Eastern Coach Works	H43/31F	1979	Ex RoadCar, 1994
784	YBF684S	Bristol VRT/SL3/501	Eastern Coach Works	H43/31F	1978	Ex Happy Days, Woodseaves, 1992
787	LAK937W	Bristol VRT/SL3/6LXB	Eastern Coach Works	H43/31F	1981	Ex Yorkshire Traction, 1992
788	LAK938W	Bristol VRT/SL3/6LXB	Eastern Coach Works	H43/31F	1981	Ex Yorkshire Traction, 1992

The Yorkshire Bus Handbook

Following privatisation, East Yorkshire was one of the first companies to place orders for new vehicles, choosing the Olympian/Northern Counties combination. First of the 1991 delivery was 554, H154BKH, seen in York while heading back to Hull. *Malc McDonald*

Optare's current double-deck bus is the Spectra based on a DAF chassis. At the time of its launch both manufacturers were part of the United Bus group. The vehicle was aimed at the UK market, and has sold mostly to London Buses, Reading and Wilts & Dorset, though many are now also operated in Turkey. East Yorkshire took delivery of their only example in 1992. 571, A1EYD, is seen in Hull. *Tony Wilson*

Open top services are provided at Scarborough where 637, DRB307H is seen in overall advert livery apart from the vehicle front. This example is the only mark 1 version of the VR still in the fleet, and was new to Midland General in 1969. *Tony Wilson*

The East Yorkshire Routemaster operation in Hull is being scaled down as we go to press and no doubt a number of these vehicles will be withdrawn. No.811, ALD990B, was at one time operated by Gash of Newark and was obtained by East Yorkshire from RoadCar in 1989. It displays the midnight blue and primrose livery carried by all Routemasters within the fleet. *David Cole*

KSA186P is number 878 in the East Yorkshire fleet, It was obtained from a coach operator near Bridgend but was originally in the Grampian fleet. This Alexander-bodied Leyland Atlantean still carries a dual doorway body but the middle door has been sealed up as can be seen in this view at Hull bus station shortly before the vehicle was placed in store. *David Cole*

789	MWG939X	Bristol VRT/SL3/6LXB	Eastern Coach Works	H43/31F	1981	Ex Yorkshire Traction, 1992
790	RUA450W	Bristol VRT/SL3/6LXB	Eastern Coach Works	H43/31F	1980	Ex Yorkshire Woollen, 1994
791	MWG941X	Bristol VRT/SL3/6LXB	Eastern Coach Works	H43/31F	1981	Ex Yorkshire Traction, 1992
792w	BRF692T	Bristol VRT/SL3/501	Eastern Coach Works	H43/31F	1978	Ex PMT, 1992
793	SGR793V	Bristol VRT/SL3/6LXB	Eastern Coach Works	H43/31F	1980	Ex United, 1986
794	GRF694V	Bristol VRT/SL3/501	Eastern Coach Works	H43/31F	1979	Ex Southend, 1992
795	HWJ930W	Bristol VRT/SL3/501(6LXB)	Eastern Coach Works	H43/31F	1981	Ex Yorkshire Traction, 1992
796	HWJ931W	Bristol VRT/SL3/501(6LXB)	Eastern Coach Works	H43/31F	1981	Ex Yorkshire Traction, 1993
797	HWJ932W	Bristol VRT/SL3/501(6LXB)	Eastern Coach Works	H43/31F	1981	Ex Yorkshire Traction, 1993
798	GRF698V	Bristol VRT/SL3/501	Eastern Coach Works	H43/31F	1979	Ex PMT, 1992
799	JYG433V	Bristol VRT/SL3/6LXB	Eastern Coach Works	H43/31F	1979	Ex Yorkshire Woollen, 1994

801-805

		AEC Routemaster R2RH	Park Royal	H36/28R	1961	Ex London Buses, 1988

801	NRH801A	802	NRH802A	803	NRH803A	804	NVS804	805	NRH805A

806	RSK254	AEC Routemaster 2R2RH	Park Royal	H36/28R	1962	Ex London Buses, 1988
807	NKH807A	AEC Routemaster 2R2RH	Park Royal	H36/28R	1962	Ex London Buses, 1988
808	VLT188	AEC Routemaster R2RH	Park Royal	H36/28R	1960	Ex Kingston-upon-Hull, 1989
809	PAG809A	AEC Routemaster R2RH	Park Royal	H36/28R	1963	Ex Kingston-upon-Hull, 1989
810	NVS855	AEC Routemaster R2RH	Park Royal	H36/28R	1961	Ex RoadCar, 1989
811	ALD990B	AEC Routemaster R2RH	Park Royal	H36/28R	1964	Ex RoadCar, 1989
812	ALM65B	AEC Routemaster R2RH	Park Royal	H36/28R	1964	Ex RoadCar, 1989
813	LDS335A	AEC Routemaster R2RH	Park Royal	H36/28R	1959	Ex Western Scottish, 1992
814	LDS237A	AEC Routemaster R2RH	Park Royal	H36/28R	1960	Ex Western Scottish, 1992
815	LDS337A	AEC Routemaster R2RH	Park Royal	H36/28R	1960	Ex Western Scottish, 1992
816	CUV210C	AEC Routemaster R2RH	Park Royal	H36/28R	1965	Ex Black Prince, 1992
817	LDS239A	AEC Routemaster R2RH	Park Royal	H36/28R	1961	Ex Western Scottish, 1992
818	EDS117A	AEC Routemaster R2RH	Park Royal	H36/28R	1960	Ex Blue Triangle, Rainham, 1994
819	EDS221A	AEC Routemaster R2RH	Park Royal	H36/28R	1962	Ex Blue Triangle, Rainham, 1994
820	SHE820M	Bristol VRT/SL2/6G	Eastern Coach Works	H43/34F	1974	Ex Yorkshire Traction, 1990
821	MEF821W	Bristol VRT/SL3/6LXB	Eastern Coach Works	H43/31F	1981	Ex United, 1986
871	PRH244G	Leyland Atlantean PDR1A/1	Roe	H44/31F	1968	Ex Connor & Graham, 1994
872	PRH246G	Leyland Atlantean PDR1A/1	Roe	H44/31F	1968	Ex Connor & Graham, 1993
874	OTO556M	Leyland Atlantean AN68/1R	East Lancashire	H47/34F	1974	Ex Thornton Dale, Pickering, 1992
875	OTO564M	Leyland Atlantean AN68/1R	East Lancashire	H47/34F	1974	Ex Thornton Dale, Pickering, 1992
877w	KSA182P	Leyland Atlantean AN68A/1R	Alexander AL	H45/29F	1976	Ex GM, Cefn Cribwr, 1992
878w	KSA186P	Leyland Atlantean AN68A/1R	Alexander AL	H45/29D	1976	Ex GM, Cefn Cribwr, 1992
880	SRP818N	Bristol VRT/SL2/6G	Eastern Coach Works	H43/31F	1974	Ex Metro, Hull, 1992
881	GAK481N	Bristol VRT/SL2/6G	Eastern Coach Works	H43/31F	1974	Ex Yorkshire Traction, 1990
882	GAK482N	Bristol VRT/SL2/6G	Eastern Coach Works	H43/31F	1974	Ex Yorkshire Traction, 1990
889	VFT189T	Leyland Atlantean AN68/2R	MCW	H49/37F	1979	Ex Thornton Dale, Pickering, 1992
894	MLK656L	Daimler Fleetline CRL6	Park Royal	H45/31F	1973	Ex Connor & Graham, 1994
895	KUC915P	Daimler Fleetline CRL6	MCW	H44/29F	1975	Ex Connor & Graham, 1994
902	ANC918T	Leyland Atlantean AN68A/1R	Park Royal	H43/32F	1978	Ex GM Buses, 1992
909	MPT309P	Leyland Atlantean AN68/1R	Eastern Coach Works	H45/27F	1976	Ex Go-Ahead Northern, 1986
911	MPT311P	Leyland Atlantean AN68/1R	Eastern Coach Works	H45/27F	1976	Ex Go-Ahead Northern, 1986
912	JJG4P	Leyland Atlantean AN68/1R	Eastern Coach Works	H43/31F	1976	Ex Rhodes, Wawne, 1992
913	JJG7P	Leyland Atlantean AN68/1R	Eastern Coach Works	H43/31F	1976	Ex Rhodes, Wawne, 1992
914	JJG11P	Leyland Atlantean AN68/1R	Eastern Coach Works	H43/31F	1976	Ex Rhodes, Wawne, 1992
915	JJG14P	Leyland Atlantean AN68/1R	Eastern Coach Works	H43/31F	1976	Ex Rhodes, Wawne, 1992
917	NJI1250	Leyland Atlantean PDR1A/1R	Northern Counties (1984)	H43/31F	1970	Ex Cleveland Transit, 1990
918	NJI1251	Leyland Atlantean PDR1A/1R	Northern Counties (1984)	H43/31F	1970	Ex Cleveland Transit, 1990
919	NJI1252	Leyland Atlantean PDR1A/1R	Northern Counties (1986)	H43/31F	1970	Ex Cleveland Transit, 1990
920	NJI1253	Leyland Atlantean PDR1A/1R	Northern Counties (1985)	H43/31F	1970	Ex Cleveland Transit, 1990
921	NJI1254	Leyland Atlantean PDR1A/1R	Northern Counties (1984)	H43/31F	1970	Ex Cleveland Transit, 1990
922	LOD722P	Bristol VRT/SL3/501	Eastern Coach Works	H43/31F	1976	Ex Devon General, 1986
926	RHC726S	Leyland Atlantean AN68A/1R	East Lancashire	H43/32F	1978	Ex Stagecoach South, 1993
931	FBZ2931	Leyland Atlantean PDR1A/1	Northern Counties (1984)	H43/31F	1970	Ex Cleveland Transit, 1990
932	FBZ2932	Leyland Atlantean PDR1A/1	Northern Counties (1984)	H43/31F	1970	Ex Cleveland Transit, 1990
933	FBZ2933	Leyland Atlantean PDR1A/1	Northern Counties (1985)	H43/31F	1970	Ex Cleveland Transit, 1990
940	UNA861S	Leyland Atlantean AN68A/1R	Park Royal	H43/32F	1978	Ex GM Buses, 1993
942	JJG2P	Leyland Atlantean AN68/1R	Eastern Coach Works	H43/31F	1976	Ex Eastbourne, 1992
943	JJG3P	Leyland Atlantean AN68/1R	Eastern Coach Works	H43/31F	1976	Ex Eastbourne, 1992
947	RRH244M	Leyland Atlantean AN68B/1R	Park Royal	H43/30F	1974	Ex Metro, Hull, 1992
951	RRH233M	Leyland Atlantean AN68B/1R	Park Royal	H43/30F	1974	Ex Metro, Hull, 1992
952	TIJ952	Leyland Atlantean AN68B/1R	Park Royal	H43/30F	1974	Ex Metro, Hull, 1992
958	PVO821R	Bristol VRT/SL3/501(6LXB)	Eastern Coach Works	H43/31F	1977	Ex Trent, 1991
959	RAU807R	Bristol VRT/SL3/501(6LXB)	Eastern Coach Works	H43/31F	1976	Ex Trent, 1991
960	RAU810R	Bristol VRT/SL3/501(6LXB)	Eastern Coach Works	H43/31F	1976	Ex Trent, 1991

961-978

Bristol VRT/SL3/501 — Eastern Coach Works — H43/31F — 1976-79

961	RKH961R	965	RKH965R	970	UKH970R	973	UKH973R	976	WAG976S
962	RKH962R	967	SKH967R	971	UKH971R	974	UKH974R	977	WAG977S
963	RKH963R	968	SKH968R	972	UKH972R	975	WAG975S	978	WAG978S
964	RKH964R	969	SKH969R						

979	RTH928S	Bristol VRT/SL3/501	Eastern Coach Works	H43/31F	1978	Ex The Bee Line, 1992

980-991

Bristol VRT/SL3/501 — Eastern Coach Works — H43/31F — 1977-79

980	WAG980S	983	BKH983T	986	EKH986T	988	EKH988T	990	EKH990T
981	BKH981T	984	BKH984T	987	EKH987T	989	EKH989T	991	EKH991T
982	BKH982T	985	EKH985T						

992	BTU327S	Bristol VRT/SL3/501	Eastern Coach Works	H43/31F	1978	Ex PMT, 1992
993	BRF688T	Bristol VRT/SL3/501	Eastern Coach Works	H43/31F	1978	Ex PMT, 1992
994	FTU394T	Bristol VRT/SL3/501	Eastern Coach Works	H43/31F	1979	Ex PMT, 1992
995	WTU487W	Bristol VRT/SL3/501(6LXB)	Eastern Coach Works	H43/31F	1981	Ex PMT, 1992
996	GRF696V	Bristol VRT/SL3/501	Eastern Coach Works	H43/31F	1979	Ex PMT, 1992
997	PPH462R	Bristol VRT/SL3/501(6LXB)	Eastern Coach Works	H43/31F	1977	Ex Badgerline, 1992
998	PPH464R	Bristol VRT/SL3/501(6LXB)	Eastern Coach Works	H43/31F	1977	Ex Badgerline, 1992
999	PPH470R	Bristol VRT/SL3/501(6LXB)	Eastern Coach Works	H43/31F	1977	Ex Badgerline, 1992

Operating Companies:
East Yorkshire Travel: 9, 11/9, 20/1/6, 31-3, 46-50, 65/6, 214/31/82, 353.
East Yorkshire: Remainder.

Previous Registrations:

165DKH	A106MKH	IIL2156	BRH180T
1918KH	NPD124L	IIL2157	AYR326T
202YTE	From new	IIL2158	EAT185T
271CLT	C178BFE, 2732RH	IIL2159	EAT186T
3277KH	A107OKH	IIL2160	EAT187T
32CHY	BAJ639Y,9975VT,DFP495Y	KSU381	SS7376, 1949MN
334EYL	B108LPH	LDS237A	WLT416
39EYD	PNW331W	LDS239A	WLT727
421CKH	A521EVN	LDS335A	VLT81
46EYB	B109UAG	LDS337A	WLT364
508DKH	B108UAG	MIJ999	OWF691X
546EYB	B110LPH	NJI1250	SDC138H
571XKN	D31OKH, 931GTA	NJI1251	SXG50H
665EYL	C118FKH	NJI1252	SXG52H
741DYE	A607UGD	NJI1253	SDC144H
787EYC	C120GKH	NJI1254	SDC145H
794EYD	B111WAT	NJI1255	BGR4S, 334EYL, BAG96S
80EYC	B932MLN	NKH807A	366CLT
8225KH	GKH190T	NRH801A	WLT732
834EYD	B930MLN, B931MLN	NRH802A	WLT798
926BWV	C113GKH	NRH803A	WLT871
95EYM	B902SPR	NRH805A	41CLT
A10EYD	A106FVN	NVS804	WLT982
A573SRH	A105MKH, 95EYM	NVS855	WLT757
B111WAT	B107LPH	OJI7078	E906LVE
C310JAT	C115DRH, 39EYD	PAG809A	741DYE
CRM182X	OHE278X, 6253VC	RRH211M	PAT950M
CYC658A	VNB108L	RRH233M	PAT951M
DDZ236	PNW336W	RRH244M	PAT947M
EGV267Y	HHC365Y, RPN11	RSK254	271CLT
EYD1T	D32OKH	SIB6614	XAG206X
EYD2T	D33OKH	SIB6615	UGR510R
FAZ2781	UTN954Y	TIJ952	PAT952M
FBZ2931	SXG48H	VKH44	From new
FBZ2932	SXG49H	VLT188	From new
FBZ2933	SDC143H	WLT694	A403HRJ
GRH2Y	GRH528Y	YOI7898	VAB829R
GRH3Y	A529MAT	YUU556	B931MLN, B930MNL
IIL2155	BRH179T		

Named Vehicles: 22 *Ryedale Star;* 188 *Mrs Marjorie Graham.*

Liveries: Red and grey (crimson and cream from April 1995); light grey and red (East Yorkshire Travel); red, cream and blue (Connor and Graham); National Express (54-64, 67/8).

As we go to press the first vehicles to carry the new East Yorkshire livery have emerged from the paintshop. First to emmerge into the sunlight was 555, H155BKH, a Leyland Olympian with Northern Counties bodywork. Gold fleetnames are added to the crimson and cream livery and feature an EY motif in dark red. *Andrew Jarosz*

Numerically the final vehicle in the East Yorkshire fleet is 999, PPH470R. This high-bridge VRT is one of six now in the East Yorkshire fleet which originated with London Country in 1977 and have arrived in Yorkshire after a period in the West Country. *Keith Grimes*

EDDIE BROWN

Eddie Brown Tours Ltd, Coach Garage, Brafferton, Helperby, North Yorkshire, YO6 2NY

WIJ551	Volvo B10M-61	Van Hool Alizée	C53F	1987	Ex Park's, 1992
NJI5510	Volvo B10M-61	Van Hool Alizée	C50FT	1987	
D895SWM	Mercedes-Benz L307D	Whittaker Europa	M12	1987	Ex Selwyn's, Runcorn, 1994
MIB658	Volvo B10M-61	Van Hool Alizée	C53F	1988	Ex Park's, 1994
551ALW	Volvo B10M-60	Van Hool Alizée	C49FT	1989	
NIB5457	Fiat Ducato	Fiat	M15	1989	Ex BMT Travel, Harrogate, 1994
G840VAY	Dennis Javelin 8.5SDL1903	Duple 320	C34F	1989	Ex Selwyn's, Runcorn, 1994
G732YAC	Volvo B10M-60	Plaxton Paramount 3500 III	C49FT	1989	Ex Volvo demonstrator, 1990
H551SWY	Scania K113CRB	Van Hool Alizée	C51FT	1991	
J551BWW	Scania K113CRB	Van Hool Alizée	C52FT	1992	
J869JNS	Volvo B10M-60	Van Hool Alizée	C52FT	1992	Ex Clyde Coast, Ardrossan, 1993
L551OUM	Scania K113CRB	Van Hool Alizée	C48FT	1994	
M51WWT	Volvo B10M-60	Plaxton Première 350	C53F	1995	
M551WWT	Volvo B10M-60	Plaxton Première 350	C53F	1995	

Previous Registrations:

46AEW	NYS57Y	MIB658	E628UNE, LSK807
551ALW	F51BWY	NJI5510	D51LWW

Livery: White, brown, red and orange

Three Scania K113s are operated by Eddie Brown, all with Van Hool Alizée bodies. Built at Lier, south west of Antwerp in Belgium, it is one of that countries two popular bodybuilders, the other is Jonckheere based at Roeselare, south of Brugge. Local regulations require the bodywork to endure some 18 years service and have become popular with British operators in recent times. *David Donati*

FAIRWAY RIDER

B L Barnett, 308 Wincolmlee, Kingston-upon-Hull, North Humberside, HU2 0QE

Depot: 308 Wincolmlee, Kingston-upon-Hull

TMU846Y	Leyland Leopard PSU3E/4R	Duple Dominant IV(1983)	C53F	1972	Ex Capitol, Cwmbran, 1992
GUG539N	Leyland Atlantean AN68/1R	Roe	H43/33F	1974	Ex Yorkshire Rider, 1994
GUG558N	Leyland Atlantean AN68/1R	Roe	H43/33F	1975	Ex Yorkshire Rider, 1994
HWT28N	Leyland Atlantean AN68/1R	Roe	H43/33F	1975	Ex Yorkshire Rider, 1994
LUG84P	Leyland Atlantean AN68/1R	Roe	H43/33F	1975	Ex Yorkshire Rider, 1994
LUG99P	Leyland Atlantean AN68/1R	Roe	H43/33F	1975	Ex Yorkshire Rider, 1994
SFV434P	Leyland Atlantean AN68/1R	Eastern Coach Works	H43/31F	1976	Ex Woodward, Glossop, 1994
NDH6P	Ford R1014	Duple Dominant	C45F	1976	Ex Davies, Pantydwr, 1993
SUA136R	Leyland Atlantean AN68/1R	Roe	H43/33F	1977	Ex Yorkshire Rider, 1994
WNW151S	Leyland Atlantean AN68/1R	Roe	H43/33F	1977	Ex Yorkshire Rider, 1994
VBH606S	Bedford YMT	Duple Dominant	C53F	1978	Ex White, Hull, 1993
RBE22S	Ford R1114	Plaxton Supreme III	C53F	1978	Ex White, Hull, 1993
PDN236T	Ford R1114	Duple Dominant II	C53F	1979	Ex Barnett & Lord, Bilton, 1992
JDG283V	Leyland Leopard PSU5C/4R	Duple Dominant II	C50F	1980	Ex Greenslades, Exeter, 1992
AAC966X	Bedford YNT	Plaxton Supreme V	C53F	1982	Ex Simons, Hanslope, 1994
EIL3018	Leyland Tiger TRCTL11/3R	Plaxton Paramount 3500	C46FT	1983	Ex Thomas, Wokingham, 1992
A337HNX	Ford R1115	Plaxton Paramount 3200	C53F	1983	Ex Streetly Coaches, 1993
C209PPE	Leyland Tiger TRCTL11/3RH	Plaxton Paramount 3500 II	C51F	1985	Ex Grangeburn, Motherwell, 1994
C365GAT	Mercedes-Benz L608D	Reeve Burgess	C19F	1986	Ex Marr, Hull, 1993
E778TPW	Mercedes-Benz L307D	??	M12	1988	Ex Skoda GB, Kings Lynn, 1993
G402CRD	Renault Master T35D	Jubilee	C16F	1990	Ex van conversion, 1992

Livery: Cream and red (Fairway Rider) double-decks; grey and red (Fairway Rhodes) remainder.

Previous Registrations:

AAC966X	XVC12X, CEC147		EIL3018	A512HVT	
				TMU846Y	JRK618K

Named vehicles:
GUG539N *Tanya Grace*; HWT28N *Emma Caroline*; LUG99P *Benjamin*.

No longer in the fleet, but illustrating the days of Charles Rhodes is AAC966X photographed in Manchester while on an excursion. The livery here is grey with red, orange and yellow stripes.
Phillip Stephenson

FRODINGHAM COACHES

Frodingham Coaches Ltd, 52 Main Street, North Frodingham,
North Humberside, YO25 8LG

Depot: Kelleythorpe Industrial Estate, Driffield

36	E36VKP	Iveco Daily 49.10	Dormobile Routemaker	B25F	1988	Ex Dalybus, Eccles, 1995
513	B513HHH	Leyland Tiger TRCTL11/3R(Volvo)	Duple Laser 2	C55F	1984	Ex Holmeswood Coaches, 1994
521	H521VWA	Mercedes-Benz 811D	Whittaker	B31F	1991	
567	D567MVR	Volvo B10M-61	Plaxton Paramount 3200 III	C53F	1987	Ex Longstaff, Mirfield, 1994
585	IIL8585	Bedford YNT	Duple Dominant II	C53F	1982	Ex Luton & District, 1988
587	D587MVR	Leyland Tiger TRCTL11/3RZ	Plaxton Paramount 3200 III	C53F	1987	Ex Shearings, 1993
698	DSV698	Volvo B10M-61	Berkhof Esprite 350	C53F	1985	Ex Wallace Arnold, 1991

Previous Registrations:
IIL8585   ABH773X

Livery: White, grey and blue

GLENN COACHES

J T Dudding & J Wreglesworth, 58 The Village, Wiggington, York
North Yorkshire, YO3 8PS

Depot: Cleveland Industrial Estate, Sutton-on-the-Forest

LEU273P	Leyland Leopard PSU3C/4R	Plaxton Elite III Express	C49F	1976	Ex Stephenson, Easingwold, 1993
UWW772R	Leyland Leopard PSU3E/4R	Plaxton Supreme III	C49F	1977	Ex Ingleby's, York, 1994
UAV965S	Leyland Leopard PSU3E/4R	Plaxton Supreme III Express	C53F	1978	Ex Cook, Biggleswade, 1990
PJO8T	Leyland Leopard PSU3E/4R	Duple Dominant II Express	C49F	1978	Ex City of Oxford, 1989
GWY970T	Leyland Leopard PSU3E/4R	Duple Dominant II	C53F	1979	Ex Ford, Ackworth, 1986
TFG154	Volvo B58-56	Duple Dominant II	C53F	1980	Ex Irvine, Law, 1992
TWP999V	Leyland Leopard PSU3E/4R	Duple Dominant II Express	C53F	1979	Ex Bodman, Worton, 1991
ETH101V	Leyland Leopard PSU5C/4R	Duple Dominant II	C50F	1980	Ex Brewers, 1994
NOI1425	Volvo B58-61	Duple Dominant II Express	C53F	1980	Ex Coachlines, Warrington, 1992
GGM74W	Leyland Leopard PSU3F/4R	Plaxton Supreme IV Express	C49F	1981	Ex Ladyline, Rawmarsh, 1993
PNW333W	Leyland Leopard PSU3F/4R	Plaxton Supreme IV Express	C53F	1981	Ex Scarborough & District, 1993
RPE556X	Leyland Tiger TRCTL11/3R	Plaxton Supreme IV	C53F	1981	Ex Frost & Heath, Leigh-on-Sea, 1990
YKR702	Volvo B10M-61	Plaxton Paramount 3500	C49FT	1984	Ex Wallace Arnold, 1990

Previous Registrations:

ETH101V	JDG287V, MKH774A	TFG154	FWJ820V
NOI1425	EYH803V	YKR702	From new

Livery: Red, cream and yellow

Bridlington railway station is the location of this view of Frodingham Coaches H521VWA a Whittaker bodied Mercedes Benz 811D. Interestingly, this vehicle carries Frodingham Bus markings following the number of times passengers have asked 'Is this the Frodingham bus?' *Keith Grimes*

The City Walls of York can be seen in this view of GWY970T. The vehicle is a Duple Dominant II bodied Leyland Leopard which is now in the Glenn Coaches fleet but for some time was operated by Ford of Ackworth near Pontefract. *Mike Fowler*

GLOBE

Globe Luxury Coaches Ltd, 19 Wellington Street, Barnsley, South Yorkshire S70 1EW
Barnsley Bus Company Ltd, Rosa Garage, Wakefield Road, Barnsley,
South Yorkshire, S71 1NN

Depot: Wakefield Road, Barnsley

WDR675M	Leyland National 1151/2R/0202		B23DL	1974	Ex Tanet Valley, Pentrefelin, 1988
JOX527P	Leyland National 11351A/1R		B49F	1976	Ex Western National, 1990
MTV756P	Leyland Leopard PSU3C/4R	Duple Dominant	C49F	1976	Ex Moffat & Williamson, Gauldry, 1994
PTT87R	Leyland National 11351A/1R		B50F	1977	Ex Western National, 1990
CPT821S	Leyland Leopard PSU3E/4R	Plaxton Supreme III Express	C53F	1978	Ex Kingston-upon-Hull, 1993
YRY7T	Leyland Leopard PSU3E/4R	Plaxton Supreme III Express	C53F	1978	Ex Singh, Coventry, 1993
AYJ90T	Leyland National 11351A/1R		B50F	1979	Ex Sovereign, 1993
A908LWU	Leyland Tiger TRCTL11/3R	Plaxton Paramount 3200 E	C44F	1983	Ex Dorset Travel Services, 1991
A134EPA	Leyland Tiger TRCTL11/2R	Plaxton Paramount 3200	C53F	1984	Ex Ace, Mansfield, 1991
B265AMG	Mercedes-Benz L608D	Reeve Burgess	C19F	1984	Ex Rover, Chesham, 1993
B897DTU	Mercedes-Benz L608D	PMT Hanbridge	C25F	1985	Ex Schofield, Shepshed, 1987
C685WNX	Freight Rover Sherpa	Carlyle	B16F	1985	Ex Rialto Travel, Marple, 1993
C363KGG	Mercedes-Benz L608D	Reeve Burgess	B20F	1986	Ex North Mymms, Potters Bar, 1989
C65BWR	Fiat 35-8		M12	1986	Ex , 1994
C803KBT	Leyland Cub CU335	Optare	DP33F	1986	Ex Aidobourne, Chester-le-Street, 1991
C839CBU	Renault-Dodge S56	Northern Counties	B18F	1986	Ex Robin Hood, Rudyard, 1994
D105OWG	Renault-Dodge S56	Reeve Burgess	B25F	1986	Ex Moffat & Williamson, Gauldry, 1994
D108OWG	Renault-Dodge S56	Reeve Burgess	B25F	1986	Ex Glossopdale, 1993
D114OWG	Renault-Dodge S56	Reeve Burgess	B25F	1986	Ex Moffat & Williamson, Gauldry, 1994
D171LTA	Renault-Dodge S56	Reeve Burgess	B23F	1986	Ex Markham, Birmingham, 1994
D677SEM	Renault-Dodge S56	Northern Counties	B22F	1986	Ex Merseybus, 1994
D140RAK	Renault-Dodge S56	Reeve Burgess	B25F	1987	Ex Mainline, 1994
D851KWR	Freight Rover Sherpa	Dormobile	B20F	1987	Ex Yorkshire Rider, 1991

One of the early examples of Optare bodywork can be found on a batch of Leyland Cubs new to West Yorkshire PTE. Now widely dispersed, C803KBT is almost back home as it enters Eldon Street, Barnsley now in the livery of Globe. *Tony Wilson*

	D374JUM	Volkswagen LT55	Optare City Pacer	B25F	1987	Ex London Buses, 1992
w	D903MDB	Renault-Dodge S56	Northern Counties	B18F	1987	Ex Merseybus, 1994
	D312RVR	Renault-Dodge S56	Northern Counties	B22F	1987	Ex James Aughton, 1994
w	D975TKC	Renault-Dodge S56	Alexander AM	B23F	1987	Ex Merseybus, 1994
	D976TKC	Renault-Dodge S56	Alexander AM	B23F	1987	Ex Merseybus, 1994
	D701THF	Renault-Dodge S56	Alexander AM	B23F	1987	Ex Merseybus, 1994
	D703UEM	Renault-Dodge S56	Alexander AM	B23F	1987	Ex Merseybus, 1994
w	D822RYS	Renault-Dodge S56	Alexander AM	B25F	1987	Ex West Midland Road Car, 1994
	E704UEM	Renault-Dodge S56	Alexander AM	B23F	1987	Ex Merseybus, 1995
	E180UWF	Renault-Dodge S56	Reeve Burgess	B25F	1987	Ex Mainline, 1994
	E184UWF	Renault-Dodge S56	Reeve Burgess	B25F	1987	Ex Mainline, 1994
	E518PWR	Volkswagen LT55	Optare City Pacer	B25F	1987	Ex County Bus, 1992
	E520PWR	Volkswagen LT55	Optare City Pacer	B25F	1987	Ex County Bus, 1992
	E588EHD	Ford R1114	Plaxton Elite III	C53F	1987	Ex Stott, New Mill, 1994
	E700HLB	Mercedes-Benz 709D	Reeve Burgess Beaver	DP23F	1988	Ex Golden Coaches, Llandow, 1995
	F888URP	Volvo B10M-61	Caetano Algarve	C49FT	1989	
	F889URP	Volvo B10M-61	Caetano Algarve	C53F	1988	
	F890URP	Volvo B10M-61	Caetano Algarve	C53F	1988	
	F891URP	Volvo B10M-61	Caetano Algarve	C49FT	1989	
	F892URP	Volvo B10M-61	Caetano Algarve	C49FT	1989	
	F893URP	Volvo B10M-61	Caetano Algarve	C49FT	1989	
	F894URP	Volvo B10M-61	Caetano Algarve	C49FT	1989	
	F896URP	Volkswagen LT50	G C Smith Sprinter	C23F	1989	
	F248HDB	Peugeot-Talbot Pullman	Talbot	B22F	1989	Ex Mancunian, Bradford, 1993
	G963VBC	Toyota Coaster HB31R	Caetano Optimo	C18F	1989	Ex Grady, Didsbury, 1991
	G901WAY	Volvo B10M-60	Caetano Algarve	C57F	1990	

Photographed in Barnsley is ANA456Y, a Plaxton-bodied Leyland Tiger no longer in the fleet but showing the name as BBC. It is seen with Barnsley Bus & Coach titles. *Andrew Jarosz*

GORDONS

D J & R Gordon, Chesterton Road, Eastwood Trading Estate, Rotherham,
South Yorkshire, S65 1SU
Billies Coaches Ltd, 100 Doncaster Road, Mexborough
South Yorkshire, S64 0JS

w	CRO684K	AEC Reliance 6U3ZR	Plaxton Elite III	C44DL	1972	Ex Jacob, Southampton, 1988
	ANS67S	AEC Reliance 6U3ZR	Plaxton Supreme III	C51F	1978	Ex Hutchison, Overtown, 1980
	BFX746T	Bedford YMT	Plaxton Supreme IV	C51DL	1979	Ex Rendall, Parkstone, 1983
B	EKU75V	Bedford YMT	Duple Dominant II	C53F	1980	
B	FAK230V	Volvo B58-61	Caetano Alpha	C57F	1980	
	JLS456V	Volvo B58-61	Plaxton Supreme IV	C57F	1980	Ex Rennie, Dunfermline, 1981
	HAS716X	Volvo B58-56	Plaxton Supreme VI	C46FT	1981	Ex Skill, Nottingham, 1988
	NDW139X	Leyland Tiger TRCTL11/3R	Plaxton Supreme V Express	C53F	1982	Ex Butler Bros, Kirkby-in-Ashfield, 1992
	ACX785Y	AEC Reliance 6U2R	Plaxton Supreme IV	C45FT	1982	Ex Traject, Halifax, 1991
	VET721Y	Leyland Tiger TRCTL11/3R	Plaxton Paramount 3200	C51F	1983	Ex Hague, Sheffield, 1985
	FIL7486	Volvo B10M-61	Plaxton Paramount 3500	C53FT	1984	
B	A445YWG	Volvo B10M-61	Plaxton Paramount 3200	C57FT	1984	
	B910UPW	Leyland Tiger TRCTL11/3R	Plaxton Paramount 3500	C53F	1985	Ex Ambassador, 1992
B	C354FBO	Bedford YNV	Plaxton Paramount 3200 II	C57F	1985	Ex Capitol, Cwmbran, 1992
	D813SHE	Bedford YMP	Plaxton Paramount 3200 III	C35F	1987	
	FIL7485	Volvo B10M-61	Van Hool Alizée	C49FT	1987	Ex Premier Travel, 1989
	E316UUB	Volvo B10M-61	Plaxton Paramount 3500 III	C48FT	1988	Ex Wallace Arnold, 1991
B	E770HJF	Volvo B10M-61	Plaxton Paramount 3200 III	C57F	1988	
	F370MUT	Dennis Javelin 12SDA1906	Plaxton Paramount 3200 III	C53F	1988	Ex Patterson, Birmingham, 1994
	F743LOD	Dennis Javelin 8.5SDL1903	Plaxton Paramount 3200 III	C35F	1989	Ex Seward, Dalwood, 1992
	G513EFX	Volvo B10M-60	Plaxton Paramount 3200 III	C57F	1990	Ex Excelsior, 1991
	G344OWE	Volvo B10M-60	Plaxton Paramount 3200 III	C55DL	1990	
B	G303RJA	Dennis Javelin 12SDA1907	Plaxton Paramount 3200 III	C53F	1990	Ex Star Line, Knutsford, 1994
B	G964WNR	Toyota Coaster HB31R	Caetano Optimo	C21F	1990	
	H660AST	Dennis Javelin 11SDL1905	Plaxton Paramount 3200 III	C53F	1991	Ex Mayne, Buckie, 1993
	H688UAK	Dennis Javelin 8.5SDA1926	Plaxton Paramount 3200 III	C33FT	1991	
	H157HAC	Dennis Javelin 8.5SDA1926	Plaxton Paramount 3200 III	C35F	1991	Ex Supreme, Coventry, 1994
	H689UAK	Volvo B10M-60	Plaxton Paramount 3200 III	C55DL	1991	
	J1EXC	Volvo B10M-60	Plaxton Excalibur	C49F	1992	Ex Anderson, Horsforth, 1993

Previous Registrations:

ACX785Y	TVH138X	FIL7486	A910AHE
FIL7485	D849KVE	HAS716X	WJS840X, 3692NT

Livery: Red and cream

Centenary Way in Rotherham provides a good location for pictures of buses from several operators. Pictured in October 1994 was Gordons 35-seat Plaxton Paramount 3200 D813SHE. Based on a Bedford YMP chassis, this example is one of the last before Bedford ceased production of full-size PSVs.
Tony Wilson

HARROGATE & DISTRICT

Harrogate & District Travel Ltd, Petroleum House, Camwall Road, Starbeck, Harrogate, North Yorkshire HG1 4PT

A subsidiary of Blazefield Holdings Ltd.

Depots: Petroleum House and Dairycrest Yard, Camwall Road, Starbeck; Manse Lane, Knaresborough and Nidderdale High School, Pateley Bridge.

172	F172SMT	Leyland Swift LBM6T/2RA	Wadham Stringer Vanguard II	B39F	1988	Ex County, 1992
173	F173SMT	Leyland Swift LBM6T/2RA	Wadham Stringer Vanguard II	B39F	1988	Ex County, 1992
201	E961NMK	Leyland Swift LBM6T/2RS	Wadham Stringer Vanguard	B37F	1987	Ex Harrogate Independent, 1993
202	E962NMK	Leyland Swift LBM6T/2RS	Wadham Stringer Vanguard	B37F	1987	Ex Harrogate Independent, 1993
203	E963NMK	Leyland Swift LBM6T/2RS	Wadham Stringer Vanguard	B37F	1987	Ex Harrogate Independent, 1993
204	G111VMM	Leyland Swift LBM6T/2RA	Wadham Stringer Vanguard II	B37F	1989	Ex Harrogate Independent, 1993
206	G113VMM	Leyland Swift LBM6T/2RA	Wadham Stringer Vanguard II	B37F	1989	Ex Harrogate Independent, 1993
207	G114VMM	Leyland Swift LBM6T/2RA	Wadham Stringer Vanguard II	B37F	1989	Ex Harrogate Independent, 1993
222	G922WGS	Mercedes-Benz 709D	Reeve Burgess Beaver	B23F	1990	Ex Welwyn-Hatfield Line, 1993
223	G923WGS	Mercedes-Benz 709D	Reeve Burgess Beaver	B23F	1990	Ex Welwyn-Hatfield Line, 1993
224	F402XWR	Mercedes-Benz 811D	Optare StarRider	DP33F	1988	Ex Rover, Bromsgrove, 1994
249	G449LKW	Iveco Daily 49-10	Reeve Burgess Beaver	B25F	1989	Ex Yorkshire Coastliner, 1993
275	G275MWU	Iveco Daily 49-10	Reeve Burgess Beaver	B25F	1990	Ex Keighley & District, 1993
279	G279MWU	Iveco Daily 49-10	Reeve Burgess Beaver	B25F	1990	Ex Keighley & District, 1995
281	H12SDW	Iveco Daily 49-10	Reeve Burgess Beaver	B25F	1990	Ex Keighley & District, 1994
305	B263KPF	Leyland Tiger TRCTL11/2RH	Plaxton Paramount 3200 II	DP49F	1985	Ex Keighley & District, 1993
314	B514UWW	Leyland Olympian ONLXB/1R	Eastern Coach Works	DPH41/29F	1985	Ex Keighley & District, 1993
315	A605NYG	Leyland Olympian ONLXB/1R	Eastern Coach Works	DPH41/29F	1984	Ex Keighley & District, 1994
316	B516UWW	Leyland Olympian ONLXB/1R	Eastern Coach Works	H45/32F	1985	Ex York City & District, 1990
324	E324SWY	Leyland Lynx LX112LXCTZR1R	Leyland Lynx	B49F	1987	Ex York City & District, 1990
325	E325SWY	Leyland Lynx LX112LXCTZR1R	Leyland Lynx	B49F	1987	Ex York City & District, 1990

306   JIL2214

York rail station provides the background for this picture of Harrogate & District 202, E962NMK. A Wadham Stringer-bodied Leyland Swift, it is a late example of the early Vanguard style of bodywork from 1987. *Tony Wilson*

Vehicles often move between the northern area fleets within the Blazefield Holdings group. Harrogate & District 275, G275MWU, was previously with Keighley & District and is a Reeve Burgess Beaver-bodied Iveco Daily. *Phillip Stephenson*

330w	UWY70X	Leyland National 2 NL116AL11/1R		B52F	1981	Ex Keighley & District, 1993
336	SWX536W	Leyland National 2 NL116AL11/1R		B52F	1981	Ex Keighley & District, 1992
338	UWY64X	Leyland National 2 NL116AL11/1R		B52F	1981	Ex Keighley & District, 1992
339	SWX539W	Leyland National 2 NL116AL11/1R		B52F	1981	Ex York City & District, 1990
340	UWY67X	Leyland National 2 NL116AL11/1R		B52F	1981	Ex Keighley & District, 1992

361-365

		Volvo B10B-58	Alexander Strider	B51F	1995	

361	M388VWX	**362**	M389VWX	**363**	M390VWX	**364**	M391VWX	**365**	M392VWX

381	G381MWU	Leyland Lynx LX112L10ZR1R	Leyland Lynx	DP47F	1990	
382	G382MWU	Leyland Lynx LX112L10ZR1R	Leyland Lynx	DP47F	1990	
383	G383MWU	Leyland Lynx LX112L10ZR1R	Leyland Lynx	DP47F	1990	
384	G384MWX	Leyland Lynx LX112L10ZR1R	Leyland Lynx	DP47F	1990	
385	G297KWY	Leyland Lynx LX112L10ZR1R	Leyland Lynx	B49F.	1989	Ex Keighley & District, 1994
391	C482YWY	Leyland Olympian ONLXB/1R	Eastern Coach Works	H45/32F	1985	Ex Keighley & District, 1994
392	C481YWY	Leyland Olympian ONLXB/1R	Eastern Coach Works	DPH42/29F	1985	Ex Yorkshire Coastliner, 1994

645-654

		Volvo B6-9.9M	Alexander Dash	B40F	1994	

645	L645OWY	**647**	L647OWY	·649	L649OWY	**651**	L651OWY	**653**	L653OWY
646	L646OWY	**648**	L648OWY	**650**	L650OWY	**652**	L652OWY	**654**	L654OWY

664	M384VWX	Volvo B6-9.9M	Alexander Dash	B40F	1995
665	M385VWX	Volvo B6-9.9M	Alexander Dash	B40F	1995
666	M386VWX	Volvo B6-9.9M	Alexander Dash	B40F	1995
667	M387VWX	Volvo B6-9.9M	Alexander Dash	B40F	1995

Previous Registrations:
H12SDW   H281SWW

Livery: Red and cream

Vehicles are interchanged within the Blazefield group to meet service requirements, though no common numbering system exists between the various operations. Harrogate & District received four Leyland Lynx with high-back seating in 1990. In 1994 385, G297KWY, a bus-seated example was transferred from Keighley & District, and is seen arriving in Leeds. *Tony Wilson*

The Blazefield Group have recently invested heavily in Volvo B6 chassis with Alexander Dash bodies. Currently there are 14 such vehicles in the Harrogate and District fleet. No.645, L645OWY displays route branding for services 1 and 2. *Phillip Stephenson*

INDEPENDENT / THORNES

Thornes Motor Services Ltd, Derwent Garage, Bubwith, Selby,
North Yorkshire, YO8 7LT
Independent Coachways Ltd, Low Fold Garage, New Road Side, Horsforth,
Leeds, West Yorkshire, LS18 4DR
Edwards Coachways Ltd, Low Fold Garage, New Road Side, Horsforth,
Leeds, West Yorkshire, LS18 4DR

Depot: Derwent Garage, Bubwith and Low Fold Garage, Horsforth.

24	SMV24	Volvo B58-56	Plaxton Supreme V	C53F	1979	
32w	OKP980	Beadle-Leyland	Beadle	B39F	1952	Ex Maidstone & District, 1960
35	VHO200	Seddon Mk19	Harrington Wayfarer	C41F	1959	Ex Liss & District, 1961
43	UEL564J	Bristol RELL6G	Eastern Coach Works	DP50F	1971	Ex Hampshire Bus, 1984
44	UEL562J	Bristol RELL6G	Eastern Coach Works	DP50F	1970	Ex Hampshire Bus, 1984
46	GSL906N	Daimler Fleetline CRG6LXB	Alexander AL	H49/34D	1975	Ex Tayside, 1985
48	VOD101K	Bristol RELL6G	Eastern Coach Works	B53F	1971	Ex Devon General, 1985
49	UTT560J	Bristol RELL6G	Eastern Coach Works	B53F	1971	Ex Devon General, 1985
55	OWC719M	Bristol RELL6L	Eastern Coach Works	B53F	1973	Ex Colchester, 1988
57	THL261H	Bristol RELL6G	Eastern Coach Works	B53F	1970	Ex Farnell Instruments, 1989
71w	EWT386C	Bristol SUL4P	Eastern Coach Works	B36F	1965	Ex West Yorkshire Road Car, 1974
74	JCV385N	Bristol LHS6L	Plaxton Supreme III	C35F	1975	Ex Pollard, Ruan Minor, 1991
76w	MBO1F	Bristol LHS6L	Weymann	B30F	1968	Ex Western Welsh, 1977
78w	BAG150S	Bedford YMT	Plaxton Supreme III	C53F	1978	
79	VBT379V	Bedford YMT(Perkins)	Plaxton Supreme V Express	C53F	1979	
81w	JHP810N	Bedford YRT	Plaxton Elite III	C53F	1975	Ex Parr, Liverpool, 1981
85	B385JVY	Volvo B10M-61	Plaxton Paramount 3500	C49FT	1984	
86	LBT380N	AEC Reliance 6U3ZR	Plaxton Derwent	B66F	1975	Ex Premier, Stainforth, 1984

Thornes of Bubwith's VHO200 was obtained second-hand in 1961 and has since been maintained to full PSV standard by the operator. It is an unusual Harrington Wayfarer-bodied Seddon and is a regular participant at rallies throughout the North of England over the summer months. This view was taken on one of the vehicle's forays to Sandtoft. *Phillip Stephenson*

Seen passing Selby Minster is a former Tayside, Alexander-bodied Daimler Fleetline. Fleet number 46, GSL906N is now in Thornes blue, grey and red livery. Some eight years after its arrival from Dundee, it was joined by sister GSL907N which came via a more circuitous route. *David Cole*

93	VFN53	Volvo B10M-46	Plaxton Paramount 3200 II	C43F	1987	Ex Courtlands, Horley, 1989
94	F467WFX	Volvo B10M-60	Plaxton Paramount 3200 III	C53F	1989	Ex Excelsior, 1990
101	G27HKY	Scania K93CRB	Plaxton Paramount 3200 III	C57F	1990	Ex Premier Coaches, Dunnington, 1992
102	F427DUG	Volvo B10M-60	Plaxton Paramount 3200 III	C53F	1989	Ex Wallace Arnold, 1992
103	HBT378S	Freight Rover Sherpa	Carlyle	B18F	1987	Ex Ribble, 1992
104	BBT380V	Leyland National 2 NL116L11/1R		DP48F	1980	Ex West Riding, 1993
107	K500TMS	Volvo B10M-60	Plaxton Paramount 3200 III	C53F	1993	
109	NFA12M	Daimler Fleetline CRG6LX	Willowbrook	H44/33F	1973	Ex Circle Line, Gloucester, 1993
110	GSL907N	Daimler Fleetline CRG6LXB	Alexander AL	H49/38F	1975	Ex Cedar Coaches, Bedford, 1993
111	M600TMS	Volvo B10M-62	Plaxton Premiére 320	C53F	1995	
112	M700TMS	Volvo B10M-62	Plaxton Premiére 320	C53F	1995	
113	KNT815W	Bedford CFL	Plaxton Mini Supreme	C17F	1980	Ex Jervis Bros, Margam, 1994
114	NHN260K	Daimler Fleetline CRG6LX	Park Royal	B48D	1972	Ex Darlington, 1995
135	M200VHO	Volvo B10M-62	Plaxton Excalibur	C49FT	1995	

Operating companies: Independent 43/4/8/9, 55/7, 107/11/12; Edwards: 94, 102/4; Thornes: remainder

Previous Registrations:

BAG150S	HBT378S	LBT380N	HUM951N
BBT380V	CCY818V	SMV24	FNW24T
HBT378S	D829PUK	VFN53	D866YPH
JCV385N	LBT380N, KKH101N, WRL270		

Livery: Blue, grey and red

Named vehicles: 79 *Derwent Phaser*; 135 *Derwent Excalibur*

INGLEBY'S

Ingleby's Luxury Coaches Ltd, 24 Hospital Fields Road, Fulford, York,
North Yorkshire, YO1 4DZ

TRN731	Leyland Leopard PSU3/3R	Plaxton Panorama	C49F	1964	Ex Ribble, 1975
FAV8Y	Volvo B10M-61	Van Hool Alizée	C48FT	1983	Ex Kenzie, Shepreth, 1989
A71OUG	Volvo B10M-61	Plaxton Paramount 3200	C53F	1984	
B872FWA	Volvo B10M-61	Plaxton Paramount 3500 II	C53F	1985	Ex Clarke's of London, 1989
C486HAK	Volvo B10M-61	Plaxton Paramount 3500 II	C53F	1985	Ex Clarke's of London, 1992
C352DND	Volvo B10M-61	Plaxton Paramount 3200 II	C53F	1986	Ex Shearings, 1994
C180LWB	Volvo B10M-61	Plaxton Paramount 3500 II	C53F	1986	Ex Clarke's of London, 1993
E515CDS	Volvo B10M-60	Van Hool Alizée	C53F	1988	Ex Park's, 1994
M948JJU	Volvo B6-9M	Jonckheere Deauville Ascot	C35F	1995	

Previous Registrations:

C486HAK	C484HAK	E515CDS	E640UNE, UOT648

Livery: Light blue and cream

Photographed outside York rail station is UWR712R, a Plaxton Supreme-bodied Leyland Leopard. Now withdrawn from the fleet in favour of more Volvo B10Ms, it typifies the model so popular with operators in recent times. *Andrew Jarosz*

JARONDA TRAVEL

R, JM & CS Barwick, 15 Park Lane, Barlow, Selby, North Yorkshire, YO8 8JW

Depot: 32 Wistowgate, Cawood

OFB968R	Bristol LH6L	Eastern Coach Works	B43F	1977	Ex Bristol, 1985
DTL544T	Bristol LH6L	Eastern Coach Works	B43F	1978	Ex RoadCar, 1989
PVY767T	Bedford YMT	Duple Dominant	B63F	1979	Ex Munro, Uddingston, 1993
SVY500T	Bedford YMT	Duple Dominant II	C53F	1979	
G140GOL	Dennis Dart 9SDL3002	Duple Dartline	B39F	1990	
H878LOX	Dennis Dart 9SDL3002	Carlyle Dartline	B39F	1990	
K601HWR	Dennis Dart 9SDL3017	Plaxton Pointer	B43F	1992	

Livery: White and two-tone blue

The seven-vehicle fleet of Jaronda Travel may often be found in Selby where they wait time in the turning circle. However, OFB968R, a Bristol LH, is seen in nearby Cawood, the village where the depot is located.
Tony Wilson

Jaronda Travel operate a service from Selby to York through the village of Cawood. Here the service passes over a bridge across the River Ouse which is subject to a weight limit. The largest vehicle which can pass over this bridge is the Dart and three examples have been purchased for the service including H878LOX a Carlyle Dartline-bodied example built in 1992.
Phillip Stephenson

JOLLY ROGER

R G Flatt, 6 Birch Close, New Earswick, North Yorkshire YO3 8BH

Depot: Willow Tree Farm, Gowthorpe, Humberside and Townend Business Park, New Road, Newport, Humberside

SOE975H	Daimler Fleetline CRG6LX	Park Royal	H47/33D	1970	Ex Partridge, Hadleigh, 1992
PRG141J	Daimler Fleetline CRG6LX	Alexander L	H48/32D	1971	Ex Partridge, Hadleigh, 1992
NHN259K	Daimler Fleetline SRG6LX	Roe	B48D	1972	Ex Darlington, 1994
PYJ460L	Daimler Fleetline CRG6LX	Alexander AL	H49/34D	1972	Ex Partridge, Hadleigh, 1992
MTU666L	Bedford YRT	Plaxton Elite III	C53F	1973	Ex ??, Hull, 1993
RUR119M	Bedford YRT	Plaxton Elite III	C53F	1974	Ex Sampson, Hoddesdon, 1988
ONL923M	Bedford YRT	Plaxton Elite III	C53F	1974	Ex Bell, Stamfordham, 1989
NSJ200M	Bedford YRT	Plaxton Elite III Express	C53F	1974	Ex Maye, Astley, 1994
RMO495M	Bedford YRT	Plaxton Elite III	C53F	1974	Ex Hirst Brothers, New Earswick, 1994
GOG560N	Daimler Fleetline CRL6(6LXB)	Park Royal	H43/33F	1975	Ex Curtis Coaches, 1992
KUC989P	Leyland Fleetline FE30ALR	MCW	H44/24D	1976	Ex Red & Green Cs, Chislehurst, 1994
OJD128R	Leyland Fleetline FE30AGR	Park Royal	H43/32F	1976	Ex Hornsby, Ashby, 1994
OJD175R	Leyland Fleetline FE30AGR	MCW	H44/24D	1976	Ex Eddie Brown, Helperby, 1993
PVY769T	Bedford YMT	Plaxton Supreme IV	C53F	1979	Ex Hirst Brothers, New Earswick, 1994

Livery: Two-tone green

Named vehicles: SOE975H *Batholomue Roberts*; PRG141J *John Paul Jones*; PYJ460L *Nathaniel Gordon*; MTU666L *Long John Silver*; RUR119M *Captain Pugwash*; ONL923M *Captain Blood*; RMO495M *Captain Blackbeard*; GOG560N *Captain Morgan*; KUC989P *Captain Drake*; OJD128R *Captain Hook*; OJD175R *Captain Billy Bones*; PVY769T *Captain Kidd*.

Using famous pirate's names on all vehicles, Jolly Roger the Pocklington Pirate operates from two bases in Humberside. Seen here is Captain Blood ONL923M, a Bedford YRT with Plaxton Elite III bodywork, in the two-tone green livery used. On this vehicle the window surrounds are painted red.
Andrew Jarosz

K-LINE / TAYLORS

K-Line Travel Ltd, Unit 14, Whitehall Road Industrial Estate, Leeds
West Yorkshire, LS12 5JB

Depots: St Johns Road, Birkby, Huddersfield and Whitehall Road Industrial Estate, Leeds.

JJG905P	Leyland National 10351/1R		B41F	1975	Ex Pride of the Road, Huddersfield, 1994
PJT255R	Leyland National 10351A/1R		B41F	1976	Ex Pride of the Road, Huddersfield, 1994
EPD504V	Leyland National 10351B/1R		B41F	1979	Ex Sovereign, 1994
LRB211W	Leyland National 2 NL116L11/1R		DP48F	1981	Ex Independent, Horsforth, 1995
HLG50X	Bedford YNT	Plaxton Supreme V	C53F	1982	Ex Bostock, Congleton, 1989
G155NJX	MCW MetroRider MF154/1	MCW	DP26F	1990	
H512YCX	DAF SB220LC550	Optare Delta	DP48F	1991	Ex The Wright Company, Wrexham, 1994
L511EHD	DAF SB220LC550	Ikarus CitiBus	B48F	1993	
L512EHD	DAF SB220LC550	Ikarus CitiBus	B48F	1993	
M811RCP	DAF SB220LT550	Ikarus CitiBus	B49F	1994	
M812RCP	DAF SB220LT550	Ikarus CitiBus	B49F	1994	
M813RCP	DAF SB220LT550	Ikarus CitiBus	B49F	1994	
M814RCP	DAF SB220LT550	Ikarus CitiBus	B49F	1994	
M815RCP	DAF SB220LT550	Ikarus CitiBus	B49F	1994	
M816RCP	DAF SB220LT550	Ikarus CitiBus	B49F	1994	
M817RCP	DAF SB220LT550	Ikarus CitiBus	B49F	1994	
M818RCP	DAF SB220LT550	Ikarus CitiBus	B49F	1994	
M819RCP	DAF SB220LT550	Ikarus CitiBus	B49F	1994	

Livery: Cream, green and yellow.

The K-Line fleetname is gradually giving way to Taylors in this joint operation based in Leeds. The standard vehicle is the DAF SB220 with most examples having Hungarian built Ikarus CitiBus bodies supplied new. The exception is H512YCX, an Optare-bodied Delta aquired from The Wright Company, and seen here in Huddersfield. *Tony Wilson*

KEIGHLEY & DISTRICT

Keighley & District Travel Ltd, 20 Devonshire Street, Keighley, West Yorkshire, BD21 2AU

A subsidiary of Blazefield Holdings Ltd
Depots: Sureness Road, Keighley and Gargrave Road, Skipton

101-108
Mercedes-Benz 711D   Plaxton Beaver   B25F   1993

| 101 | L652MYG | 103 | L654MYG | 105 | L656MYG | 107 | L658MYG | 108 | L659MYG |
| 102 | L653MYG | 104 | L655MYG | 106 | L657MYG | | | | |

121	L660MYG	Mercedes-Benz 811D	Plaxton Beaver	B33F	1993	
122	L661MYG	Mercedes-Benz 811D	Plaxton Beaver	B33F	1993	
123	L662MYG	Mercedes-Benz 811D	Plaxton Beaver	B33F	1993	
124	L663MYG	Mercedes-Benz 811D	Plaxton Beaver	B33F	1993	
125	L664MYG	Mercedes-Benz 811D	Plaxton Beaver	B33F	1993	
194	G278MWU	Iveco Daily 49-10	Reeve Burgess Beaver	B25F	1990	Ex Harrogate & District, 1992
197	G277MWU	Iveco Daily 49-10	Reeve Burgess Beaver	B25F	1990	Ex Harrogate & District, 1995
198	G276MWU	Iveco Daily 49-10	Reeve Burgess Beaver	B25F	1990	Ex Harrogate & District, 1994

201-208
Leyland Lynx LX112L10ZR1R   Leyland Lynx   B49F   1989

| 201 | G293KWY | 203 | G295KWY | 206 | G298KWY | 207 | G299KWY | 208 | G300KWY |
| 202 | G294KWY | 204 | G296KWY | | | | | | |

221	L642OWY	Volvo B6-9.9M	Alexander Dash	B40F	1994
222	L643OWY	Volvo B6-9.9M	Alexander Dash	B40F	1994
223	L644OWY	Volvo B6-9.9M	Alexander Dash	B40F	1994

Opposite: **The latest liveries for Keighley & District are seen here. The popular midibus, here in the form of 221, L642OWY, a Volvo B6 with Alexander Dash bodywork is seen in Keighley, while route branding is seen on 902, L649MYG.** *Lee Whitehead/Tony Wilson*

Below: **1993 saw the introduction of thirteen Plaxton Beaver-bodied Mercedes vehicles into the Keighley & District fleet. No.106, L657MYG seats twenty-five on a 711D chassis and is seen loading in Keighley bus station for Riddlesden.** *Lee Whitehead*

240	G62RGG	Volvo B10M-60	Plaxton Paramount 3500 III	C49FT	1990	Ex Bryan, Leicester, 1994
241	F884RFP	Volvo B10M-61	Plaxton Paramount 3500 III	C49FT	1989	Ex Cambridge Coach Services, 1994
243	A906LWU	Leyland Tiger TRCTL11/3R	Plaxton Paramount 3200 E	C53F	1983	Ex West Yorkshire, 1989
244	JIL2215	Leyland Tiger TRCTL11/3R	Plaxton Paramount 3200 E	C49F	1983	Ex West Yorkshire, 1989
246	B264KPF	Leyland Tiger TRCTL11/2RH	Plaxton Paramount 3200 II E	C49F	1985	Ex Sovereign, 1992
247	HIL2395	Leyland Tiger TRCTL11/3R	Plaxton Paramount 3200	C50F	1983	Ex Ingfield-Northern Rose, 1994
248	JIL2216	Leyland Tiger TRCTL11/3RH	Plaxton Paramount 3200 E	C53F	1983	Ex Lancaster, 1993
250	G435MWU	Leyland Tiger TRCL10/3RZA	Plaxton Paramount 3200 III	C55F*	1990	Ex Yorkshire Coastliner, 1994

251-262

Leyland National 10351B/1R — B44F — 1978-79 Ex West Yorkshire, 1989

251	DNW839T	253	DNW841T	256	DNW844T	258	FUG320T	261	FUG325T
252	DNW840T	254	DNW842T	257	DNW845T	260	FUG324T	262	FUG326T

263	EPD542V	Leyland National 10351B/1R		B41F	1979	Ex Sovereign, 1992
272	PWY584W	Leyland National 2 NL106AL11/1R		B44F	1980	Ex Harrogate & District, 1994

331-336

Leyland Olympian ON2R50G13Z4 Northern Counties Palatine H43/30F — 1990

331	H513RWX	333	H515RWX	334	H516RWX	335	H517RWX	336	H519RWX
332	H514RWX								

347	A604NYG	Leyland Olympian ONLXB/1R	Eastern Coach Works	DPH41/29F	1984	Ex Harrogate & District, 1992
348	A602NYG	Leyland Olympian ONLXB/1R	Eastern Coach Works	DPH41/29F	1984	Ex Harrogate & District, 1992
349	B517UWW	Leyland Olympian ONLXB/1R	Eastern Coach Works	H45/32F	1985	Ex Harrogate & District, 1992
350	FUM485Y	Leyland Olympian ONLXB/1R	Eastern Coach Works	H45/32F	1983	Ex Harrogate & District, 1992

351-373

Leyland Olympian ONLXB/1R Eastern Coach Works H45/32F 1982-85 Ex West Yorkshire, 1989
*361/8-70 are DPH41/29F

351	DWW926Y	356	DWW931Y	360	FUM488Y	364	FUM500Y	369	A603NYG
352	DWW927Y	357	DWW932Y	361	FUM490Y	365	A92KWW	370	B91SWX
353	DWW928Y	358	FUM483Y	362	FUM493Y	367	A95KWW	371	B515UWW
354	DWW929Y	359	FUM484Y	363	FUM497Y	368	A96KWW	373	C484YWY
355w	DWW930Y								

381-388

Leyland Olympian ONLXB/1R Eastern Coach Works H45/32F 1983-84 Ex York City & District, 1990
*384 is DPH41/29F

381	A683MWX	383	A685MWX	385	B92SWX	387	A94KWW	388	FUM496Y
382	A684MWX	384	B90SWX	386	A93KWW				

389-393

Leyland Olympian ONLXB/1R Eastern Coach Works DPH42/29F 1985 Ex Yorkshire Coastliner, 1992-94

389	B521UWW	390	B522UWW	391	B524UWW	392	C479YWY	393	C480YWY

901	L648MYG	Leyland Olympian ON2R50C13Z4 Alexander RH	H45/29F	1993	
902	L649MYG	Leyland Olympian ON2R50C13Z4 Alexander RH	H45/29F	1993	
903	L650MYG	Leyland Olympian ON2R50C13Z4 Alexander RH	H45/29F	1993	
904	L651MYG	Leyland Olympian ON2R50C13Z4 Alexander RH	H45/29F	1993	
905	K2YCL	Leyland Olympian ON2R50C13Z4 Northern Counties Palatine	DPH43/27F	1992	Ex Yorkshire Coastliner, 1995
906	K6YCL	Leyland Olympian ON2R50C13Z4 Northern Counties Palatine	DPH43/27F	1992	Ex Yorkshire Coastliner, 1995
907	K7YCL	Leyland Olympian ON2R50C13Z4 Northern Counties Palatine	DPH43/27F	1992	Ex Yorkshire Coastliner, 1995
972	BPF131Y	Leyland Olympian ONTL11/1R	Roe	H43/29F	1983	Ex Sovereign, 1993
973	BPF134Y	Leyland Olympian ONTL11/1R	Roe	H43/29F	1983	Ex Sovereign, 1992

974-980

Leyland Olympian ONTL11/1R Eastern Coach Works H43/29F 1985 Ex County, 1990

974	B261LPH	976	B265LPH	977	B266LPH	979	B268LPH	980	B269LPH
975	B264LPH								

KDG26	CWX671	Bristol K5G	Roe (1950)	L27/28R	1938	Ex preservation, 1993

Livery: White, red and blue (buses); dark blue (coaches).

Previous Registrations:

HIL2395	JNM756Y	JIL2215	A910LWU	JIL2216	A621ATV

The number of Leyland Nationals in the Keighley & District fleet continues to dwindle, however several 44 seat examples are still in service including 263, EPD542V, which was obtained from fellow Blazefield subsidiary Sovereign in 1992. *Phillip Stephenson*

In 1990 a major exchange of vehicles occurred within the Blazefield group resulting in several Leyland Olympians moving north from the former London Country fleets. From the County fleet came 976, B265LPH, a high-bridge version of the Eastern Coach Works/Leyland Olympian supplied to National Bus. It is seen in Keighley bus station. *Paul Wigan*

KHCT

Kingston-upon-Hull City Transport Ltd, Lombard Street, Kingston-upon-Hull, North Humberside, HU2 8QN

A subsidiary of Stagecoach Holdings plc

42	BUT24Y	Dennis Dorchester SDA801	Plaxton Paramount 3200	C49F	1983	Ex Leicester, 1987
43	BUT25Y	Dennis Dorchester SDA801	Plaxton Paramount 3200	C49F	1983	Ex Leicester, 1987
50	IIL1319	Volvo B10M-61	Plaxton Paramount 3200 II	C50FT	1986	
51	IIL1321	Volvo B10M-61	Plaxton Paramount 3200 III	C50FT	1986	
52	E52WAG	Volvo B10M-61	Plaxton Paramount 3200 III	C50FT	1988	
53	F53EAT	Dennis Javelin SDA1907	Plaxton Paramount 3200 III	C48FT	1989	
55	F55EAT	Dennis Javelin SDA1907	Plaxton Paramount 3200 III	C49FT	1989	
56	G56SAG	Volvo B10M-61	Plaxton Paramount 3500 III	C48FT	1990	
60	B60WKH	Leyland National 2 NL116HLXCT/1R		B24DL	1984	
61	YAY21Y	Dennis Lancet SD506	Duple Dominant	B25DL	1982	Ex Leicester, 1987
71	H71XKH	Leyland Swift ST2R44C97A4	Reeve Burgess Harrier	C34FT	1990	

106-110   Dennis Dominator DDA904   Alexander RL   H43/32F   1984

106	B106UAT	107	B107UAT	108	B108UAT	109	B109UAT	110	B110UAT

111	C111CAT	Dennis Dominator DDA1007	East Lancashire	H43/28F	1985
112	C112CAT	Dennis Dominator DDA1007	East Lancashire	H43/28F	1985
113	C113CAT	Dennis Dominator DDA1007	East Lancashire	DPH43/28F	1985

122-131   Dennis Dominator DDA1006   East Lancashire   H45/30F   1985

122	C122CAT	124	C124CAT	128	C128CAT	129	C129CAT	131	C131CAT
123	C123CAT	125	C125CAT						

132	E132SAT	Dennis Dominator DDA1014	East Lancashire (1992)	H45/21D	1987

133-141   Dennis Dominator DDA1014   East Lancashire   H45/32F   1987

133	E133SAT	135	E135SAT	137	E137SAT	139	E139SAT	141	E141SAT
134	E134SAT	136	E136SAT	138	E138SAT	140	E140SAT		

142-151   Dennis Dominator DDA1016   East Lancashire   H45/31F   1988

142	F142BKH	144	F144BKH	146	F146BKH	148	F148BKH	150	F150BKH
143	F143BKH	145	F145BKH	147	F147BKH	149	F149BKH	151	F151BKH

152-157   Dennis Dominator DDA1027   East Lancashire   H47/33F   1989

152	F152HAT	154	F154HAT	155	F155HAT	156	F156HAT	157	F157HAT
153	F153HAT								

204	J204JKH	Volvo B10M-60	Plaxton Paramount 3500 III	C51FT	1991	Ex York Pullman, 1993
205	J205JKH	Volvo B10M-60	Plaxton Paramount 3500 III	C51FT	1991	Ex York Pullman, 1993

506-515   MCW Metrobus DR102/7   MCW   H43/32F   1980

506	LAT506V	509	LAT509V	511	LAT511V	513	LAT513V	515	LAT515V
507	LAT507V	510	LAT510V	512	LAT512V	514	LAT514V		

516-530   MCW Metrobus DR102/17   MCW   H43/32F   1981

516	SAG516W	519	SAG519W	522	SAG522W	525	SAG525W	528	SAG528W
517	SAG517W	520	SAG520W	523	SAG523W	526	SAG526W	529	SAG529W
518	SAG518W	521	SAG521W	524	SAG524W	527	SAG527W	530	SAG530W

601-615   Iveco Daily 49-10   Robin Hood City Nippy   B25F*   1987   *602 is B18F

601	D601MKH	605	D605MKH	609	D609MKH	612	D612MKH	614	D614MKH
602	D602MKH	608	D608MKH	611	D611MKH	613	D613MKH	615	D615MKH
603	D603MKH								

Kingston-upon-Hull became a member of the Stagecoach group in 1994, and is to retain the white, blue and yellow livery for some time as part of the purchase agreement. Seen in the city is Dennis Dominator 113, C113CAT, one of a trio added to the fleet in 1985. It now features high-back seating as seen in this 1995 view. *Tony Wilson*

The standard double-deck in the Kingston-upon-Hull fleet is the Dennis Dominator. Most have East Lancashire bodywork with many featuring Alexander-influenced styling like 139, E139SAT. *Tony Wilson*

701-706

Scania N112CRB		East Lancashire		DP49F*		1988	*703 is B50F	

701	F701BAT	**703**	F703BAT	**704**	F704BAT	**705**	F705BAT	**706** F706CAG
702	F702BAT							

707-718

Volvo B10M-55   Northern Counties Paladin   B48F   1995

707	M707KRH	**710**	M710KRH	**713**	M713KRH	**715**	M715KRH	**717** M717KRH
708	M708KRH	**711**	M711KRH	**714**	M714KRH	**716**	M716KRH	**718** M718KRH
709	M709KRH	**712**	M712KRH					

801-816

Scania N113DRB   East Lancashire   H51/37F   1989-90   *809-16 are H47/37F

801	G801JRH	**805**	G805JRH	**808**	G808LAG	**811**	H811WKH	**814** H814WKH
802	G802JRH	**806**	G806JRH	**809**	H809WKH	**812**	H812WKH	**815** H815WKH
803	G803JRH	**807**	G807LAG	**810**	H810WKH	**813**	H813WKH	**816** H816WKH
804	G804JRH							

817	M817KRH	Volvo Olympian YN2RV18Z4	Northern Counties Palatine	H47/29F	1995
818	M818KRH	Volvo Olympian YN2RV18Z4	Northern Counties Palatine	H47/29F	1995
819	M819KRH	Volvo Olympian YN2RV18Z4	Northern Counties Palatine	H47/29F	1995

Previous Registrations:

IIL1319	C50FRH	IIL1321	D51ORH	KKH650	From new

Livery: Blue and white

Latest deliveries to KHCT are twelve Volvo B10Ms from the 1995 Stagecoach investment programme. Forty of the type have been supplied with Northern Counties bodywork including those allocated to Hull, Cleveland and Hartlepool. Photographed on its first weekends work is 707, M707KRH. One all twelve are in service the loaned examples from Stagecoach Manchester are to be returned to Ribble.
Lee Whitehead

LEON

Leon Motor Services Ltd, Finningley House, Old Bawtry Road, Finningley,
South Yorkshire, DN9 3DD

96	XKU903T	Leyland Fleetline FE30ALR(6LXB)	Northern Counties	H43/32F	1978	
97	BKW580T	Bedford YMT	Plaxton Supreme IV Express	C53F	1979	
99	GWF571V	Bedford YMT	Duple Dominant II Express	C53F	1980	
101	HKU361W	Leyland Fleetline FE30AGR	Alexander AD	H44/31F	1980	
102	BGY606T	Bedford YMT	Duple Dominant II	C53F	1979	Ex National Travel London, 1982
103	MHE50P	Leyland Fleetline FE30AGR	Roe	H44/34F	1976	Ex South Yorkshire PTE, 1983
104	LEO163	Leyland Tiger TRCTL11/3R	Van Hool Alizée	C48F	1983	
108	MPL135W	Leyland Leopard PSU3E/4R	Duple Dominant IV Express	C53F	1981	Ex London Country, 1986
109	D734PWF	Mercedes-Benz 609D	Reeve Burgess	DP19F	1987	
110	D736PWF	Mercedes-Benz 609D	Reeve Burgess	DP19F	1987	
111	PRJ500R	Daimler Fleetline CRG6LXB	Northern Counties	H43/32F	1976	Ex Greater Manchester, 1987
112	C809KBT	Leyland Cub CU435	Optare	B33F	1986	Ex Yorkshire Rider, 1987
113	C811KBT	Leyland Cub CU435	Optare	B33F	1986	Ex Yorkshire Rider, 1987
116	4395EL	Leyland Tiger TRCTL11/3R	Duple Caribbean	C51F	1983	Ex Hirdle, Boscombe, 1988
117	GSD723V	Leyland Fleetline FE30AGR	Alexander AL	H45/33F	1980	Ex AA (Dodds), Troon, 1988
118	GSD724V	Leyland Fleetline FE30AGR	Alexander AL	H45/33F	1980	Ex AA (Dodds), Troon, 1988
119	CHL619V	Leyland Atlantean AN68A/1R	Roe	H43/34F	1979	Ex South Yorkshire, 1989
120	MSU174	Leyland Tiger TRCTL11/3R	Van Hool Alizée	C53F	1983	Ex BRC, Tockington, 1989
121	NAK322R	Leyland Atlantean AN68A/1R	East Lancashire	H43/32F	1976	Ex South Yorkshire, 1989
122	C171AWK	Leyland Royal Tiger RT	Van Hool Alizée	C49FT	1986	Ex Harry Shaw, Coventry, 1990
123	NOC435R	Leyland Fleetline FE30AGR	MCW	H43/33F	1977	Ex West Midlands Travel, 1990
124	NOC465R	Leyland Fleetline FE30AGR	MCW	H43/33F	1977	Ex West Midlands Travel, 1990
125	NOC391R	Leyland Fleetline FE30ALR	MCW	H43/33F	1976	Ex West Midlands Travel, 1990
126	SDA561S	Leyland Fleetline FE30AGR	MCW	H43/33F	1978	Ex West Midlands Travel, 1990
127	GDZ885	Leyland Tiger TRCTL11/3RZ	Van Hool Alizée	C51D	1985	Ex Travellers, Hounslow, 1991

Leon operate two of the batch of Optare-bodied Leyland Cubs new to West Yorkshire PTE and purchased from its successor, Yorkshire Rider. Photographed while on lay-over at the south bus station in Doncaster is 112, C809KBT. *Tony Wilson*

128	TWH700T	Leyland Fleetline FE30AGR	Northern Counties	H43/32F	1979	Ex GM Buses, 1991
129	ANA49T	Leyland Fleetline FE30AGR	Northern Counties	H43/32F	1979	Ex GM Buses, 1991
130	F101RTR	Leyland Lynx LX112L10ZR1S	Leyland Lynx	B49F	1989	Ex Southampton, 1991
131	F103RTR	Leyland Lynx LX112L10ZR1S	Leyland Lynx	B49F	1989	Ex Southampton, 1991
132	FIL4145	Leyland Tiger TRCTL11/3R	Van Hool Alizée	C50FT	1984	Ex Beeston, Hadleigh, 1992
133	FIL4146	Leyland Tiger TRCTL11/3R	Van Hool Alizée	C50FT	1984	Ex Beeston, Hadleigh, 1992
134	TSJ34S	Leyland Fleetline FE30AGR	Northern Counties	H44/31F	1978	Ex Western Scottish, 1992
135	G473PGE	Leyland Lynx LX112L10ZR1R	Leyland Lynx 2	B51F	1989	Ex Whitelaw, Stonehouse, 1993
136	M926TYG	Optare MetroRider	Optare	B31F	1994	
137	M927TYG	Optare MetroRider	Optare	B31F	1994	
138	ASA24T	Leyland Fleetline FE30AGR	Eastern Coach Works	H43/32F	1978	Ex Western, 1995
139	ASA26T	Leyland Fleetline FE30AGR	Eastern Coach Works	H43/32F	1978	Ex Western, 1995
140	LMS160W	Leyland Fleetline FE30AGR	Alexander AD	H44/31F	1980	Ex Western, 1995

Previous Registrations:

4395EL	KGS482Y	FIL4146	B331ANY		LEO163	VKY541Y
C171AWK	HS8882	GDZ885	B327AMH		MSU174	NYS61Y
FIL4145	B332ANY					

Livery: Two-tone blue and grey.

New double-deck deliveries to Leon have featured Northern Counties bodywork, and so do two acquired from GM Buses in 1991. New to Lancashire United, 128, TWH700T is seen in St Sepulchre Gate, Doncaster.
Tony Wilson

The first new buses for Leon Motor Services for sometime have been two 31-seat Optare MetroRiders. Hatfield and Stainford station is the location of this view of 136 M926TYG. A Regional Railways Alexander-bodied Pacer train can be seen in the background.
Mike Fowler

LONGSTAFF

J J Longstaff & Sons Ltd, 2 Shillbank Lane, Mirfield, West Yorkshire, WF13 1LH

Depot: Eastfield Garage, Stoney Lane, Ravensthorpe

YHD599V	Volvo B58-56	Duple Dominant	B63F	1979	
D51YVH	Volvo B10M-61	Plaxton Paramount 3500 III	C53F	1987	
E479UOF	MCW Metrobus DR102/65	MCW	H43/30F	1988	Ex London Buses, 1991
E447LCX	Volvo B10M-61	Van Hool Alizée	C53F	1988	
F694ACX	Volvo B10M-60	Van Hool Alizée	C53F	1989	
M123SKY	Volvo B10M-62	Van Hool Alizée	C49F	1994	

Livery: Blue, grey and white

The only double-decker now with Longstaff is E479UOF, a MCW Metrobus new to London Buses at Harrow in 1988 and released when only three years old. It is seen in Dewsbury on its normal haunt, route 205 to Mirfield.
John Robinson

Longstaff of Mirfield operate one service together with a number of top line coaches. D51YVH is a Plaxton Paramount 3500 bodied Volvo B10M which was purchased new in 1987 and carries the blue, grey and white Longstaff livery.
Phillip Stephenson

MAINLINE

Mainline Group Ltd, 8 Riverside Court Newhall Road, South Yorkshire, S9 1BX
Sheffield United Transport Ltd, 8 Riverside Court Newhall Road, South Yorkshire, S9 1BX

Depots: Leger Way, Doncaster; Bootham Lane, Dunscroft; Station Road, Halfway; Midland Road, Rotherham; Greenland Road, Sheffield and Olive Grove, Sheffield.

10	AAK110T	Leyland National 10351B/1R		B44F	1979	
19	JKW219W	Leyland Leopard PSU3G/4R	Duple Dominant	C53F	1981	
20	JKW220W	Leyland Leopard PSU3G/4R	Duple Dominant	C53F	1981	

22-29

Leyland National 2 NL116L11/1R — B48F* — 1980 — *26 is B22DL; 25/7 are B52F

22	KWA22W	25	KWA25W	26	KWA26W	27	KWA27W	29	KWA29W
23	KWA23W								

62	YPD122Y	Leyland Tiger TRCTL11/2R	Duple Dominant IV Express	C53F	1983	Ex Sheafline, Sheffield, 1990
63	YPD103Y	Leyland Tiger TRCTL11/2R	Duple Dominant IV Express	C53F	1983	Ex Sheafline, Sheffield, 1990
69	KIB6110	Leyland Leopard PSU3D/4R	Plaxton Derwent (1987)	B55F	1977	Ex Compass, Wakefield, 1989
98	FWA498V	Leyland Leopard PSU3E/4R	Duple Dominant II Express	DP53F	1980	
147w	D147RAK	Renault-Dodge S56	Reeve Burgess	B25F	1987	
165	D165RAK	Renault-Dodge S56	Reeve Burgess	B25F	1987	
171u	E171UWF	Renault-Dodge S56	Reeve Burgess	B25F	1987	
175u	E175UWF	Renault-Dodge S56	Reeve Burgess	B25F	1987	
177	E177UWF	Renault-Dodge S56	Reeve Burgess	B25F	1987	

190-219

Renault-Dodge S56 — Reeve Burgess Beaver — B25F — 1988

190	E190XWG	196	E196XWG	202	E202XWG	208	E208XWG	214	E214XWG
191	E191XWG	197	E197XWG	203	E203XWG	209	E209XWG	215	E215XWG
192	E192XWG	198	E198XWG	204	E204XWG	210	E210XWG	216	E216XWG
193	E193XWG	199	E199XWG	205	E205XWG	211	E211XWG	217	E217XWG
194	E194XWG	200	E200XWG	206	E206XWG	212	E212XWG	218	E218XWG
195	E195XWG	201	E201XWG	207	E207XWG	213	E213XWG	219	E219XWG

220-239

Renault-Dodge S56 — Northern Counties — B23F* — 1989 — *228-39 are B25F

220	F220EWG	224	F224EWG	228	F228EWG	232	F232EWG	236	F236EWG
221	F221EWG	225	F225EWG	229	F229EWG	233	F233EWG	237	F237EWG
222	F222EWG	226	F226EWG	230	F230EWG	234	F234EWG	238	F238EWG
223	F223EWG	227	F227EWG	231	F231EWG	235	F235EWG	239	F239EWG

240-254

Renault-Dodge S56 — Reeve Burgess Beaver — B25F — 1988 — Ex Lincoln, 1989

240	E425XKU	243	E403BCT	246	E406BCT	249	E409BCT	252	E412BCT
241	E401BCT	244	E404BCT	247	E407BCT	250	E410BCT	253	E413BCT
242	E402BCT	245	E405BCT	248	E408BCT	251	E411BCT	254	E414BCT

255	E415BCT	Iveco Daily 49-10	Reeve Burgess Beaver	B21F	1988	Ex Lincoln, 1989
256	E416BCT	Iveco Daily 49-10	Reeve Burgess Beaver	B21F	1988	Ex Lincoln, 1989
257	E417BCT	Iveco Daily 49-10	Reeve Burgess Beaver	B21F	1988	Ex Lincoln, 1989
258	E418BCT	Iveco Daily 49-10	Reeve Burgess Beaver	B21F	1988	Ex Lincoln, 1989
287	SWB287L	Leyland Atlantean AN68/1R	Alexander AL	O43/31F	1973	

In 1988 Lincoln City Transport started an operation called Betta Bus in Scunthorpe which only lasted nine months. The vehicles used in Scunthorpe are now operated by Mainline and include four Iveco Daily minibuses with Reeve Burgess Beaver bodies. No.258 E418BCT is one of these vehicles. *Phillip Stephenson*

Mainline's open-top Leyland Atlantean 287, SWB287L, was used on local bus services between June and August 1994. Taking advantage of the fine weather in July were several passengers heading for Intake. *Lee Whitehead*

301-350 — Renault-Dodge S56 — Reeve Burgess Beaver — B23F — 1990

301	G301NWB	311	G311NWB	321	G321NWB	331	G331NWB	341	G341NWB
302	G302NWB	312	G312NWB	322	G322NWB	332	G332NWB	342	G342NWB
303	G303NWB	313	G313NWB	323	G323NWB	333	G333NWB	343	G343NWB
304	G304NWB	314	G314NWB	324	G324NWB	334	G334NWB	344	H344RKU
305	G305NWB	315	G315NWB	325	G325NWB	335	G335NWB	345	H345RKU
306	G306NWB	316	G316NWB	326	G326NWB	336	G336NWB	346	H346RKU
307	G307NWB	317	G317NWB	327	G327NWB	337	G337NWB	347	H347RKU
308	G308NWB	318	G318NWB	328	G328NWB	338	G338NWB	348	H348RKU
309	G309NWB	319	G319NWB	329	G329NWB	339	G339NWB	349	H349RKU
310	G310NWB	320	G320NWB	330	G330NWB	340	G340NWB	350	H569SWJ

351-389 — Renault-Dodge S56 — Reeve Burgess Beaver — B23F — 1991 — 386-9 are B21F

351	H351UWB	359	H359UWB	367	H367UWB	375	H375UWB	383	H383UWB
352	H352UWB	360	H390UWB	368	H368UWB	376	H376UWB	384	H384UWB
353	H353UWB	361	H361UWB	369	H369UWB	377	H377UWB	385	H385UWB
354	H354UWB	362	H362UWB	370	H370UWB	378	H378UWB	386	H386UWB
355	H355UWB	363	H363UWB	371	H371UWB	379	H379UWB	387	H387UWB
356	H356UWB	364	H364UWB	372	H372UWB	380	H380UWB	388	H388UWB
357	H357UWB	365	H365UWB	373	H373UWB	381	H381UWB	389	H389UWB
358	H358UWB	366	H366UWB	374	H374UWB	382	H382UWB		

401	K401EDT	Volvo B6-8.5M	Plaxton Pointer	B34F	1992
402	K402EDT	Dennis Dart 9SDL3016	Northern Counties Paladin	B35F	1992
403	L456JCK	Volvo B10L	Säffle Karosseri	B40D	1994 — Volvo development vehicle

411-440 — Volvo B6-9.9M — Plaxton Pointer — B40F — 1995

411	M411VHE	417	M417VHE	423	M423VHE	429	M429VHE	435	M435VHE
412	M412VHE	418	M418VHE	424	M424VHE	430	M430VHE	436	M436VHE
413	M413VHE	419	M419VHE	425	M425VHE	431	M431VHE	437	M437VHE
414	M414VHE	420	M420VHE	426	M426VHE	432	M432VHE	438	M438VHE
415	M415VHE	421	M421VHE	427	M427VHE	433	M433VHE	439	M439VHE
416	M416VHE	422	M422VHE	428	M428VHE	434	M434VHE	440	M440VHE

The latest arrivals with Mainline are thirty Volvo B6s built in Scotland. These follow evaluation of similar vehicle 401, K401EDT which was built at the Volvo-owned Steyr plant outside Vienna. It is seen on service 70 passing along Charter Row in Sheffield. *Tony Wilson*

In addition to the B6, Mainline also took delivery in 1992 of a Dennis Dart. This example, 402, K402EDT was bodied by Northern Counties with dutch-inspired Paladin design and is seen in the Haymarket part of Sheffield. *Tony Wilson*

One of the thirty B6s currently on delivery is 413, M413VHE, seen here in Pond Street, Sheffield. Also due are a further twenty-five Volvo B10Ms which are to receive Alexander's PS-style of bodywork. The seating on this latest batch may differ, as the latest chassis variant of the B10M features its radiator positioned between axles on the nearside. *Tony Wilson*

The mainstay of the Mainline single-deck fleet is the Volvo B10M with Alexander's PS-type bodywork, the first being delivered in 1990. The latest twenty-five now in build may require a change in seating capacity as the radiator on the latest variant of the chassis is now located between axles on the nearside. Photographed with Rotherham Mainline titles is 655, H655THL. *Tony Wilson*

601-650

Volvo B10M-55   Alexander PS   B51F   1990

601	G601NWA	611	G611NWA	621	G621NWA	631	G631NWA	641	G641NWA
602	G602NWA	612	G612NWA	622	G622NWA	632	G632NWA	642	H642RKU
603	G603NWA	613	G613NWA	623	G623NWA	633	G633NWA	643	H643RKU
604	G604NWA	614	G614NWA	624	G624NWA	634	G634NWA	644	H644RKU
605	G605NWA	615	G615NWA	625	G625NWA	635	G635NWA	645	H645RKU
606	G606NWA	616	G616NWA	626	G626NWA	636	G636NWA	646	H646RKU
607	G607NWA	617	G617NWA	627	G627NWA	637	G637NWA	647	H647RKU
608	G608NWA	618	G618NWA	628	G628NWA	638	G638NWA	648	H648RKU
609	G609NWA	619	G619NWA	629	G629NWA	639	G639NWA	649	H649RKU
610	G610NWA	620	G620NWA	630	G630NWA	640	G640NWA	650	H650RKU

651-690

Volvo B10M-55   Alexander PS   B51F   1991

651	H651THL	659	H659THL	667	H667THL	675	H675THL	683	H683THL
652	H652THL	660	H660THL	668	H668THL	676	H676THL	684	H684THL
653	H653THL	661	H661THL	669	H669THL	677	H677THL	685	H685THL
654	H654THL	662	H662THL	670	H670THL	678	H678THL	686	H686THL
655	H655THL	663	H663THL	671	H671THL	679	H679THL	687	H687THL
656	H656THL	664	H664THL	672	H672THL	680	H680THL	688	H688THL
657	H657THL	665	H665THL	673	H673THL	681	H681THL	689	J689XAK
658	H658THL	666	H691THL	674	H674THL	682	H682THL	690	J690XAK

691-715

Volvo B10M-55   Alexander PS   B51F   1992

691	J691AWF	696	J696AWF	701	J701AWF	706	K706EDT	711	K711EDT
692	J692AWF	697	J697AWF	702	J702AWF	707	K707EDT	712	K712EDT
693	J693AWF	698	J698AWF	703	J703AWF	708	K708EDT	713	K713EDT
694	J694AWF	699	J699AWF	704	J704AWF	709	K709EDT	714	K714EDT
695	J695AWF	700	J794AWF	705	J705AWF	710	K710EDT	715	K715EDT

716-740

Volvo B10M-55   Alexander PS   B..F   1995

716	M716VET	721	M421VET	726	M726VET	731	M731VET	736	M736VET
717	M717VET	722	M422VET	727	M727VET	732	M732VET	737	M737VET
718	M718VET	723	M423VET	728	M728VET	733	M733VET	738	M738VET
719	M719VET	724	M424VET	729	M729VET	734	M734VET	739	M739VET
720	M720VET	725	M425VET	730	M730VET	735	M735VET	740	M740VET

Two integral Auwaerter Neoplan N416s are operated by Mainline arriving in the SUT fleet who were also the UK importers and dealers for the product. Now numbered 803 with Mainline, F616CWJ was photographed in Doncaster. *Tony Wilson*

800u	JKW315W	Leyland Atlantean AN68B/1R	Marshall	H45/29D	1981	
802	E101VWA	Auwaerter Neoplan N416/SLII	Auwaerter	B50F	1987	Ex Carlton demonstrator, 1988
803	F616CWJ	Auwaerter Neoplan N416/SLII	Auwaerter	B50F	1988	
804	TVP853S	Leyland National 11351A/1R		DP45F	1978	Ex West Midlands Travel, 1992
805	NOE595R	Leyland National 11351A/1R	East Lancs Greenway (1992)	B48F	1977	Ex London & Country, 1992
806	CWX669T	Leyland National 11351A/1R	East Lancs Greenway (1992)	B48F	1979	Ex West Riding, 1990
809	CWX666T	Leyland National 11351A/1R		B49F	1979	Ex Sheafline, 1990
810	EUM896T	Leyland National 11351A/1R		B49F	1979	Ex Sheafline, 1990
811	EUM898T	Leyland National 11351A/1R		B49F	1979	Ex Sheafline, 1990
813	TUG809R	Leyland National 11351A/1R		B49F	1977	Ex Sheafline, 1990
814	TUG810R	Leyland National 11351A/1R		B49F	1977	Ex Sheafline, 1990
815	VNO735S	Leyland National 11351A/1R		B49F	1977	Ex Eastern National, 1992
817w	CWX663T	Leyland National 11351A/1R		B49F	1979	Ex Sheafline, 1991
818	CWX665T	Leyland National 11351A/1R		B49F	1979	Ex Sheafline, 1990
819	CWX668T	Leyland National 11351A/1R		B49F	1979	Ex West Riding, 1990
820	LMA414T	Leyland National 11351A/1R(6LXB)		B49F	1979	Ex Crosville Wales, 1988
821	UTU982R	Leyland National 11351A/1R(6LXB)		B49F	1977	Ex Crosville Wales, 1988
822	CWX664T	Leyland National 11351A/1R		B49F	1979	Ex Sheafline, 1990
823	EUM888T	Leyland National 11351A/1R		B49F	1979	Ex West Riding, 1990
825	GUB178N	Leyland National 11351/1R		B50F	1974	Ex Sheafline, 1990
827	PWW717R	Leyland National 11351A/1R		B50F	1976	Ex Sheafline, 1990
828	RWX150R	Leyland National 11351A/1R		B50F	1976	Ex Compass Buses, 1989
831	NHL564M	Leyland National 1151/2R/0502		B50F	1973	Ex Sheafline, 1990
833	NHL568M	Leyland National 1151/2R/0502		B50F	1974	Ex Sheafline, 1989
835w	MUA881P	Leyland National 11351A/1R		B50F	1976	Ex Sheafline, 1989
836	MUA884P	Leyland National 11351A/1R		B50F	1976	Ex Sheafline, 1990
839	NHL563M	Leyland National 1151/2R/0502		B50F	1973	Ex Sheffield & District, 1988
843	MUA879P	Leyland National 11351A/1R		B50F	1976	Ex Compass Buses, 1989
844	HNL158N	Leyland National 11351/1R		B52F	1975	Ex West Riding, 1989
845	HNL159N	Leyland National 11351/1R		B52F	1975	Ex West Riding, 1989
847	HNL164N	Leyland National 11351/1R		B52F	1975	Ex West Riding, 1989
848	OWF424R	Leyland National 11351A/1R		B52F	1977	Ex RoadCar, 1990
849	VAK448S	Leyland National 11351A/1R		B52F	1978	Ex RoadCar, 1990
850w	XAK452T	Leyland National 11351A/1R		B52F	1978	Ex RoadCar, 1990
852	NPK236R	Leyland National 10351A/1R		B41F	1976	Ex London Country NW, 1990
853	PJJ348S	Leyland National 10351A/1R		B41F	1977	Ex Sheffield United, 1990
854	VCW135L	Leyland National 1051/1R/2801		B44F	1973	Ex Sheafline, 1991

855	GMB653T	Leyland National 10351B/1R		B44F	1978	Ex Sheafline, 1991
856	JTU581T	Leyland National 10351B/1R		B44F	1979	Ex Sheafline, 1991
857	AAK111T	Leyland National 10351B/1R		B44F	1979	Ex Sheafline, 1991
858	AKU166T	Leyland National 10351B/1R		B44F	1979	Ex West Riding, 1989
859	TUG806R	Leyland National 11351A/1R		B49F	1977	Ex Sheafline, 1990
860	CWX667T	Leyland National 11351A/1R		B49F	1977	Ex Sheafline, 1990
862	GUB185N	Leyland National 11351A/1R		B50F	1975	Ex Sheffield & District, 1989
863	MUA877P	Leyland National 11351A/1R		B50F	1976	Ex Sheffield & District, 1989
866	PUM676P	Leyland National 11351A/1R		B50F	1976	Ex Sheffield & District, 1989
867	PWW710R	Leyland National 11351A/1R		B50F	1976	Ex Sheffield & District, 1989
868	PWW718R	Leyland National 11351A/1R		B50F	1976	Ex Sheffield & District, 1989
870	TCY730M	Leyland National 11351/1R		B52F	1974	Ex Sheffield & District, 1990
871w	GBF74N	Leyland National 11351/1R		B52F	1974	Ex Sheffield & District, 1989
873	SWE435S	Leyland National 11351A/1R		B52F	1977	Ex Sheafline, 1990
874	SWE447S	Leyland National 11351A/1R		B52F	1977	Ex Sheafline, 1990
875	WWA121S	Leyland National 11351A/1R		B52F	1978	Ex Sheafline, 1990
879	DMS17V	Leyland National 2 NL116L11/1R		B52F	1980	Ex Trimdon, 1988
880	SNS823W	Leyland National 2 NL116L11/1R		B52F	1980	Ex Trimdon, 1988
881	KWA21W	Leyland National 2 NL116L11/1R		B49F	1980	
882	SFA286R	Leyland National 11351A/1R		B52F	1977	Ex PMT, 1993
883	PJT270R	Leyland National 11351A/1R		B49F	1976	Ex Stagecoach South, 1993
884	SFJ135R	Leyland National 11351A/1R		B49F	1977	Ex Southern National, 1993
885	UHG728R	Leyland National 11351A/1R		B49F	1976	Ex Ribble, 1993
1001	YPD126Y	Leyland Tiger TRCTL11/2R	Duple Dominant IV Express	C53F	1983	Ex Lonodn Country, 1991
1002	YPD142Y	Leyland Tiger TRCTL11/2R	Duple Dominant IV Express	C53F	1983	Ex London Country, 1991
1003	3910WE	Leyland Tiger TRCTL11/3R	Plaxton Paramount 3500	C51F	1983	Ex South Yorkshire, 1991
1004	3913WE	Leyland Tiger TRCTL11/3R	Plaxton Paramount 3500	C49FT	1984	Ex South Yorkshire, 1991
1005	475HDT	Dennis Dorchester SDA808	Plaxton Paramount 3200	C44FT	1984	Ex South Yorkshire, 1991
1006	476HDT	Dennis Dorchester SDA808	Plaxton Paramount 3200	C44FT	1984	Ex South Yorkshire, 1991
1007	477HDT	Dennis Dorchester SDA808	Plaxton Paramount 3200	C44FT	1984	Ex South Yorkshire, 1991
1008	F78FWG	Dennis Javelin SDA1907	Duple 320	C53F	1989	Ex South Yorkshire, 1991
1009	F79FWG	Dennis Javelin SDA1907	Duple 320	C53F	1989	Ex South Yorkshire, 1991
1010	E306UUB	Volvo B10M-61	Plaxton Paramount 3500 III	C48FT	1988	Ex Wallace Arnold, 1991
1011	E307UUB	Volvo B10M-61	Plaxton Paramount 3500 III	C48FT	1988	Ex Wallace Arnold, 1991
1012	C452OFL	Leyland Tiger TRCTL11/3RH	Plaxton Paramount 3500 II	C49F	1986	Ex Premier Travel, 1994
1021	PWK10W	Leyland Leopard PSU3F/5R	Duple Dominant II	C53F	1981	
1064	AKU164T	Leyland National 10351B/1R		B44F	1979	
1156	3156WE	Leyland Titan PD2/30	Roe	H33/26RD	1958	

1686-1702

Leyland Atlantean AN68A/1R — Alexander AL — H45/29D — 1979

1686	CWG686V	1695	CWG695V	1700	CWG700V	1701	CWG701V	1702	CWG702V
1693	CWG693V	1697	CWG697V						

1750-1773

Leyland Atlantean AN68A/1R — Roe — H45/29D — 1979

1750	CWG750V	1755	CWG755V	1756	CWG756V	1766w	CWG766V	1773	CWG773V
1752	CWG752V								

1777-1806

Leyland Atlantean AN68B/1R — Alexander AL — H45/29D — 1981

1777	JKW277W	1782	JKW282W	1800	JKW300W	1802	JKW302W	1805	JKW305W
1778	JKW278W	1784	JKW284W	1801	JKW301W	1803	JKW303W	1806	JKW306W
1780	JKW280W								

1807-1834

Leyland Atlantean AN68B/1R — Marshall — H45/29D* — 1981 — *1812 is H41/29D

1807	JKW307W	1820	JKW320W	1825	JKW325W	1828	JKW328W	1832u	JKW332W
1808	JKW308W	1821u	JKW321W	1826u	JKW326W	1830	JKW330W	1833	JKW333W
1812	JKW312W	1823	JKW323W	1827	JKW327W	1831	JKW331W	1834	JKW334W
1818	JKW318W	1824	JKW324W						

1854-1887

MCW Metrobus DR104/6 — MCW — H46/31F — 1981

1854	JHE154W	1859	JHE159W	1866	JHE166W	1874	JHE174W	1883	JHE183W
1855	JHE155W	1861	JHE161W	1868	JHE168W	1876	JHE176W	1887	JHE187W
1858	JHE158W	1865	JHE165W						

The number of Alexander bodied Atlanteans within the Mainline fleet is slowly shrinking. 1802 JKW302W is one of the remaining members of the 1981 batch It is seen in the recently revamped Pond Street bus station in central Sheffield. *Lee Whitehead*

Mainline still operate a number of Leyland Atlanteans fitted with unusual Marshall bodies. In common with all Mainline Atlanteans this vehicle is fitted with a Voyce gearbox . *Lee Whitehead*

Over the period 1981 to 1986 small batches of MCW Metrobuses were bought by Mainlines predecessor SYT. King Street in Sheffield is the location of this view of 1915, A115XWE, one of 20 examples purchased in 1983. *Lee Whitehead*

1901-1920
MCW Metrobus DR104/11 MCW H47/33F 1983

1901	UKY901Y	1905	A105XWE	1909	A109XWE	1913	A113XWE	1917	A117XWE
1902	UKY902Y	1906	A106XWE	1910	A110XWE	1914	A114XWE	1918	A118XWE
1903	UKY903Y	1907	A107XWE	1911	A111XWE	1915	A115XWE	1919	A119XWE
1904	UKY904Y	1908	A108XWE	1912	A112XWE	1916	A116XWE	1920	A120XWE

1921-1940
MCW Metrobus DR104/12 MCW H47/33F 1984-85

1921	B921CDT	1925	B925CDT	1929	B929CDT	1933	B933CDT	1937	B937CDT
1922	B922CDT	1926	B926CDT	1930	B930CDT	1934	B934CDT	1938	B938CDT
1923	B923CDT	1927	B927CDT	1931	B931CDT	1935	B935CDT	1939	B939CDT
1924	B924CDT	1928	B928CDT	1932	B932CDT	1936	B936CDT	1940	B940CDT

1941-1950
MCW Metrobus DR102/50 MCW DPH42/28F 1985

1941	B941FET	1943	B943FET	1945	B945FET	1947	C947HWF	1949	C949HWF
1942	B942FET	1944	B944FET	1946	B946FET	1948	C948HWF	1950	C950HWF

1951-1960
MCW Metrobus DR104/53 MCW DPH42/28F* 1986 * 1951 is DPH42/24F

1951	C951LWJ	1953	C953LWJ	1955	C955LWJ	1957	C957LWJ	1959	C959LWJ
1952	C952LWJ	1954	C954LWJ	1956	C956LWJ	1958	C958LWJ	1960	C960LWJ

Opposite, top: Gelenken (or Bendi) buses are still more popular on the continent though there have been attemps to bring this versatile unit into the UK market. Illustrating the vertical flexibility is mainline 2003, C103HDT, a Leyland model built in Denmark. *Lee Whitehead*
Opposite, Bottom: The latest single-deck model from Volvo is the B10L, a low-floor rear-engined chassis still undergoing development trials. Mainline have used an example built by the Swedish bodybuilder Säffle. Numbered 403, L456JCK is seen on its normal sevice, 52 to Crooks. *Tony Wilson*

501 BATEMOOR
MAINLINE
MAINLINE
2003
Leyland
C103 HDT

52 Woodhouse
The Volvo Ultra Low Floor Concept Bus : Easy Access, No Steps
VOLVO
MAINLINE
403
L456 JCK

2001-2010

	Leyland-DAB 07-1735B-222054	DAB	AB60T	1985			

2001	C101HDT	2003	C103HDT	2005	C105HDT	2007	C107HDT	2009	C109HDT
2002	C102HDT	2004	C104HDT	2006	C106HDT	2008	C108HDT	2010	C110HDT

2011	C111HDT	Leyland-DAB 07-1735L-222054	DAB		ADP67D	1985
2012	C112HDT	Leyland-DAB 07-1735L-222054	DAB		ADP67D	1985
2013	C113HDT	Leyland-DAB 07-1735L-222054	DAB		ADP67D	1985

2101-2140

	Dennis Dominator DDA133	Alexander RH	H46/32F	1981

2101	KKU101W	2109	KKU109W	2117	KKU117W	2125	KKU125W	2133	MWB853W
2102	KKU102W	2110	KKU110W	2118	KKU118W	2126	KKU126W	2134	MWB854W
2103	KKU103W	2111	KKU111W	2119	KKU119W	2127	KKU127W	2135	MWB855W
2104	KKU104W	2112	KKU112W	2120	KKU120W	2128	KKU128W	2136	MWB856W
2105	KKU105W	2113	KKU113W	2121	KKU121W	2129	MWB849W	2137	OWE137X
2106	KKU106W	2114	KKU114W	2122	KKU122W	2130	MWB850W	2138	OWE138X
2107	KKU107W	2115	KKU115W	2123	KKU123W	2131	MWB851W	2139	OWE139X
2108	KKU108W	2116	KKU116W	2124	KKU124W	2132	MWB852W	2140	OWE140X

2141-2220

	Dennis Dominator DDA133	Alexander RH	H46/32F	1981-82

2141	NKU141X	2157	NKU157X	2173	NKU173X	2189	NKU189X	2205	NKU205X
2142	NKU142X	2158	NKU158X	2174	NKU174X	2190	NKU190X	2206	NKU206X
2143	NKU143X	2159	NKU159X	2175	NKU175X	2191	NKU191X	2207	NKU207X
2144	NKU144X	2160	NKU160X	2176	NKU176X	2192	NKU192X	2208	NKU208X
2145	NKU145X	2161	NKU161X	2177	NKU177X	2193	NKU193X	2209	NKU209X
2146	NKU146X	2162	NKU162X	2178	NKU178X	2194	NKU194X	2210	NKU210X
2147	NKU147X	2163	NKU163X	2179	NKU179X	2195	NKU195X	2211	NKU211X
2148	NKU148X	2164	NKU164X	2180	NKU180X	2196	NKU196X	2212	NKU212X
2149	NKU149X	2165	NKU165X	2181	NKU181X	2197	NKU197X	2213	NKU213X
2150	NKU150X	2166	NKU166X	2182	NKU182X	2198	NKU198X	2214	NKU214X
2151	NKU151X	2167	NKU167X	2183	NKU183X	2199	NKU199X	2215	NKU215X
2152	NKU152X	2168	NKU168X	2184	NKU184X	2200	NKU200X	2216	NKU216X
2153	NKU153X	2169	NKU169X	2185	NKU185X	2201	NKU201X	2217	NKU217X
2154	NKU154X	2170	NKU170X	2186	NKU186X	2202	NKU202X	2218	NKU218X
2155	NKU155X	2171	NKU171X	2187	NKU187X	2203	NKU203X	2219	NKU219X
2156	NKU156X	2172	NKU172X	2188	NKU188X	2204	NKU204X	2220	NKU220X

2221-2274

	Dennis Dominator DDA133	Alexander RH	H46/32F	1982-83

2221	SDT221Y	2232	SDT232Y	2243	SDT243Y	2254	SDT254Y	2264	SDT264Y
2222	SDT222Y	2233	SDT233Y	2244	SDT244Y	2255	SDT255Y	2265	SDT265Y
2223	SDT223Y	2234	SDT234Y	2245	SDT245Y	2256	SDT256Y	2266	SDT266Y
2224	SDT224Y	2235	SDT235Y	2246	SDT246Y	2257	SDT257Y	2267	SDT267Y
2225	SDT225Y	2236	SDT236Y	2247	SDT247Y	2258	SDT258Y	2268	SDT268Y
2226	SDT226Y	2237	SDT237Y	2248	SDT248Y	2259	SDT259Y	2270	SDT270Y
2227	SDT227Y	2238	SDT238Y	2249	SDT249Y	2260	SDT260Y	2271	SDT271Y
2228	SDT228Y	2239	SDT239Y	2250	SDT250Y	2261	SDT261Y	2272	SDT272Y
2229	SDT229Y	2240	SDT240Y	2251	SDT251Y	2262	SDT262Y	2273	SDT273Y
2230	SDT230Y	2241	SDT241Y	2252	SDT252Y	2263	SDT263Y	2274	SDT274Y
2231	SDT231Y	2242	SDT242Y	2253	SDT253Y				

2275-2304

	Dennis Dominator DDA165	Alexander RH	H46/32F*	1983	*2275 is H46/33F

2275	UWJ275Y	2281	UWJ281Y	2287	UWJ287Y	2293	UWJ293Y	2299	A299XAK
2276	UWJ276Y	2282	UWJ282Y	2288	UWJ288Y	2294	UWJ294Y	2300	A300XAK
2277	UWJ277Y	2283	UWJ283Y	2289	UWJ289Y	2295	A295XAK	2301	A301XAK
2278	UWJ278Y	2284	UWJ284Y	2290	UWJ290Y	2296	A296XAK	2302	A302XAK
2279	UWJ279Y	2285	UWJ285Y	2291	UWJ291Y	2297	A297XAK	2303	A303XAK
2280	UWJ280Y	2286	UWJ286Y	2292	UWJ292Y	2298	A298XAK	2304	A304XAK

2311-2320

	Dennis Dominator DDA165	Northern Counties	H47/33F	1983

2311	A311XAK	2313	A313XAK	2315	A315XAK	2317	A317XAK	2319	A319XAK
2312	A312XAK	2314	A314XAK	2316	A316XAK	2318	A318XAK	2320	A320XAK

2351-2365 Dennis Dominator DDA901 East Lancashire H46/33F 1984

2351	B351CDT	2354	B354CDT	2357	B357CDT	2360	B360CDT	2363	B363CDT
2352	B352CDT	2355	B355CDT	2358	B358CDT	2361	B361CDT	2364	B364CDT
2353	B353CDT	2356	B356CDT	2359	B359CDT	2362	B362CDT	2365	B365CDT

2401-2449 Dennis Dominator DDA901 Alexander RH H46/32F 1984

2401	A401YAK	2410	A410YAK	2419	A419YAK	2430	A430YAK	2439	A439YAK
2402	A402YAK	2411	A411YAK	2421	A421YAK	2431	A431YAK	2441	B441CKW
2403	A403YAK	2412	A412YAK	2423	A423YAK	2432	A432YAK	2442	B442CKW
2404	A404YAK	2413	A413YAK	2424	A424YAK	2433	A433YAK	2445	B445CKW
2405	A405YAK	2414	A414YAK	2425	A425YAK	2434	A434YAK	2446	B446CKW
2406	A406YAK	2415	A415YAK	2426	A426YAK	2435	A435YAK	2447	B447CKW
2407	A407YAK	2416	A416YAK	2427	A427YAK	2436	A436YAK	2448	B448CKW
2408	A408YAK	2417	A417YAK	2428	A428YAK	2437	A437YAK	2449	B449CKW
2409	A409YAK	2418	A418YAK	2429	A429YAK	2438	A438YAK		

2451-2470 Dennis Dominator DDA910 Alexander RH H46/32F 1985-86

2451	C871JWE	2455	C875JWE	2459	C879JWE	2463	C883JWE	2467	C887JWE
2452	C872JWE	2456	C876JWE	2460	C880JWE	2464	C884JWE	2468	C888JWE
2453	C873JWE	2457	C877JWE	2461	C881JWE	2465	C885JWE	2469	C889JWE
2454	C874JWE	2458	C878JWE	2462	C882JWE	2466	C886JWE	2470	C890JWE

2471-2485 Dennis Dominator DDA1011 Alexander RH DPH45/33F* 1986 *2471/3-6/9/80 are DPH41/33F

2471	D471OWE	2474	D474OWE	2477	D477OWE	2480	D480OWE	2483	D483OWE
2472	D472OWE	2475	D475OWE	2478	D478OWE	2481	D481OWE	2484	D484OWE
2473	D473OWE	2476	D476OWE	2479	D479OWE	2482	D482OWE	2485	D485OWE

2486	D486OWE	Dennis Dominator DDA1013	Alexander RH	DPH45/24F	1986
2487	D486OWE	Dennis Dominator DDA1013	Alexander RH	DPH45/20F	1986
2488	D486OWE	Dennis Dominator DDA1013	Alexander RH	DPH45/24F	1986
2489	D486OWE	Dennis Dominator DDA1013	Alexander RH	DPH45/33F	1986
2490	D486OWE	Dennis Dominator DDA1013	Alexander RH	DPH45/24F	1986
8001	G351FOP	Freight Rover Sherpa	Carlyle Citybus 2	B15FL	1989
8002	G352FOP	Freight Rover Sherpa	Carlyle Citybus 2	B15FL	1989
8003	G353FOP	Freight Rover Sherpa	Carlyle Citybus 2	B15FL	1989
8004	G354FOP	Freight Rover Sherpa	Carlyle Citybus 2	B15FL	1989
8005	G355FOP	Freight Rover Sherpa	Carlyle Citybus 2	B15FL	1989
8006	G356FOP	Leyland DAF 400	Carlyle Citybus 2	B15FL	1989
8007	G357FOP	Leyland DAF 400	Carlyle Citybus 2	B15FL	1989
8008	G358FOP	Leyland DAF 400	Carlyle Citybus 2	B15FL	1989
8009	G349FOP	Freight Rover Sherpa	Carlyle Citybus 2	B15FL	1989
8010	G350FOP	Freight Rover Sherpa	Carlyle Citybus 2	B15FL	1989

Previous Registrations:

3156WE	From new	3913WE	A67GBN	477HDT	B977DWG
3904WE	From new	475HDT	B975DWG	F253BHF	NXI5005
3910WE	A578KVU	476HDT	B976DWG	KIB6110	REL401R

Named Vehicle:
287 *Catherine Howard*

Liveries: Yellow and red; white and red (Coachline) 62/3, 1001-12/21.

Miramare Coaches are a small company operating a route between the centre of Leeds and Morley. Displaying the blue and white livery is NOC452R an MCW bodied Leyland Fleetline which although purchased from Kingfisher of Redditch started life in the large West Londons fleet. *David Cole*

Stephensons Nationwide Travel have operated the Park and Ride service in York in recent past. In addition, they operate coach services for which the Stephensons name is used. Illustrated here is PRO448W, a Leyland Leopard with the Supreme IV variant of Plaxtons bodywork. *Andrew Jarosz*

MIRAMARE COACHES

D Muffitt, 5 Bantam Close, Wide Lane, Morley, West Yorkshire, LS27 8SX

Depot: Fountain Street, Morley

NOC452R	Leyland Fleetline FE30AGR	MCW		H43/33F	1976	Ex Kingfisher, Redditch, 1994
WNO638T	Leyland National 11351A/1R			B52F	1978	Ex Hopkinson, Market Harborough, 1993

Livery: Blue and white

NATIONWIDE TRAVEL

HJ Stephenson, Nine Acre, Stillington Road, Easingwold,
North Yorkshire, YO6 3DZ

Depot & outstations: Unit 15, Moor Lane Industrial Estate, Tholthorpe; Easingwold; Helmsley and Kirkby Moorside.

	KUM520L	Leyland Leopard PSU3B/4R	Plaxton Elite III Express	C49F	1973	Ex Morse, Stillington, 1994
	PGW658L	Leyland Leopard PSU3B/4R	Plaxton Elite III Express	C49F	1973	Ex Glenn Coaches, Wigginton, 1994
w	HWY722N	Leyland Leopard PSU3B/4R	Alexander AY	DP49F	1975	Ex Rackford Cs, South Anston, 1993
	JKY945P	Leyland Leopard PSU5A/4R	Duple Dominant	C57F	1975	Ex Glenn Coaches, Wigginton, 1994
w	RMA312P	Leyland Leopard PSU3C/4R	Plaxton Supreme III Express	C49F	1976	Ex Beverley Starlights Jazz Band, 1994
	AAL992A	Leyland Leopard PSU3C/4R	Duple Dominant I	C53F	1976	Ex Tenby Bus & Coach, 1992
	HIL6233	Leyland Leopard PSU3E/4R	Duple Dominant I	C49F	1978	Ex Aldham Coaches, Wombell, 1991
	EGR707S	Leyland Leopard PSU3E/4R	Plaxton Supreme III Express	C53F	1978	Ex Go-Ahead Northern, 1991
	EGR708S	Leyland Leopard PSU3E/4R	Plaxton Supreme III Express	C53F	1978	Ex Go-Ahead Northern, 1990
	PJI9141	Leyland Leopard PSU5C/4R	Plaxton Supreme IV	C57F	1979	Ex Jones, Formby, 1993
	JUF817V	Leyland Leopard PSU3E/4R	Plaxton Supreme IV Express	C49F	1979	Ex ??, 1995
	TUP575V	Leyland Leopard PSU3E/4R	Willowbrook 003	C49F	1980	Ex Go-Ahead Northern, 1991
	TUP583V	Leyland Leopard PSU3E/4R	Willowbrook 003	C49F	1980	Ex Go-Ahead Northern, 1991
	TUP584V	Leyland Leopard PSU3E/4R	Willowbrook 003	C49F	1980	Ex Go-Ahead Northern, 1991
	TUP585V	Leyland Leopard PSU3E/4R	Willowbrook 003	C49F	1980	Ex Go-Ahead Northern, 1991
	AGR235W	Leyland Leopard PSU3F/4R	Willowbrook 003	C49F	1980	Ex Northumbria, 1991
	PRO448W	Leyland Leopard PSU3F/5R	Plaxton Supreme IV	C53F	1980	Ex Amberley Travel, Pudsey, 1994
	EUY532W	Leyland Leopard PSU5D/4R	Duple Dominant IV	C51FT	1980	Ex Amberley Travel, Pudsey, 1994
	LFT94X	Leyland Leopard PSU3F/4R	Willowbrook 003	C49F	1981	Ex Go-Ahead Northern, 1991
	LFT95X	Leyland Leopard PSU3F/4R	Willowbrook 003	C49F	1981	Ex Go-Ahead Northern, 1991
	SSO448X	Fiat 60F10	Asco	C25F	1981	Ex Wold Travel, North Dalton, 1994
	PJI9142	MCW Metroliner HR131/3	MCW	C49FT	1985	Ex Northern Bus, North Anston, 1991
	D830RYS	Renault-Dodge S56	Alexander AM	B25F	1987	Ex Victoria Travel, Earlestown, 1994
	D898DSF	Renault-Dodge S56	Alexander AM	B25F	1987	Ex Victoria Travel, Earlestown, 1994
	D686SEM	Renault-Dodge S56	Alexander AM	B23F	1987	Ex Walker & Hutchinson, Pudsey, 1994

Previous Registrations:

AAL992A	MDF117P	PJI9141	DDG267T, UCK529, TKC768T
EUY532W	KUX246W, YFU846	PJI9142	B606LSO
HIL6233	CFS109S		

Livery: White, orange and red. York 'Park & Ride' vehicles are white.

NORTHERN BUS

Northern Bus Co Ltd, Northern Garage, Houghton Road, North Anston,
South Yorkshire, S31 7JJ

0113r	AFM113G	Bristol RELL6G	Eastern Coach Works	B53F	1969	Ex Crosville Wales, 1990
0135	GHY135K	Bristol RELH6L	Eastern Coach Works	DP49F	1972	Ex Griffiths, Llangristiolus, 1988
0234	JFM234D	Bristol Lodekka FS6G	Eastern Coach Works	H33/27RD	1966	Ex Crosville Wales, 1994
0530	AFM105B	Bristol RELH6G	Eastern Coach Works	C47F	1964	Ex preservation, 1994
0594	HFM594D	Bristol RELL6G	Eastern Coach Works	DP50F	1966	Ex Liverpool Community, 1990
0742	PLJ742G	Bristol RELL6G	Eastern Coach Works	B45D	1969	Ex Bexhill Bus, 1994
0978	627HFM	Bristol Lodekka LD6B	Eastern Coach Works	CO33/27RD	1959	Ex Dunn-Line, Nottingham, 1991
1220	XDL122L	Bristol RELH6G	Eastern Coach Works	C47F	1972	Ex preservation, 1994
1221	RPU869M	Bristol RELH6G	Eastern Coach Works	DP47F	1974	Ex Vale, Cheetham, 1992
1222	222WFM	Bristol RELH6L	Plaxton Elite III Express	C49F	1974	Ex United Counties, 1988
1223	223FWW	Bristol RELH6L	Plaxton Elite III Express	C49F	1974	Ex United Counties, 1988
1229	929CVJ	Bristol RELH6G	Eastern Coach Works B51	C49F	1972	Ex Badgerline, 1992
1230u	WPD30Y	Leyland Leopard PSU3G/4RT	Eastern Coach Works B51	DP49F	1982	Ex The Bee Line, 1992
1231r	JOX461P	Leyland Leopard PSU3C/4R	Plaxton Supreme III Express	DP49F	1976	Ex Crosville Wales, 1994
1235u	TPC105X	Leyland Tiger TRCTL11/2R	Eastern Coach Works B51	DP53F	1982	Ex Davies Bros, Pencader, 1992
1236	WPH136Y	Leyland Tiger TRCTL11/2R	Eastern Coach Works B51	DP53F	1982	Ex Davies Bros, Pencader, 1992
1270	WWY70X	Leyland Leopard PSU3F/4R	Willowbrook 003	DP49F	1982	Ex United, 1992
1311w	SHN111L	Bristol REMH6G	Plaxton Elite III	C49F	1973	Ex Sealandair, Dublin, 1992
1316	SHN116L	Bristol REMH6G	Plaxton Elite III	C53F	1973	Ex Sealandair, Dublin, 1992
2101	RHT141G	Bristol RELL6G	Eastern Coach Works	B53F	1968	Ex Badgerline, 1992
2102w	VOD102K	Bristol RELL6G	Eastern Coach Works	B53F	1971	Ex Citybus, Belfast, 1991
2103	XAH873H	Bristol RELL6G	Eastern Coach Works	DP50F	1970	Ex Citybus, Belfast, 1991
2107w	YFM277L	Bristol RELL6G	Eastern Coach Works	DP50F	1973	Ex Crosville Wales, 1990
2108	YFM278L	Bristol RELL6G	Eastern Coach Works	DP50F	1973	Ex Crosville Wales, 1990
2112	YFM282L	Bristol RELL6G	Eastern Coach Works	B52F	1973	Ex Crosville Wales, 1990

223FWW was new to United Counties as SBD223M. This 1974 Bristol RELH6L with a Plaxton Elite III Express bodywork is one of many formerBristols which originated with National Bus Company fleets. It is seen in Dinnington en-route for Worksop. *Daniel Hill*

Northern Bus operate a pair of Bedford JJL type midibuses, a product developed in association with Marshall, whose bodywork is carried by both examples. Photographed in Dinnington is 2601, UKK335X.
Tony Wilson

Former Crosville Bristol vehicles have been purchased frequentlyby Northern Bus. One of the interesting examples is 627HFM a 1959 Bristol LD6B which was built as a convertible open top vehicle. It is seen in open-top guise carrying a livery which represents that it originally carried when built.
Daniel Hill

A number of Northern Bus vehicles carry branded liveries for specific sections of the route network. Bristol VR 3084, AET184T displays the cream, green and red livery for the services in Bradfield. It also displays the name Pashani Bebhi which with several others is taken from characters in the childrens TV series The Herbs.
Phillip Stephenson

2116	YFM286L	Bristol RELL6G	Eastern Coach Works	DP50F	1973	Ex Crosville Wales, 1991
2118	HPW518L	Bristol RELL6G	Eastern Coach Works	B53F	1972	Ex Vale, Cheetham, 1992
2120	HHW920L	Bristol RELL6G(0680)	Eastern Coach Works	B48D	1973	Ex Citybus, Belfast, 1991
2178	EFM178H	Bristol RELL6G	Eastern Coach Works	B53F	1970	Ex Citybus, Belfast, 1991
2182	SJA382K	Bristol RELL6G	Eastern Coach Works	B49F	1971	Ex Hollis Coaches, Sealand, 1993
2193	PDL493H	Bristol RELL6G	Eastern Coach Works	B53F	1970	Ex preservation, 1992
	DDM23X	Leyland Leopard PSU3F/4R	Willowbrook 003	C49F	1981	Ex Crosville Wales, 1994
	DDM32X	Leyland Leopard PSU3F/4R	Willowbrook 003	C49F	1982	Ex Crosville Wales, 1995
	SND281X	Leyland Leopard PSU5D/4R	Duple Dominant IV	C49F	1981	Ex Crosville Wales, 1995
	SND282X	Leyland Leopard PSU5D/4R	Duple Dominant IV	C49F	1981	Ex Crosville Wales, 1995
	SND283X	Leyland Leopard PSU5D/4R	Duple Dominant IV	C49F	1981	Ex Crosville Wales, 1995
2406u	NNN6M	Bristol RELH6L	Eastern Coach Works	B49F	1974	Ex Ron Lyles, Batley, 1993
2414	KRP214L	Bristol RELH6L	Eastern Coach Works	DP47F	1973	Ex Angelina Laurio, Maltby, 1993
2432u	GHY132K	Bristol RELH6L	Eastern Coach Works	DP49F	1972	Ex Citybus, Belfast, 1990
2434	GHY134K	Bristol RELH6L	Eastern Coach Works	DP49F	1972	Ex Badgerline, 1992
2438	GHY138K	Bristol RELH6L	Eastern Coach Works	DP49F	1972	Ex Badgerline, 1992
2467	NCH767M	Bristol RELH6L	Eastern Coach Works	B49F	1974	Ex Trent, 1990
2468	PCH268L	Bristol RELH6L	Eastern Coach Works	B53F	1972	Ex West Sussex, Chichester, 1992
2472	EVO292J	Bristol RELH6G	Eastern Coach Works	DP49F	1971	Ex preservation, 1990
2478r	TCH278L	Bristol RELH6L	Eastern Coach Works	B53F	1973	Ex Trent, 1990
2481	TCH281L	Bristol RELH6L	Eastern Coach Works	B49F	1973	Ex Trent, 1990
2494	BHN694N	Bristol RELH6L	Eastern Coach Works	DP49F	1974	Ex preservation, 1992
2504	HRN104N	Bristol RESL6L	Eastern Coach Works	DP44F	1975	Ex Fylde, 1993
2505	HRN105N	Bristol RESL6L	Eastern Coach Works	DP44F	1975	Ex Fylde, 1993
2506	HRN106N	Bristol RESL6L	Eastern Coach Works	DP44F	1975	Ex Fylde, 1993
2507	HRN107N	Bristol RESL6L	Eastern Coach Works	DP44F	1975	Ex Fylde, 1993
2508	HRN108N	Bristol RESL6L	Eastern Coach Works	DP44F	1975	Ex Fylde, 1993
2550	OCK350K	Bristol RESL6L	Eastern Coach Works	B47F	1972	Ex Citybus, Belfast, 1991
2554	THU354G	Bristol RESL6L	Eastern Coach Works	B43F	1969	Ex preservation, 1992
2601u	UKK335X	Bedford JJL	Marshall	B27F	1981	Ex Brighton, 1992
2602u	AVS903T	Bedford JJL	Marshall	B27F	1978	Ex Brighton, 1992
3000	CPU979G	Bristol VRT/SL/6G	Eastern Coach Works	H39/31F	1969	Ex preservation, 1994
3004	MDM284P	Bristol VRT/SL3/501 (6LXB)	Eastern Coach Works	H43/31F	1977	Ex Crosville Wales, 1994
3006	XAK906T	Bristol VRT/SL3/501	Eastern Coach Works	H43/31F	1978	Ex RoadCar, 1994
3007u	KAU327N	Bristol VRT/SL2/6G	Eastern Coach Works	H43/34F	1974	Ex Trent, 1993
3008	XAK908T	Bristol VRT/SL3/501	Eastern Coach Works	H43/31F	1978	Ex RoadCar, 1994
3009	RAU809R	Bristol VRT/SL3/501 (6LX)	Eastern Coach Works	H43/31F	1976	Ex Trent, 1992
3012r	VDV112S	Bristol VRT/SL3/6LXB	Eastern Coach Works	CO43/31F	1978	Ex Crosville Wales, 1994
3013	VDV113S	Bristol VRT/SL3/6LXB	Eastern Coach Works	H43/29F	1978	Ex Crosville Wales, 1994
3025	URB825S	Bristol VRT/SL3/501 (6LX)	Eastern Coach Works	H43/31F	1977	Ex Trent, 1992
3026	YRC126M	Bristol VRT/SL2/6G	Eastern Coach Works	H43/34F	1974	Ex Trent, 1991
3027	URB827S	Bristol VRT/SL3/501 (6LX)	Eastern Coach Works	H43/31F	1977	Ex Trent, 1992
3028	URB828S	Bristol VRT/SL3/501 (6LX)	Eastern Coach Works	H43/31F	1977	Ex Trent, 1992
3029	RCH629L	Bristol VRT/SL2/6G	Eastern Coach Works	H43/34F	1972	Ex Trent, 1991
3034	RMA434V	Bristol VRT/SL3/501	Eastern Coach Works	H43/31F	1980	Ex Crosville Wales, 1994
3041u	XMO541H	Bristol VRT/SL2/6G	Eastern Coach Works	H39/31F	1970	Ex The Bee Line, 1993
3051r	AYG851S	Bristol VRT/SL3/6LXB	Eastern Coach Works	H43/29F	1978	Ex Crosville Wales, 1994
3068	VTV168S	Bristol VRT/SL3/6XLB	Eastern Coach Works	H43/31F	1978	Ex East Midland, 1993
3070	BTU370S	Bristol VRT/SL3/501	Eastern Coach Works	H43/31F	1978	Ex East Midland, 1993
3076	XRR176S	Bristol VRT/SL3/6LXB	Eastern Coach Works	H43/31F	1978	Ex East Midland, 1993
3077	XRR177S	Bristol VRT/SL3/6XLB	Eastern Coach Works	H43/31F	1978	Ex East Midland, 1993
3078u	HKE678L	Bristol VRT/SL2/6G	Eastern Coach Works	H43/34F	1973	Ex The Bee Line, 1993
3081r	MDM281P	Bristol VRT/SL3/6LXB	Eastern Coach Works	H43/29F	1975	Ex Crosville Wales, 1994
3083	AET183T	Bristol VRT/SL3/6XLB	Eastern Coach Works	H43/34F	1979	Ex East Midland, 1993
3084	AET184T	Bristol VRT/SL3/6XLB	Eastern Coach Works	H43/34F	1979	Ex East Midland, 1993
3089	FTU389T	Bristol VRT/SL3/501	Eastern Coach Works	H43/31F	1978	Ex Crosville Wales, 1994
3095u	GRF695V	Bristol VRT/SL3/501	Eastern Coach Works	H43/31F	1979	Ex PMT, 1993
3601	HJI3292	Leyland Olympian ONTL11/2RSp	Eastern Coach Works	CH45/28F	1983	Ex The Bee Line, 1992

Named Vehicles: 0234 *Happy Dragon*; 1231 *Jack*; 2550 *Fireman Sam*; 2554 *Thug*; 2601 *Hattie*; 3000 *Good King Henry*; 3006 *Mungo*; 3007 *Mr Onion*; 3008 *Midge*; 3009 *Lady Rosemary*; 3013 *Pippin*; 3025 *Parsley*; 3026 *Sage*; 3027 *Sir Basil*; 3028 *Bayleaf*; 3029 *Dill*; 3034 *Tog*; 3041 *Constable Knapweed*; 3051 *Poggle*; 3070 *Belladonna/Andy4*; 3076 *Aunt Mint*; 3077 *Señor Solidago*; 3078 *Tarragon*; 3084 *Pashani Bebhi*; 3601 *Zorba*.

Previous Registrations:

222WFM	SBD222M	929CVJ	VHK177L	SHN111L	SHN111L, 737LZU
223FWW	SBD223M	HJI3292	YPJ502Y	SHN116L	SHN116L, 737LZU
627HFM	From new	KAU327N	ORC256N, YRC181		

Livery: Various depending on vehicle design and purpose.

INGFIELD - NORTHERN ROSE

Ingfield Northern Rose Ltd, 20 Devonshire Street, Keighley, West Yorkshire, BD21 2AH

Depot: Ingfield Garage, High Street, Settle
A subsidiary of Blazefield Holdings Ltd.

KAD358V	Leyland Leopard PSU5C/4R	Plaxton Supreme IV	C57F	1980	Ex Rover, Bromsgrove, 1992
LUA285V	Leyland Leopard PSU5D/4R	Plaxton Supreme IV	C57F	1980	Ex Rover, Bromsgrove, 1992
VAV256X	Leyland Tiger TRCTL11/3R	Plaxton Supreme V Express	C53F	1982	Ex Harrogate Independent, 1993
RUT224	Bova EL26/581	Bova Europa	C47FT	1982	Ex Ingfield Coaches, 1992
JIL2519	Bova EL26/581	Bova Europa	C53F	1982	Ex Whaites, Settle, 1994
C304CRH	Ford Transit 190D	Carlyle	B16F	1985	Ex Scarborough & District, 1992
C63LHL	Ford Transit 190D	Carlyle	DP20F	1986	Ex West Riding, 1992
C380YNE	Peugeot-Talbot Express	Made-to-Measure	M12	1985	Ex Holme, Austwick, 1992
D558HNW	Iveco Daily 49-10	Robin Hood City Nippy	DP21F	1986	Ex Harrogate & District, 1994
D130DRV	Iveco Daily 49-10	Robin Hood City Nippy	B21F	1986	Ex Harrogate & District, 1993
D31TKA	Freight Rover Sherpa	Dormobile	B16F	1987	Ex Whaites, Settle, 1994
E367NEG	Volvo B10M-61	Plaxton Paramount 3200 III	C53F	1988	Ex Cambridge Coach Services, 1995
E446TYG	Iveco Daily 49.10	Robin Hood City Nippy	DP25F	1988	Ex Keighley & District, 1992

Previous Registrations:

JIL2519	XUA33X, WWW33, BUA387X, 951BOV	RUT224	PHE647X

Livery: White and blue

Infield - Northern Rose is the Settle operation of the Blazefield Group and features full-size coaches and minibuses. Photographed while visiting the National Trust property of Beningbrough Hall is RUT224, a Bova Europa. *Tony Wilson*

PENNINE

N J & M Simpson, Grouse Garage, Gargrave, Skipton,
North Yorkshire, BD23 3RB

Depots: West Close Garage, Barnoldswick; Grouse Garage, Gargrave; New Road Garage, Ingleton; White Friars Garage, Settle and Red Lion Garage, Skipton.

u	MTD235	Leyland Royal Tiger PSU1/15	Leyland	C41C	1951	Ex Leyland demonstrator, 1952
w	OWY197K	Leyland Leopard PSU3B/4R	Plaxton Elite II Express	C53F	1972	Ex Laycock, Barnoldswick, 1972
w	RWY379M	Leyland Leopard PSU3B/4R	Plaxton Elite III Express	C49F	1974	
w	JWU797N	Leyland Leopard PSU3C/4R	Plaxton Elite III Express	C49F	1975	
	JWU798N	Leyland Leopard PSU3C/4R	Plaxton Elite III Express	C49F	1975	
w	JWU799N	Leyland Leopard PSU3C/4R	Plaxton Elite III Express	C49F	1975	
	JIL7417	Leyland Leopard PSU3E/4R	Plaxton Supreme III Express	C49F	1977	
	UDW140S	Leyland Leopard PSU3E/4R	Plaxton Supreme III Express	C53F	1978	Ex Southend, 1988
	JIL7416	Leyland Leopard PSU3E/4R	Plaxton Supreme IV Express	C49F	1978	
	JIL4653	Leyland Leopard PSU3E/4R	Plaxton Supreme IV Express	C53F	1979	Ex Fishwick, Leyland, 1989
	JIL4698	Leyland Leopard PSU3E/4R	Plaxton Supreme IV Express	C49F	1980	
	JIL2427	Leyland Leopard PSU3F/4R	Plaxton Supreme IV	C49F	1981	Ex Southdown, 1990
	JIL2428	Leyland Leopard PSU3E/4R	Plaxton Supreme IV Express	C49F	1981	Ex London Country, 1986
	JIL2426	Leyland Leopard PSU3E/4R	Plaxton Supreme IV	C53F	1981	Ex Wings, Sleaford, 1984
LN1	JIL2794	Leyland National 10351A/1R(Volvo)		B41F	1977	Ex Northumbria, 1994
LN2	RIB5081	Leyland National 10351A/1R		B41F	1978	Ex R&I Buses, Milton Keynes, 1994
LN3	SPC276R	Leyland National 10351A/1R		B41F	1977	Ex Northumbria, 1994
LN4	JIL2793	Leyland National 10351A/2R		B36D	1977	Ex London Buses, 1994
LN5	JIL2795	Leyland National 1051/1R/0501		B44F	1973	Ex Executive Minibuses, Greasby, 1994
LN6	JIL8353	Leyland National 2 NL106L11/1R		B44F	1980	Ex Harrogate & District, 1995
LN7	HPF311N	Leyland National 1151/1R/SC		B44F	1975	Ex Kingsman, Sheffield, 1995
LN8	HHU636N	Leyland National 10351/1R		B44F	1975	Ex Yorkshire Terrier, 1995
LN9	JNA589N	Leyland National 10351/1R		B41F	1975	Ex Kingsman, Sheffield, 1995

Previous Registrations:

JIL2426	BTL485X	JIL2793	OJD879R	JIL7417	UWR712R
JIL2427	MAP347W, 400DCD, OUF50W	JIL4653	OCK452T	JIL7422	SPC278R
JIL2428	NPA220W	JIL4698	NWT839V	JIL8353	PWY583W
JIL2794	SPC282R	JIL7416	AUA965S	RIB5081	YPF767T
JIL2795	XDL800L				

Livery: Orange, white and black

Pennine have recently added Leyland Nationals to their fleet, breaking a tradition which has seen the Leyland Leopard as the sole type for several years. Painted in the black and orange scheme is LN2, RIB5081, its registration bears testiment to its time with R&I Buses though it was new to London Country as SNB367 in 1987.
Mike Fowler

PONTEFRACT COACHES

S Stringer, 102 Southgate, Pontefract, West Yorkshire, WF8 1PN

	IBZ5893	Daimler Fleetline CRL6	Northern Counties	H44/31F	1975	Ex Nottingham, 1993
	MTV758P	Leyland Leopard PSU3C/4R	Duple Dominant E	DP53F	1976	Ex Nottingham, 1991
	63XMD	Leyland Leopard PSU3C/4R	Plaxton Supreme III	C53F	1976	
	MOU748R	Bristol VRT/SL3/6LXB	Eastern Coach Works	H43/27D	1976	Ex City Line, 1993
	NFB115R	Bristol VRT/SL3/6LXB	Eastern Coach Works	H43/27D	1976	Ex City Line, 1993
w	SGR130R	Leyland National 11351A/1R		B49F	1977	Ex Four Seasons, Allerton Bywater, 19.93
w	XAK454T	Leyland National 11351A/1R		B52F	1978	Ex Clyde Coast, Ardrossan, 1993
	BUH229V	Bristol VRT/SL3/501	Eastern Coach Works	DPH40/27F	1980	Ex Red & White, 1993
	XOI5903	Leyland Tiger TRCTL11/3R	Plaxton Paramount 3500	C53F	1984	
	TJI2804	Volvo B10M-61	Duple Caribbean	C53F	1985	Ex ??, 1995
	C512BFB	Ford Transit 190D	Dormobile	B16F	1986	Ex Badgerline, 1994
	C530BFB	Ford Transit 190D	Dormobile	B16F	1986	Ex Badgerline, 1994
	TJI2806	Bedford YMP	Plaxton Paramount 3200 II	C41F	1986	Ex Newbury Coaches, Ledbury, 1995
	TJI2807	Bedford YNV Venturer	Plaxton Paramount 3200 III	C57F	1987	Ex Cedar, Bedford, 1995
	TJI2805	DAF SB2305DHTD585	Plaxton Paramount 3200 III	C55F	1987	Ex Nelson, Glyn Neath, 1995
	F64SMC	Mercedes-Benz 407D	Reeve Burgess	M15	1988	
	F356BWU	Mercedes-Benz 811D	Reeve Burgess Beaver	C25F	1988	
	F706ENE	Leyland Tiger TRCL10/3ARZM	Plaxton Paramount 3200 III	C53F	1989	Ex Shearings, 19.93

Previous Registrations:

63XMD	PYG581R	TJI2804	C437LOJ	TJI2807	D101PBM
IBZ5892	HRC788N	TJI2805	E350EVH, PJI3548, E552WEP	XOI5903	B252AMG
IBZ5893	HRC789N	TJI2806	D95ALR		

Livery: White, red and black

Wearing Stringers' white red and black livery is Leyland National XAK454T, an example new to Yorkshire Traction in 1978 and returned to the area after a spell on the Ayrshire coast. It is seen working service 477 to Selby. *Phillip Stephenson*

PRIDE OF THE ROAD

Pride of the Road (Travel) Ltd, 31 St John's Road, Huddersfield, West Yorkshire, LS..

Depots: St John's Road, Huddersfield and Century Road, Newfields Industrial Estate, Heaton Road, Hull.

1	PTF761L	Leyland National 1151/2R/0401		B52F	1973	Ex Yorkshire Rider, 1992
3	OJD901R	Leyland National 10351A/2R		B36D	1977	Ex London Buses, 1990
8	EGB85T	Leyland National 11351A/1R		B52F	1978	Ex Wirralbus, Birkenhead, 1991
9	MTJ774S	Leyland National 11351A/1R		B49F	1977	Ex Yorkshire Rider, 1993
12	JJG889P	Leyland National 11351A/1R		B52F	1976	Ex Yorkshire Rider, 1993
15	EFN170L	Leyland National 1151/1R/2402		B49F	1973	Ex East Kent, 1988
18	ORP475M	Leyland National 1151/1R/0401		B52F	1974	Ex Cumberland, 1990
24	KIW5201	Bova EL28/581	Duple Calypso	C53F	1985	Ex McCabe, Douglas Water, 1990
25	GDZ9114	DAF MB230DKFL615	Van Hool Alizée	C44FT	1986	
26	D665TCX	DAF SB2300DHTD585	Plaxton Paramount 3200 II	C53F	1986	
30	E319EVH	DAF SB2305DHTD585	Plaxton Paramount 3200 III	C55F	1988	
31	H196TCP	DAF SB2305DHTD585	Plaxton Paramount 3200 III	C53F	1990	
32	H197TCP	DAF SB2305DHTD585	Plaxton Paramount 3200 III	C53F	1990	
33	H198TCP	DAF SB2305DHTD585	Plaxton Paramount 3200 III	C53F	1990	
36	RKA866T	Leyland National 11351A/1R		B49F	1978	Ex Merseybus, 1991
39	J797KHD	DAF SB2305DHS585	Plaxton Paramount 3200 III	C57F	1992	
40	J798KHD	DAF MB230LT615	Van Hool Alizeé	C51FT	1992	
41	NJI3653	Bova EL28/581	Duple Calypso	C53F	1984	Ex Crusader, Barnsley, 1992
42	FSU359	DAF MB230LB615	Caetano Algarve	C53F	1988	Ex Catteralls, Southam, 1992
46	RBU171R	Leyland National 11351A/1R		B49F	1977	Ex Blue Bus, Horwich, 1992
48	JNA590N	Leyland National 10351/1R		B41F	1975	Ex Blue Bus, Horwich, 1992
49	OKJ514M	Leyland National 1151/1R		B49F	1974	Ex Good News Travel, 1993
50	SEO210M	Leyland National 11351/1R		B49F	1974	Ex Good News Travel, 1993

Having sold the network of routes established in South and West Yorkshires Pride of the Road have now expanded their operations into Humberside and established a route network within Hull. Bound for the Boothferry estate is THX164S a Leyland National which started life with London Buses but came to Pride of the Road from Armstrong of Castle Douglas in 1992 and has recently been sold to AJC Coaches. *Phillip Stephenson*

The latest arrivals with Pride of the Road are a half dozen DAF SB220s with Ikarus CitiBus bodywork. Two are seen together outside Hull rail station shortly after delivery. Nearest the camera is M835RCP.
Tony Wilson

51	EPT876S	Leyland National 11351A/1R		B49F	1978	Ex Good News Travel, 1993
52	GCY746N	Leyland National 11351/1R		B52F	1974	Ex Good News Travel, 1993
53	MFN119R	Leyland National 11351A/1R		B49F	1976	Ex Good News Travel, 1993
54	AYR305T	Leyland National 10351A/2R		B36D	1979	Ex K-Line, Kirkburton, 1993
55	NFM827M	Leyland National 1151/1R/0405		B48F	1973	Ex Mancunian, Bradford, 1993
56	UPB339S	Leyland National 10351A/1R		B41F	1977	Ex Mancunian, Bradford, 1993
57	MMB968P	Leyland National 11351/1R/SC		B48F	1975	Ex Mancunian, Bradford, 1993
58	J411NCP	DAF SB220LC550	Ikarus CitiBus	B49F	1992	Ex Liverline, Liverpool, 1993
59	J412NCP	DAF SB220LC550	Ikarus CitiBus	B49F	1992	Ex Liverline, Liverpool, 1993
61	F237RJX	DAF MB230LB615	Caetano Algarve	C53F	1989	Ex Moxon, Oldcoates, 1994
62	K520RJX	DAF MB230LTF615	Van Hool Alizée	C57F	1993	Ex Landtourers, Farnham, 1994
63	K529RJX	DAF MB230LTF615	Van Hool Alizée	C57F	1993	Ex Landtourers, Farnham, 1994
64	NEL129P	Leyland National 11351A/1R		B49F	1976	Ex Quickstep Travel, 1994
	M831RCP	DAF SB220LT550	Ikarus CitiBus	B49F	1995	
	M832RCP	DAF SB220LT550	Ikarus CitiBus	B49F	1995	
	M833RCP	DAF SB220LT550	Ikarus CitiBus	B49F	1995	
	M834RCP	DAF SB220LT550	Ikarus CitiBus	B49F	1995	
	M835RCP	DAF SB220LT550	Ikarus CitiBus	B49F	1995	
	M836RCP	DAF SB220LT550	Ikarus CitiBus	B49F	1995	
	D365OSU	Dodge Commando GO8	Wright	B24FL	1986	Ex Yorkshire Rider, 1994
	WPT722R	Leyland National 11351A/1R		B49F	1977	Ex K-Line, Kirkburton, 1993

Previous Registrations:

229ASV	SMY619X	KIW5201	C661GUS
FSU359	F877TNH	KIW8611	D903VVH
GDZ9114	C761CWX	NJI3653	A215YAB, 5516PP, A333KRT

Livery: White and orange

RELIANCE

JH & M Duff, The Garage, Wigginton Road, Sutton-on-the-Forest,
North Yorkshire, YO6 1ES

CWG761V	Leyland Atlantean AN68A/1R	Roe	H45/29D	1979	Ex Your Bus, Alcester, 1993
CWG770V	Leyland Atlantean AN68A/1R	Roe	H45/29D	1979	Ex Your Bus, Alcester, 1993
SND352X	Leyland Tiger TRCTL11/3R	Plaxton Supreme VI Express	C53F	1982	Ex Premier Coaches, Dunnington, 1993
C76XWK	Leyland Tiger TRCTL11/3RZ	Plaxton Paramount 3200 III	C51F	1986	Ex Midland Red South, 1993
C630PAU	DAF MB230DKFL615	Plaxton Paramount 3200 II	C53F	1986	Ex Midland Fox, 1990
F992BFR	Leyland Swift LBM6T/1RS	Elme Orion	C27F	1989	Ex Kinnaird, Edinburgh, 1992

Livery: Green and cream

Two MCW MetroRiders MF150 are operated by Ross both with high-back seating. The model ceased production with MCW and moved to Optare's Leeds factory where an improved version of this popular product is now built. Seen in Pontefract is E262VHE. *Mike Fowler*

ROSS TRAVEL

P E Ross, The Garage, Allinson Street, Station Road, Featherstone
West Yorkshire, WF7 5BC

1	HSC163X	Leyland Cub CU435	Duple Dominant	B31F	1981	Ex Lothian, 1993
2	HSC170X	Leyland Cub CU435	Duple Dominant	B31F	1981	Ex Lothian, 1993
3	HSC169X	Leyland Cub CU435	Duple Dominant	B31F	1981	Ex Lothian, 1993
4	HSC159X	Leyland Cub CU435	Duple Dominant	B31F	1981	Ex Lothian, 1993
5	HSC173X	Leyland Cub CU435	Duple Dominant	B31F	1981	Ex Lothian, 1993
6	E262VHE	MCW MetroRider MF150/32	MCW	DP25F	1987	Ex K-Line, Kirkburton, 1993
7	E413EVH	MCW MetroRider MF150/36	MCW	DP25F	1988	Ex K-Line, Kirkburton, 1993
	GGB640L	Bedford J2SZ10	Plaxton Embassy	C20F	1972	Ex Sutton, Sunderland, 1986
	BKW81T	Bedford YMT	Plaxton Supreme IV	C49FT	1979	Ex Pontefract Disabled Miners, 1988
	KIJ2632	Volvo B58-61	Irizar	C46FT	1980	Ex Garforth Coachways, 1993
	FTH996W	Volvo B58-61	Plaxton Supreme IV	C53F	1981	Ex United Welsh Coaches, 1989
	EOI5357	Volvo B58-61	Jonckheere Bermuda	C49FT	1982	Ex Volvoverland, Robin Hood, 1984
	BPJ77H	Van Hool T815H	Van Hool Alicron	C54F	1984	Ex Wood, Billericay, 1993
	A63FNU	Bova FHD12.280	Bova Futura	C36DT	1984	Ex Nottigham CC, 1995
	B649FWE	Bedford YNT	Duple Laser	C49FT	1985	Ex Beetlestone, Coventry, 1991
	HIL7643	Bova FHD12.280	Bova Futura	C53F	1986	
	D506GEN	Volvo B10M-61	Plaxton Paramount 3200 III	C53F	1987	Ex Shearings, 1992
	HIL7642	Volvo B10M-61	Duple 340	C49FT	1987	Ex Bleanch, Hetton le Hole, 1988
	HIL7644	Scania K92CRB	Plaxton Paramount 3200 II	C53F	1987	Ex Aston, Kempsey, 1991
	E507YSU	Mercedes-Benz L307D	North West Coach Sales	M15	1988	
	HIL7641	LAG G355Z	LAG Panoramic	C49FT	1989	Ex Wood, Buckfastleigh, 1992
	G836RDS	Mercedes-Benz 609D	North West Coach Sales	C24F	1990	

Previous Registrations:

BPJ77H	A103TVW	HIL7641	F620VNH	HIL7644	D662XCT
D506GEN	D571MVR, ESU121	HIL7642	D530YCX	KIJ2632	PFD119W
EOI5357	BBD849X	HIL7643	D202XUT		

Livery: Blue and white

Five Leyland Cubs, all fitted with Duple Dominant bodywork and previously operating in Edinburgh are the mainstay of the Ross bus fleet. Seen here is number 1, HSC163X, complete with side names proclaiming *The Featherstone Rover*. *Phillip Stephenson*

SHEFFIELD OMNIBUS

Basichour Ltd, Green Lane Depot, Ecclesfield, Sheffield, South Yorkshire, S30 3WY

Part of theYorkshire Traction group

1028	PKA728S	Leyland Atlantean AN68A/1R	MCW	H43/32F	1978	Ex Merseybus, 1992
1090	OEM790S	Leyland Atlantean AN68A/1R	MCW	H43/32F	1978	Ex Merseybus, 1993
1098	OEM798S	Leyland Atlantean AN68A/1R	MCW	H43/32F	1978	Ex Merseybus, 1993
1099	OEM799S	Leyland Atlantean AN68A/1R	MCW	H43/32F	1978	Ex Merseybus, 1993

1111-1130

Leyland Atlantean AN68A/2R — East Lancashire — H50/32D — 1976-77 Ex Preston, 1991

1111	UFV111R	1118	UFV118R	1122	CRN122S	1125	CRN125S	1128	CRN128S
1112	UFV112R	1119	UFV119R	1123	CRN123S	1126	CRN126S	1129	CRN129S
1114	UFV114R	1121	CRN121S	1124	CRN124S	1127	CRN127S	1130	CRN130S
1115	UFV115R								

1131-1140

Leyland Atlantean AN68A/2R — East Lancashire — H50/32D — 1979 Ex Preston, 1992

1131	NCK131T	1133	NCK133T	1135	NCK135T	1137	NCK137T	1139	NCK139T
1132	NCK132T	1134	NCK134T	1136	NCK136T	1138	NCK138T	1140	NCK140T

1307	URN207V	Leyland Atlantean AN68A/2R	East Lancashire	H45/33F	1979	Ex Lancaster, 1992
1308	URN208V	Leyland Atlantean AN68A/2R	East Lancashire	H45/33F	1979	Ex Lancaster, 1993
1309	URN209V	Leyland Atlantean AN68A/2R	East Lancashire	H45/33F	1979	Ex Lancaster, 1993
1332	YJK932V	Leyland Atlantean AN68A/2R	East Lancashire	H47/35F	1979	Ex Thames Transit, 1991

1345-1354

Leyland Atlantean AN68A/1R — East Lancashire — H46/31F* — 1980 Ex Thames Transit, 1991
*1346 is DPH46/27F, 1345/53 are H46/27D

1345	CPO345W	1347	CPO347W	1350	CPO350W	1352	CPO352W	1354	CPO354W
1346	CPO346W	1348	CPO348W	1351	CPO351W	1353	CPO353W		

1401	KCK201W	Leyland Atlantean AN68C/2R	East Lancashire	H50/36F	1981	Ex Lancaster, 1993
1402	KCK202W	Leyland Atlantean AN68C/2R	East Lancashire	H50/36F	1981	Ex Lancaster, 1992
1403	KCK203W	Leyland Atlantean AN68C/2R	East Lancashire	H50/36F	1981	Ex Lancaster, 1993
1404	KCK204W	Leyland Atlantean AN68C/2R	East Lancashire	H50/36F	1981	Ex Lancaster, 1993

With the wind down of Olympian production at the Volvo plant near Workington the opportunity was taken to build a number of Alexander-bodied Olympians for dealer's stock. These were offered to various operators and five were purchased by Sheffield Omnibus. This Alexander RH-bodied Olympian is seen at Thorpe Hesley near Rotherham on its first day in service. It is numbered 1602, L602NOS.
Lee Whitehead

Sheffield Omnibus run a trio of Alexander PS bodied Volvo B10M single decks. These vehicles are of a similar build to the substantial fleet operated by Mainline. Since this photograph was taken K235MAP has been renumbered 2235. *Lee Whitehead*

1410	DHG210W	Leyland Atlantean AN68B/1R		East Lancashire		H45/33F	1980	Ex Lancaster, 1993	
1411	DHG211W	Leyland Atlantean AN68B/1R		East Lancashire		H45/33F	1980	Ex Lancaster, 1992	
1434	LEO734Y	Leyland Atlantean AN68D/1R		Northern Counties		H43/32F	1983	Ex Ribble, 1994	
1440	VCX340X	Leyland Atlantean AN68C/2R		Northern Counties		H47/36F	1982	Ex Black Prince, Morley, 1993	

1467-1479

		Leyland Atlantean AN68A/1R		Eastern Coach Works		H43/31F	1979-80	Ex Ribble, 1994	
1467	TRN467V	1471	TRN471V	1473	TRN473V	1475	TRN475V	1479	TRN479V
1468	TRN468V	1472	TRN472V						

1482	LRB582W	Leyland Atlantean AN68C/1R		Eastern Coach Works		H43/31F	1981	Ex Trent, 1994	
1538	VRP38S	Bristol VRT/SL3/6LXB		Alexander AL		H45/27D	1977	Ex Nottingham Omnibus, 1992	
1568	VVV68S	Bristol VRT/SL3/6LXB		Alexander AL		H45/27D	1977	Ex Nottingham Omnibus, 1992	
1569	VVV69S	Bristol VRT/SL3/6LXB		Alexander AL		H45/27D	1977	Ex Nottingham Omnibus, 1992	

1601-1605

		Leyland Olympian ON2R56C16Z4 Alexander LH				H45/29F	1993		
1601	L601NOS	1602	L602NOS	1603	L603NOS	1604	L604NOS	1605	L605NOS

2018	DMS18V	Leyland National 2 NL116L11/1R				B52F	1980	Ex West Riding, 1993	
2023	DMS23V	Leyland National 2 NL116L11/1R				B49F	1980	Ex West Riding, 1993	
2025	DMS25V	Leyland National 2 NL116L11/1R				B49F	1980	Ex West Riding, 1993	
2031	KWA31W	Leyland National 2 NL116L11/1R				B52F	1981	Ex West Riding, 1993	

2082-2087

		Leyland National 2 NL116L11/1R				B49F	1980-81	Ex United Counties, 1993	
2082	NRP582V	2083	NRP583V	2084	NRP584V	2085	NRP585V	2087	NRP587V

2128	A128EPA	Leyland Tiger TRCTL11/2R		Plaxton Paramount 3200		DP53F	1983	Ex Nottingham, 1994	
2137	A137EPA	Leyland Tiger TRCTL11/2R		Plaxton Paramount 3200		DP53F	1983	Ex Nottingham, 1994	

2201-2208

		Volvo B6-9.9M		Alexander Dash		B40F	1995		
2201	M201EUS	2203	M203EUS	2205	M205EUS	2207	M207EUS	2208	M208EUS
2202	M202EUS	2204	M204EUS	2206	M206EUS				

With the demise of the Lancaster undertaking Sheffield Omnibus snapped up a number of youthful Leyland Atlanteans in order to expand its Sheffield operations. 1411 DHG211W is a 78 seat East Lancashire-bodied example which was built for Lancaster in 1980.
Lee Whitehead

Having initially standardised on double deck vehicles, in recent times Sheffield Omnibus have favoured single decks for vehicle purchases. One of eight Alexander Dash-bodied Volvo B6 vehicles purchased in 1995 is 2201 M201EUS.
Lee Whitehead

2235	K235MAP	Volvo B10M-55	Alexander PS	B51F	1992	
2236	K236MAP	Volvo B10M-55	Alexander PS	B51F	1992	
2237	K237MAP	Volvo B10M-55	Alexander PS	B51F	1992	

2270-2274

		Volvo B6-9.9M	Alexander Dash	B40F	1992	Ex Cumberland, 1994
2270	K270ERM	2271	K271ERM	2272	K272ERM	2273	K273ERM	2274	J704BRM

2278	L478TDU	Volvo B6R	Alexander Dash	B40F	1993	Ex Volvo demonstrator, 1994
2501	IIL2501	Leyland Atlantean AN68A/1R	East Lancashire Sprint (1992) B47F		1976	Ex Hyndburn, 1991
2505	XRF26S	Leyland Atlantean AN68A/1R	East Lancashire Sprint (1993) B47F		1978	Ex Liverline, 1992

Previous Registrations:
IIL2501   LJA645P

Livery: Cream and blue

SOUTH YORKSHIRE SUPERTRAM

South Yorkshire Supertram Ltd, 11 Arundel Gate, Sheffield, S1 2PN.

Depot: Nunnery, Sheffield

01-25		Siemans		Duewag		B88T	1993-94			
01	04	07	10	13	16	18	20	22	24
02	05	08	11	14	17	19	21	23	25
03	06	09	12	15					

Livery: Silver

1994 saw the opening of the South Yorkshire Supertram with the first section of route being established between Meadowhall Interchange and Fitzalan Square, Sheffield. The network has continued to expand in 1995. A fleet of 25 bi-directional four-bogie cars have been supplied from Germany to operate the network. Tram 01 remained in Düsseldorf for commssioning trials for some time, though it is now delivered, here seen in central Sheffield. *David Cole*

SS SUNCRUISERS

J Stephenson and C E Spalding, 74 Scalby Road, Scarborough,
North Yorkshire, YO12 5QN

1	KON327P	Leyland Fleetline FE30ALR	MCW	O43/33F	1976	Ex West Midlands Travel, 1991
SS2	MOM573P	Leyland Fleetline FE30ALR	Park Royal	O43/33F	1976	Ex West Midlands Travel, 1991
4	HPK507N	Bristol VRT/SL/6G	Eastern Coach Works	O43/31F	1975	Ex Alder Valley, 1991
SS5	NHR165M	Daimler Fleetline CRG6LX	MCW	O43/31F	1973	Ex Thamesdown, 1991
SS7	KBE108P	Daimler Fleetline CRG6LX	Roe	O43/31F	1976	Ex Grimsby-Cleethorpes, 1993
	LFS296F	Bristol VRT/LL/6G	Eastern Coach Works	O43/31F	1968	Ex Holmes & Allsop, Scarborough, 1992

Livery: Turquoise and yellow

Competition for passengers on Scarborough sea front is intense with three operators serving this market. SS Suncruisers runs a fleet of six open-top vehicles including KON327P a MCW-bodied Leyland Fleetline which was formerly with West Midlands Travel in closed top form. *David Longbottom*

SOUTH RIDING

Tanport Ltd, Upper Sheffield Road, Barnsley, South Yorkshire, S70 4PP
South Yorkshire, S61 2DW

Depot: 20 Acreshill Road, Darnall, Sheffield

Part of the Yorkshire Traction Group

1w	GOL421N	Leyland National 11351/1R	B49F	1975	Ex Northumbria, 1992
2	KRE282P	Leyland National 11351/1R	B52F	1976	Ex PMT, 1992
3w	JBR693T	Leyland National 11351A/1R	B49F	1978	Ex Northumbria, 1992
4	JJG884P	Leyland National 11351/1R	B49F	1976	Ex PMT, 1992
5	MLG960P	Leyland National 11351/1R/SC	B52F	1975	Ex Halton, 1992
6	RFM882M	Leyland National 1151/1R/0402	B49F	1974	Ex Halton, 1992
7	LMB947P	Leyland National 11351/1R/SC	B52F	1975	Ex Halton, 1992
8w	NTC638M	Leyland National 1151/1R/0402	B49F	1974	Ex Northumbria, 1992
9w	SGR110R	Leyland National 11531A/1R	B49F	1976	Ex Northumbria, 1992
10	RFM878M	Leyland National 1151/1R/0402	B49F	1974	Ex Halton, 1992
11w	VPT947R	Leyland National 11351A/1R	B49F	1977	Ex Northumbria, 1992
12	RFM885M	Leyland National 1151/1R/0402	B49F	1974	Ex Halton, 1992
14	JBR688T	Leyland National 11351A/1R	B49F	1978	Ex Northumbria, 1992
16	KRE276P	Leyland National 11351/1R	B52F	1976	Ex PMT, 1992
17	SGR117R	Leyland National 11351A/1R	B49F	1976	Ex Northumbria, 1992
18w	RFM893M	Leyland National 1151/1R/0402	B49F	1974	Ex Halton, 1992
19w	CUP659S	Leyland National 11351A/1R	B49F	1978	Ex Northumbria, 1992
20w	SGR120R	Leyland National 11351A/1R	B49F	1976	Ex Northumbria, 1992
21	SKG913S	Leyland National 11351A/1R	B49F	1978	Ex Barnard, Kirton-in-Lindsey, 1992
22	SKG926S	Leyland National 11351A/1R	B49F	1978	Ex Barnard, Kirton-in-Lindsey, 1992
23	SKG922S	Leyland National 11351A/1R	B49F	1978	Ex Barnard, Kirton-in-Lindsey, 1992

The South Riding operation was set up by two former NBC managers to compete with Mainline. The livery chosen was based on that carried by Halton Transport vehicles but with a green band added. Displaying this livery is 30, PTF729L, a former Ribble Leyland National which came from Pride of the Road in 1994. *Lee Whitehead*

The all-Leyland National fleet of South Riding was acquired by the Yorkshire Traction group in 1994 and recently the premises at Blackburn near Rotherham have been vacated with the fleet now sharing premises with Andrews of Sheffield. Leyland National SKG926S is a former National Welsh vehicle which came via Barnards of Curton in Lyndsey.

Keith Grimes

RFM882M is a former Crosville Leyland National which joined South Riding from Halton Transport. This vehicle is seen in Castle Square Sheffield enroute for Henswick. It is expected that South Riding will be merged with Andrews in due course, three vehicles have recently been repainted into Andrews livery.

Keith Grimes

24	VPT948R	Leyland National 11351A/1R	B49F	1975	Ex Northumbria, 1992
25	GOL433N	Leyland National 11351/1R	B49F	1977	Ex Northumbria, 1992
27	UTU979R	Leyland National 11351A/1R	B49F	1977	Ex East Midland, 1993
28w	RAU600R	Leyland National 11351A/1R	B49F	1976	Ex East Midland, 1993
29	LRB591P	Leyland National 11351/1R	B49F	1975	Ex East Midland, 1993
30	PTF729L	Leyland National 1151/2R/0401	B52F	1972	Ex Pride of the Road, 1994
31w	NEV680M	Leyland National 1151/2R/0402	B49F	1973	Ex Pride of the Road, 1994
32w	EGB83T	Leyland National 11351A/1R	B49F	1979	Ex Pride of the Road, 1994
33	EFN164L	Leyland National 1151/1R/2402	B49F	1973	Ex Pride of the Road, 1994
34	EFN163L	Leyland National 1151/1R/2402	B49F	1973	Ex Pride of the Road, 1994
35w	HPF323N	Leyland National 10351/1R/SC	DP39F	1975	Ex Barnsley & District, 1994
36w	HPF302N	Leyland National 10351/1R/SC	DP39F	1975	Ex Barnsley & District, 1994
37	VPT591R	Leyland National 11351A/1R	B48F	1977	Ex Barnsley & District, 1994
38	SWE444S	Leyland National 11351A/1R	B52F	1977	Ex Yorkshire Traction, 1994
39	SWE446S	Leyland National 11351A/1R	B52F	1977	Ex Yorkshire Traction, 1994
40	YWG462T	Leyland National 11351A/1R	B52F	1978	Ex Yorkshire Traction, 1994
41	HEU123N	Leyland National 11351/1R	B52F	1975	Ex Halton, 1992

Livery: Red, cream and green; blue yellow & white (Andrews) 22, 38, 40.

Named Vehicles: 22 *Charles Peace*, 40 *Friar Tuck*

The Yorkshire Bus Handbook

SWIFTS HAPPY DAYS

SJ & JE Swift, Happy Days, Thorne Road, Blaxton, Doncaster,
South Yorkshire, DN9 3AX

VUJ23Y	Ford R1114	Duple Dominant IV	C53F	1983	Ex Andrews, Sheffield, 1990
PIA233	DAF SB2005DHU605	Jonckheere Bermuda	C49F	1983	Ex Bennett, Warrington, 1993
YEL92Y	Leyland Leopard PSU5E/4R	Eastern Coach Works B51	DP57F	1982	Ex Northern Bus, North Anston, 1994
CIW708	Dennis Dorchester SDA807	Duple Caribbean	C53FT	1984	Ex Turner, Rossington, 1995
844FKX	DAF MB200DKTL600	Jonckheere Jubilee	C57F	1982	Ex Smith, High Wycombe, 1994

Previous Registrations:

844FKX	WRK21X		CIW708	A767HPF		PIA233	BBD853X

Livery: Red, white and blue

Recently withdrawn from the Swifts Happy Days fleet was their only double-deck vehicle CWG720V, an Alexander-bodied Leyland Atlantean which came to Swifts from Camm of Nottingham. The vehicle was photographed in Doncaster south bus station. *Lee Whitehead*

The only double-deck in the Sykes fleet is RAH132M, a Bristol VRT with a standard Eastern Coach Works body liveried in blue and cream. Seen while parked in York, the vehicle may be found working service to it's home-base of Appleton Roebuck. *Mike Fowler.*

Although this view was taken in Chesterfield, Thompson Travel are based in Rotherham. MSF125P is one of a pair of former Lothian Alexander bodied Leyland Leopards which came into the Thompson fleet from Ladyline of Rawmarsh. *Lee Whitehead.*

SYKES

JH Sykes, Southfield, Appleton Roebuck, North Yorkshire, YO5 7DG

KNV666L	Bedford YRT	Duple Dominant	C53F	1973	Ex Head, Lutton, 1991
NTT319M	Bristol LH6L	Marshall	C37F	1973	Ex Turner, Ulleskelf, 1992
RAH132M	Bristol VRT/SL2/6G	Eastern Coach Works	H43/31F	1974	Ex The Bee Line, 1994
RGF231P	Bristol LHS6L	Plaxton Supreme III	C33F	1976	Ex Goodwin, Stockport, 1981
HCE118X	Bedford YNT	Plaxton Supreme IV	C53F	1981	Ex Rigbys Coaches, 1993
OHE273X	Volvo B10M-61	Duple Dominant IV	C50F	1982	Ex Bruton, Balham, 1993
A301KFP	Bova FHD12.250	Bova Futura	C53F	1984	Ex Stevensons, 1990
A501WGF	Volvo B10M-61	Plaxton Paramount 3500	C50F	1984	Ex Epsom Coaches, 1993
C46WLL	Volvo B10M-61	Duple Caribbean	C53F	1986	Ex Dodworth, Boroughbridge, 1994
F846YJX	DAF SB2305DHTD585	Duple 340	C57F	1989	Ex Hanson, Halifax, 1991
F958TRN	Peugeot-Talbot Express	Dormobile	M12	1988	Ex Nova Scotia, Winsford, 1993

Previous Registrations:
A301KFP   WDL142, 124YTW

Livery: Blue and cream

THOMPSON TRAVEL

H, C & M Thompson and D E Vickers , The New Depot, Naylor Street, Parkgate,
Rotherham, South Yorkshire, S62 6BP

MSF125P	Leyland Leopard PSU3C/4R	Alexander AY	DP49F	1975	Ex Ladyline, Rawmarsh, 1993
MSF130P	Leyland Leopard PSU3C/4R	Alexander AY	DP49F	1975	Ex Ladyline, Rawmarsh, 1993
YFC14R	Leyland Leopard PSU3E/4R	Duple Dominant I	C49F	1977	Ex Ladyline, Rawmarsh, 1993
WCK133V	Leyland Leopard PSU3E/4R	Duple Dominant II Express	C51F	1979	Ex Ladyline, Rawmarsh, 1993
COF707V	Leyland Leopard PSU3E/4R	Plaxton Supreme IV Express	C51F	1979	Ex Hodgkinson, Langley Mill, 1994
JNJ31V	Leyland Leopard PSU3E/4R	Plaxton Supreme IV Express	C48F	1980	Ex Armstrong, Inverkeithing, 1993
MPL133W	Leyland Leopard PSU3E/4R	Duple Dominant II Express	C53F	1980	Ex Goodwin, Stockport, 1994
SXU708	Leyland Tiger TRCTL11/3R	Plaxton Paramount 3500	C49FT	1983	Ex Greenhalgh, Ottershaw, 1994

Previous Registrations:
JNJ31V   GWV932V, YLJ332

Livery: Red, black and white.

VIKING TOURS

M Stadie & D Turner, Brockett Park Industrial Estate, Acaster Malbis, York,
North Yorkshire, YO

Depots: Brockett Park Industrial Estate, Acaster Malbis & Stainsacre Industrial Estate, Whitby.

WJY758	Leyland Atlantean PDR1/1	Metro Cammell	O44/33F	1962	Ex SS Suncruisers, Scarborough, 1992
DRX122C	Bristol Lodekka FLF6G	Eastern Coach Works	O33/8F	1965	Ex Jorvik, Market Weighton, 1992
LFS288F	Bristol VRT/LL/6G	Eastern Coach Works	O43/31F	1968	Ex SS Suncruisers, Scarborough, 1992
RNV811M	Bristol VRT/SL2/6G	Eastern Coach Works	O43/31F	1974	Ex United Counties, 1992
MDS687P	Leyland Atlantean AN68A/1R	Alexander AL	O45/31F	1976	Ex Jorvik, Market Weighton, 1992
LRA798P	Bristol VRT/SL3/501(6LXB)	Eastern Coach Works	O43/34F	1976	Ex Trent, 1992
WTH962T	Bristol VRT/SL3/501	Eastern Coach Works	O43/31F	1979	Ex Battrick & Brown, Clayton-le-Dale, 1991

Previous Registrations:
WJY758   From new

Livery: Pale blue and yellow; many carry overall advertisements.

The all-open-top fleet of Viking Tours operates in York and Whitby using a variety of vehicle types. Added to the fleet during 1991 was WTH962T, a VRT now with the centre roof removed, and seen here in York on the city tour. *Andrew Jarosz*

Viking Tours are one of 3 operators providing open-top tours of the city of York. LRA798P is a member of this fleet which started life with Trent and was purchased by Viking in 1992 and converted to open-top. This Bristol VR with ECW bodywork is also of interest in that its Leyland engine has been replaced with a Gardner example. *Mike Fowler*

Displaying a two-tone blue and yellow livery is MDS687P. This Alexander AL-bodied Leyland Atlantean has been operating city tours in York for a number of years having been previously part of the Jorvik operation, now ceased. *David Cole*

WALLACE ARNOLD

Wallace Arnold Coaches Ltd, Gelderd Road, Leeds, West Yorkshire, LS12 6DH
Wallace Arnold Coaches Ltd, Barton Hill Way, Barton, Torquay, Devon, TQ2 8JG

Note: Fleet numbers are not carried by any of the vehicles.

101	M101UWY	Volvo B10M-62		Plaxton Excalibur	C50F	1995			
102	M102UWY	Volvo B10M-62		Plaxton Premiére 350	C48FT	1995			
103	M103UWY	Volvo B10M-62		Plaxton Premiére 350	C48FT	1995			
104	M104UWY	Volvo B10M-62		Plaxton Premiére 350	C48FT	1995			
105	M105UWY	Volvo B10M-62		Plaxton Premiére 350	C48FT	1995			

106-116   Volvo B10M-62   Plaxton Premiére 320   C50F   1995

106	M106UWY	108	M108UWY	110	M110UWY	113	M113UWY	115	M115UWY
107	M107UWY	109	M109UWY	112	M112UWY	114	M114UWY	116	M116UWY

117-131   Volvo B10M-62   Plaxton Premiére 350   C50F   1995

117	M117UWY	120	M120UWY	123	M123UWY	126	M126UWY	129	M129UWY
118	M118UWY	121	M121UWY	124	M124UWY	127	M127UWY	130	M130UWY
119	M119UWY	122	M122UWY	125	M125UWY	128	M128UWY	131	M131UWY

132-136   Volvo B10M-62   Plaxton Excalibur   C50F   1995

132	M132UWY	133	M133UWY	134	M134UWY	135	M135UWY	136	M136UYG

226	D226STT	Mercedes-Benz L307D	Yeates	M12	1987	
425	BUF425C	Leyland Titan PD3/4	Northern Counties	FCO39/30F	1965	Ex Harris Bus, West Thurrock, 1994
436	CSU936	Leyland Leopard PSU4E/4R	Plaxton Paramount 3200 II(1987)	C45F	1977	
437	CSU937	Leyland Leopard PSU4E/4R	Plaxton Paramount 3200 II(1987)	C45F	1977	
438	CSU938	Leyland Leopard PSU4E/4R	Plaxton Paramount 3200 II(1987)	C45F	1977	
511	KUM511L	Leyland Leopard PSU3B/4R	Plaxton Elite III	DP53F	1973	
576	SUG576M	Leyland Atlantean AN68/2R	Roe	H45/33D	1974	Ex Yorkshire Rider, 1992

714-725   Volvo B10M-60   Plaxton Premiére 350   C48FT   1992   721 is C40FT, 723 is C26FT

714	8980WA	719	7243WA	721	WA3399	723	4030WA	725	J725CWT
715	J715CWT	720	7820WA	722	3333WA	724	J724CWT		

726-735   Volvo B10M-60   Plaxton Excalibur   C50F   1992

726	J726CWT	728	J728CWT	730	J730CWT	732	J732CWT	735	J735CWT
727	J727CWT	729	J729CWT	731	J731CWT				

736-751   Volvo B10M-60   Plaxton Premiére 350   C50F   1992

736	J736CWT	739	J739CWT	742	J742CWT	745	J745CWT	749	J749CWT
737	J737CWT	740	J740CWT	743	J743CWT	746	J746CWT	750	J750CWT
738	J738CWT	741	J741CWT	744	J744CWT	748	J748CWT	751	J751CWT

752-761   Volvo B10M-60   Plaxton Premiére 320   C50F   1992

752	J752CWT	755	J755CWT	757	K757FYG	759	K759FYG	761	K761FYG
754	J754CWT	756	K756FYG	758	K758FYG	760	K760FYG		

762	K762FYG	Dennis Javelin 12SDA2114	Plaxton Premiére 350	C50F	1992	Ex Dennis demonstrator, 1993
763	J763CWT	Mercedes-Benz 308D	Devon Conversion	C12F	1992	
764	J764CWT	Mercedes-Benz 308D	Devon Conversion	C12F	1992	
765	J765CWT	Volkswagen Transporter	Advanced Vehicle Bodies	M10	1992	
766	J766CWT	Volkswagen Transporter	Advanced Vehicle Bodies	M10	1992	
800	8665WA	Volvo B10M-60	Plaxton Excalibur	C26FT	1991	

801-820   Volvo B10M-60   Van Hool Alizée   C48FT   1993

801	K801HUM	805	K805HUM	809	K809HUM	813	K813HUM	817	K817HUM
802	K802HUM	806	K806HUM	810	K810HUM	814	K814HUM	818	K818HUM
803	K803HUM	807	K807HUM	811	K811HUM	815	K815HUM	819	K819HUM
804	K804HUM	808	K808HUM	812	K812HUM	816	K816HUM	820	K820HUM

As well as operating from its Yorkshire home base Wallace Arnold has a substantial fleet based in Devon. Providing valuable publicity for the Torquay-based touring operation as well as being used for local tours is 425, BUF425C, a Northern Counties-bodied Leyland Titan PD3/4 that was part of the large Southdown fleet. It came to Wallace Arnold from Harris Bus of West Thurrock and is now a rare example of a bus within the Wallace Arnold coaching fleet. *Phillip Stephenson*

Plaxton-bodied coaches have featured in the Wallace Arnold fleet for many years. The current top-of-the-range model is the Plaxton Excalibur here based on a Volvo B10M. J727CWT is an example new in 1992 and is seen on tour to Newquay. *David Cole*

K801HUM is one of forty Van Hool Alizée-bodied Volvo B10Ms in the Wallace Arnold fleet. It clearly shows the orange and cream livery style carried by this operator's vehicles and was photographed at South Mimms services during the summer of 1994. South Mimms is an important transfer point for Wallace Arnold and many other tour operators. *Keith Grimes*

In recent years the Jonckheere Deauville body in its 45-series style has been favoured by Wallace Arnold for purchases of Volvo B10M chassis. Shown here is 962, L962NWW, though the numbers are not displayed on the vehicles, index marks being sufficient for identification. *Keith Grimes*

821-825 — Volvo B10M-60 — Van Hool Alizée — C50F — 1993

821	K821HUM	822	K822HUM	823	K823HUM	824	K824HUM	825	K825HUM

826-845 — Volvo B10M-60 — Jonckheere Deauville 45 — C50F — 1993

826	K826HUM	830	K830HUM	834	K834HUM	838	K838HUM	842	K842HUM
827	K827HUM	831	K831HUM	835	K835HUM	839	K839HUM	843	K843HUM
828	K828HUM	832	K832HUM	836	K836HUM	840	K840HUM	844	K844HUM
829	K829HUM	833	K833HUM	837	K837HUM	841	K841HUM	845	K845HUM

846	K846HUM	Volvo B10M-60	Plaxton Premiére 320	C50F	1993
847	K847HUM	Volvo B10M-60	Plaxton Premiére 320	C50F	1993
848	K848HUM	Volvo B10M-60	Plaxton Premiére 320	C50F	1993
849	K849HUM	Volvo B10M-60	Plaxton Premiére 320	C50F	1993
850	K850HUM	Volvo B10M-60	Plaxton Excalibur	C50F	1993

901-905 — Volvo B10M-62 — Jonckheere Deauville 45 — C50FT — 1994

901	L901NWW	902	L902NWW	903	L903NWW	904	L904NWW	905	L905NWW

906-920 — Volvo B10M-60 — Van Hool Alizée — C48FT — 1994

906	L906NWW	909	L909NWW	912	L912NWW	915	L915NWW	918	L918NWW
907	L907NWW	910	L910NWW	913	L913NWW	916	L916NWW	919	L919NWW
908	L908NWW	911	L911NWW	914	L914NWW	917	L917NWW	920	L920NWW

921	L921NWW	Volvo B10M-62	Plaxton Excalibur	C48FT	1994

922-941 — Volvo B10M-60 — Plaxton Excalibur — C50F — 1994

922	L922NWW	926	L926NWW	930	L930NWW	934	L934NWW	938	L938NWW
923	L923NWW	927	L927NWW	931	L931NWW	935	L935NWW	939	L939NWW
924	L924NWW	928	L928NWW	932	L932NWW	936	L936NWW	940	L940NWW
925	L925NWW	929	L929NWW	933	L933NWW	937	L937NWW	941	L941NWW

942-946 — Volvo B10M-60 — Jonckheere Deauville 45 — C50F — 1994

942	L942NWW	943	L943NWW	944	L944NWW	945	L945NWW	946	L946NWW

947-963 — Volvo B10M-62 — Jonckheere Deauville 45 — C50F — 1994

947	L947NWW	951	L951NWW	955	L955NWW	958	L958NWW	961	L961NWW
948	L948NWW	952	L952NWW	956	L956NWW	959	L959NWW	962	L962NWW
949	L949NWW	953	L953NWW	957	L957NWW	960	L960NWW	963	L963NWW
950	L950NWW	954	L954NWW						

965	L965NWW	Volvo B12	Jonckheere Deauville 65	C50FT	1994	
966	L966RUB	Toyota Coaster HZB50R	Caetano Optimo III	C21F	1994	
967	L967RUB	Toyota Coaster HZB50R	Caetano Optimo III	C21F	1994	
8332	8332U	AEC Reliance MU3RA	Plaxton	C41C	1958	Ex preservation, 1989

Previous Registrations:

3333WA	J722CWT	8665WA	J801BWY	CSU937	WUG127S
4030WA	J723CWT	8980WA	J714CWT	CSU938	WUG128S
7243WA	J719CWT	CSU936	SWW126R	WA3399	J721CWT
7820WA	J720CWT				

Livery: Orange, cream and brown. 425 is named *Uncle Wally*

Operating companies: Torquay: 226, 425/36-9, 724/5/38/40-6, 762-6, 816-25, 916-20/2-31.; +10 new 350s

WEST RIDING

West Riding Automobile Co Ltd, 24 Barnsley Road, Wakefield,
West Yorkshire, WF1 5JX
South Yorkshire Road Transport Ltd, 24 Barnsley Road, Wakefield,
West Yorkshire, WF1 5JX
Yorkshire Woollen District Transport Co Ltd, Mill Street East, Dewsbury,
West Yorkshire, WF12 9AG
Selby & District Bus Co Ltd, 24 Barnsley Road, Wakefield, West Yorkshire, WF1 5JX

A subsidiary of British Bus plc

Depots: Wheldon Road, Castleford; Mill Street East, Dewsbury; Beck Lane, Heckmondwike; Northgate, Pontefract; Chimes Road, Selby and Belle Isle, Barnsley Road, Wakefield

5	F625OHD	DAF SBR3000DKZ570	Van Hool Astrobel	CH57/15CT	1988	
6	F626OHD	DAF SBR3000DKZ570	Van Hool Astrobel	CH57/15CT	1988	
46	E46TYG	Leyland Royal Tiger RTC	Leyland Doyen	C47FT	1988	
47	E47TYG	Leyland Royal Tiger RTC	Leyland Doyen	C47FT	1988	
48	G103ETJ	Volvo B10M-60	Plaxton Expressliner	C46FT	1990	Ex Express Travel Services, 1994
50	G105ETJ	Volvo B10M-60	Plaxton Expressliner	C46FT	1990	Ex Express Travel Services, 1994

101-105

Leyland National 2 NL116AL11/1R(6LXB) — B49F — 1982

101	XUA72X	102	XUA73X	103	XUA74X	104	XUA75X	105	XUA76X

106-115

Leyland National 2 NL116HLXB/1R — B49F — 1982-83

106	EWT206Y	108	EWT208Y	110	EWT210Y	112	EWX212Y	114	EWX214Y
107	EWT207Y	109	EWT209Y	111	EWX211Y	113	EWX213Y	115	EWX215Y

116	VBG91V	Leyland National 2 NL116L11/1R (6HLXB)	B49F	1980	Ex Lincoln, 1989
117	VBG93V	Leyland National 2 NL116L11/1R (6HLXB)	B49F	1980	Ex Lincoln, 1989
119	CCY819V	Leyland National 2 NL116L11/1R (6HLXB)	DP48F	1979	Ex Stevensons, Uttoxeter, 1990
120	VBG89V	Leyland National 2 NL116L11/1R (6HLXB)	B49F	1980	Ex Lincoln, 1989
121	VBG90V	Leyland National 2 NL116L11/1R (6HLXB)	B49F	1980	Ex Lincoln, 1989
122	VBG84V	Leyland National 2 NL116L11/1R (6HLXB)	B49F	1980	Ex Lincoln, 1989
124	VBG92V	Leyland National 2 NL116L11/1R (6HLXB)	B49F	1980	Ex Lincoln, 1989
125	BPR48Y	Leyland National 2 NL116HLXB/2R	B49F	1980	Ex Provincial, 1989
126	BPR49Y	Leyland National 2 NL116HLXB/2R	B49F	1980	Ex Provincial, 1989
127	HED204V	Leyland National 2 NL116L11/1R (6HLXB)	B49F	1980	Ex Halton, 1989
128	HED205V	Leyland National 2 NL116L11/1R (6HLXB)	B49F	1980	Ex Halton, 1989
130	CCY820V	Leyland National 2 NL116L11/1R	DP48F	1979	Ex Stevensons, Uttoxeter, 1989
·132	C103UHO	Leyland National 2 NL116HLXCT/1R	B52F	1985	Ex Stevensons, Uttoxeter, 1989
133	C104UHO	Leyland National 2 NL116HLXCT/1R	B52F	1985	Ex Stevensons, Uttoxeter, 1989
135	NAT202V	Leyland National 2 NL116L11/1R	B49F	1980	Ex Scarborough & District, 1989
137	LRB217W	Leyland National 2 NL116AL11/1R	B52F	1981	Ex Trent, 1989
139	VBG88V	Leyland National 2 NL116L11/1R (6HLXB)	B49F	1980	Ex Lincoln, 1989
141	LRB202W	Leyland National 2 NL116AL11/1R	B52F	1981	Ex Trent, 1990
142	LRB203W	Leyland National 2 NL116AL11/1R	B52F	1981	Ex Trent, 1990
144	LRB205W	Leyland National 2 NL116AL11/1R	DP50F	1981	Ex Trent, 1990
145	LRB206W	Leyland National 2 NL116AL11/1R	B52F	1981	Ex Trent, 1990
146	SNS824W	Leyland National 2 NL116L11/1R	B49F	1980	Ex Sheffield United Transport, 1989
147	CCY817V	Leyland National 2 NL116L11/1R	DP48F	1980	Ex Stevensons, Uttoxeter, 1989
153	DMS19V	Leyland National 2 NL116L11/1R	B49F	1980	Ex Airebus, Leeds, 1989
156	KWA30W	Leyland National 2 NL116L11/1R	B52F	1980	Ex South Yorkshire, 1989
252	C920FMP	Leyland Lynx LX1126LXCTFR1	Leyland Lynx	B51F	1986	Ex Leyland Bus, 1987
253	D204FBK	Leyland Lynx LX112TL11ZR1	Leyland Lynx	B51F	1986	Ex Solent Blue Line, 1987
254	E254TUB	Leyland Lynx LX1126LXCTFR2	Leyland Lynx	B50F	1986	

255-264

Leyland Lynx LX1126LXCTFR1 — Leyland Lynx — B49F — 1987-88

255	E255TUB	257	E257TUB	259	E259TUB	261	E261TUB	263	E263TUB
256	E256TUB	258	E258TUB	260	E260TUB	262	E262TUB	264	E264TUB

Recently painted into South Yorkshire's blue and white livery is 113, EWX213Y a Gardner-engined Leyland National 2 of 1982 vintage. Photographed in Pontefract, it shows the integration of the South Yorkshire operation is well underway. *Tony Wilson*

The Leyland Lynx was bought in substantial numbers by the Caldaire group before production of the type ceased in 1991. One of the 1987 delivery is 257, E257TUB, which shows the West Riding Buses green and cream livery in this view taken in Wakefield. *Daniel Hill*

265-314 — Leyland Lynx LX112L10ZR1S — Leyland Lynx — B49F — 1988

265	E265WUB	275	F275AWW	285	F285AWW	295	F295AWW	305	F305AWW
266	E266WUB	276	F276AWW	286	F286AWW	296	F296AWW	306	F306AWW
267	E267WUB	277	F277AWW	287	F287AWW	297	F297AWW	307	F307AWW
268	E268WUB	278	F278AWW	288	F288AWW	298	F298AWW	308	F308AWW
269	E269WUB	279	F279AWW	289	F289AWW	299	F299AWW	309	F309AWW
270	E270WUB	280	F280AWW	290	F290AWW	300	F300AWW	310	F310AWW
271	E271WUB	281	F281AWW	291	F291AWW	301	F301AWW	311	F311AWW
272	F272AWW	282	F282AWW	292	F292AWW	302	F302AWW	312	F312AWW
273	F273AWW	283	F283AWW	293	F293AWW	303	F303AWW	313	F313AWW
274	F274AWW	284	F284AWW	294	F294AWW	304	F304AWW	314	F314AWW

315	E116UTX	Leyland Lynx LX112L10ZR1R	Leyland Lynx	B51F	1988	Ex Merthyr Tydfil, 1989
316	F117XTX	Leyland Lynx LX112L10ZR1R	Leyland Lynx	B51F	1988	Ex Merthyr Tydfil, 1989
317	F118XTX	Leyland Lynx LX112L10ZR1R	Leyland Lynx	B51F	1988	Ex Merthyr Tydfil, 1989

318-332 — Leyland Lynx LX2R11C15Z4S — Leyland Lynx — B49F — 1990

318	G317NNW	321	G321NNW	324	G324NUM	327	G327NUM	330	G330NUM
319	G319NNW	322	G322NNW	325	G110OUG	328	G109OUG	331	G331NUM
320	G324NNW	323	G108OUG	326	G326NUM	329	G329NUM	332	G332NUM

333-337 — Leyland Lynx LX2R11C15Z4S — Leyland Lynx 2 — B49F — 1990

333	H338TYG	334	H334TYG	335	H335TYG	336	H336TYG	337	H337TYG

338-347 — Leyland Lynx LX2R11C15Z4S — Leyland Lxnx 2 — B49F — 1990-91

338	H338UWT	340	H343UWT	342	H342UWT	344	H344UWX	346	H346UWX
339	H339UWT	341	H341UWT	343	H343UWX	345	H345UWX	347	H347UWX

348	G542GAC	Leyland Lynx LX2R11C15Z4R	Leyland Lynx	B49F	1990	Ex Volvo Bus, Warwick, 1991
349w	G148CHP	Leyland Lynx LX2R11C15Z4R	Leyland Lynx	B49F	1990	Ex Volvo Bus, Warwick, 1991
350	G149CHP	Leyland Lynx LX2R11C15Z4R	Leyland Lynx	B51F	1990	Ex Volvo Bus, Warwick, 1991
351	G49CVC	Leyland Lynx LX112L10ZR1R	Leyland Lynx	B51F	1990	Ex Volvo Bus, Warwick, 1991

352-382 — Leyland Lynx LX2R11C15Z4S* — Leyland Lxnx 2 — B49F — 1991 — *378 is LX2R11V18Z4S

352	H755WWW	359	H359WWY	365	J365YWX	371	J371YWX	377	J377AWT
353	H756WWW	360	H460WWY	366	J366YWX	372	J372AWT	378	J371AWT
354	H757WWW	361	H393WWY	367	J367YWX	373	J373AWT	379	J379BWU
355	H355WWX	362	J362YWX	368	J368YWX	374	J374AWT	380	J380BWU
356	H356WWX	363	J363YWX	369	J369YWX	375	J375AWT	381	J381BWU
357	H357WWX	364	J364YWX	370	J370YWX	376	J376AWT	382	J382BWU
358	H358WWY								

The Leyland Lynx features prominently in the West Riding fleet, a type which, unlike the Leyland National, is not an integral vehicle in the accepted sense. The Lynx 2 variant has a modified front to house the radiator and features other improvements. Seen in Morley is 359, H359WWY, an example with the stepped rear section option. *Colin Lloyd.*

The successor to the Leyland Lynx is the Volvo B10B which is produced by Volvo in chassis form for others to body. The Alexander product known as the Strider is shown in this picture of Selby & District 404, K404HWW. *Phillip Stephenson*

401-405 — Volvo B10B-58 — Alexander Strider — B51F — 1993

401	K401HWW	402	K402HWW	403	K403HWW	404	K404HWW	405	K405HWX

406	L406NUA	Volvo B10B-58	Wright Endeavour	DP49F	1993
407	L407NUA	Volvo B10B-58	Wright Endeavour	DP49F	1993
408	L408NUA	Volvo B10B-58	Wright Endeavour	DP49F	1993
409	L409NUA	Volvo B10B-58	Wright Endeavour	DP49F	1993

410-433 — Volvo B10B-58 — Alexander Strider — B51F — 1994

410	M410UNW	415	M415UNW	420	M420UNW	425	M425UNW	430	M430UNW
411	M411UNW	416	M416UNW	421	M421UNW	426	M426UNW	431	M431UNW
412	M412UNW	417	M417UNW	422	M422UNW	427	M427UNW	432	M432UNW
413	M413UNW	418	M418UNW	423	M423UNW	428	M428UNW	433	M433UNW
414	M414UNW	419	M419UNW	424	M424UNW	429	M429UNW		

451-472 — Renault-Dodge S56 — Alexander AM — B25F — 1987 — Ex United, 1989-92 / *451 is B23F

451	E72KAJ	456	E523HHN	463	E582JVN	466	E69KAJ	470	E507HHN
452	E504HHN	457	E70KAJ	464	E583JVN	468	E494HHN	471	E502HHN
453	E497HHN	462	E505HHN	465	E67KAJ	469	E503HHN	472	E506HHN
454	E508HHN								

474	D158RAK	Renault-Dodge S56	Reeve Burgess	B25F	1987	Ex Mainline, 1992
504	YWX401X	Leyland Olympian ONTL11/1R	Northern Counties	H43/28F	1982	
505	YWX402X	Leyland Olympian ONTL11/1R	Northern Counties	H43/28F	1982	

Photographed in Dewsbury while heading for Leeds is 601, B601UUM a Leyland Olympian with a traditional Eastern Coach Works body. Recent arrivals from the South Yorkshire fleet have seen Olympians allocated spare fleet numbers within this batch. *Tony Wilson*

506-552

Leyland Olympian ONLXB/1R   Eastern Coach Works   H45/33F   1982-83

506	CWR506Y	515	CWR515Y	524	CWR524Y	535	EWX535Y	544	544WRA
507	CWR507Y	516	CWR516Y	527	CWR527Y	536	EWX536Y	545	EWW545Y
508	CWR508Y	517	CWR517Y	528	EWX528Y	537	EWX537Y	546	EWW546Y
509	CWR509Y	518	CWR518Y	529	EWX529Y	538	EWW538Y	547	EWW547Y
510	CWR510Y	519	CWR519Y	530	EWX530Y	539	EWW539Y	548	EWW548Y
511	CWR511Y	520	CWR520Y	531	EWX531Y	540	EWW540Y	550	EWW550Y
512	CWR512Y	521	CWR521Y	532	EWX532Y	541	EWW541Y	551	EWW551Y
513	CWR513Y	522	CWR522Y	533	EWX533Y	543	EWW543Y	552	EWW552Y
514	CWR514Y	523	CWR523Y	534	EWX534Y				

563	A103OUG	Leyland Olympian ONTL11/1R	Northern Counties	H43/28F	1984
598	A104OUG	Leyland Olympian ONTL11/1R	Northern Counties	H43/28F	1984

560-612

Leyland Olympian ONLXB/1R   Eastern Coach Works   H45/32F   1983-85   *598, 605-7/12/3 are H43/31F
608-10 are DPH42/30F; 562 is DPH42/28F; 598, 605-7/9/10/12 are DPH41/30F; 611 is H41/32F

560	A560KWY	571	A571NWX	581	A581NWX	591	B591SWX	604	B604UUM
561	A561KWY	572	A572NWX	582	A582NWX	592	B592SWX	605	B605UUM
562	A562KWY	573	A573NWX	583	A583NWX	595	B595SWX	606	B606UUM
564	A564KWY	574	A574NWX	584	A584NWX	596	B596SWX	607	B607UUM
565	A565NWX	575	A575NWX	585	A585NWX	597	B597SWX	608	B608UUM
566	A566NWX	576	A576NWX	586	A586NWX	599	B599SWX	609	B609UUM
567	A567NWX	577	A577NWX	587	A587NWX	600	B600UUM	610	C610ANW
568	A568NWX	578	A578NWX	588	A588NWX	601	B601UUM	611	C611ANW
569	A569NWX	579	A579NWX	589	A589NWX	602	B602UUM	612	C612ANW
570	A570NWX	580	A580NWX	590	A590NWX	603	B603UUM		

Opposite: **The colour illustrations of West Riding show the contrasting liveries of the Yorkshire Buses and West Riding operations, though the application of colour is consistant. Representing the Yorkshire Buses scheme is Leyland Lynx 279, F279AWW while in the green colours of West Riding is 409, L409NUA, a Volvo B10B with Wrights's Endeavour body design.** *Lee Whitehead*

While the Optare MetroRider has been favoured for midi buses within the West Riding fleet, Yorkshire Woollen have turned to Mercedes Benz. This Plaxton Beaver bodied 811D is 778, L778RWW and is seen leaving Dewsbury bus station for Rothwell. *Lee Whitehead.*

613	E205TUB	Leyland Olympian ONTL11/1RH	Northern Counties	H43/28F	1988				
614	TWY7	Leyland Olympian ONCL10/1RZ	Northern Counties	H43/28F	1988				
615	H106RWT	Leyland Olympian ON2R50C13Z4	Northern Counties	H43/28F	1990				
616	H108RWT	Leyland Olympian ON2R50C13Z4	Northern Counties	H43/28F	1990				

701-713 — Optare MetroRider MR09 — Optare — B23F — 1991

701	H701UNW	704	H704UNW	707	H707UNW	710	H710UNW	712	H712UNW
702	H702UNW	705	H705UNW	708	H708UNW	711	H711UNW	713	H713UNW
703	H703UNW	706	H706UNW	709	H709UNW				

714-729 — Optare MetroRider MR05 — Optare — B31F — 1992-93

714	J714CUM	718	J718CUM	721	J721CUM	724	K724HUG	727	K727HUG
715	J715CUM	719	J719CUM	722	J722CUM	725	K725HUG	728	K728HUG
716	J716CUM	720	J720CUM	723	K723HUG	726	K726HUG	729	K729HUG
717	J717CUM								

730-745 — Optare MetroRider MR15 — Optare — B31F — 1993-94

730	L730MWW	734	L734MWW	737	L737PUA	740	L740PUA	743	M743UUA
731	L731MWW	735	L735PUA	738	L738PUA	741	L741PUA	744	M744UUA
732	L732MWW	736	L736PUA	739	L739PUA	742	M742UUA	745	M745UUA
733	L733MWW								

771-778 — Mercedes-Benz 811D — Plaxton Beaver — B31F — 1994

771	L771RWW	773	L773RWW	775	L775RWW	777	L779RWW	778	L778RWW
772	L772RWW	774	L774RWW	776	L776RWW				

Boar Lane in Leeds is the location of this view of 825, L825NWY, an Alexander Strider-bodied Dennis Lance in the West Riding fleet. Now that the Caldaire operations have become are part of the British Bus Group it will be interesting to see what form the new vehicle intake for this fleet takes.
Lee Whitehead

801-830

801-830		Dennis Lance 11SDA3107		Alexander Strider		B47F		1993	
801	K801HWW	807	L807NNW	813	L813NNW	819	L819NWY	825	L825NWY
802	K802HWW	808	L808NNW	814	L814NNW	820	L820NWY	826	L826NYG
803	K803HWW	809	L809NNW	815	L815NNW	821	L821NWY	827	L827NYG
804	K804HWW	810	L810NNW	816	L816NWY	822	L822NWY	828	L828NYG
805	K805HWX	811	L811NNW	817	L817NWY	823	L823NWY	829	L829NYG
806	L806NNW	812	L812NNW	818	L818NWY	824	L824NWY	830	L830NYG

920	ODC470W	Bristol VRT/SL3/6LXB	Eastern Coach Works	H43/31F	1981
921w	VUA471X	Bristol VRT/SL3/6LXB	Eastern Coach Works	H43/31F	1981
923w	VUA473X	Bristol VRT/SL3/6LXB	Eastern Coach Works	H43/31F	1981
952	LWT99V	Leyland Fleetline FE30ALR	Northern Counties	H39/31F	1980
953w	LWT100V	Leyland Fleetline FE30ALR	Northern Counties	H39/31F	1980

Operating Companies:
Selby & District: 401-5/21/2/52-5/68/70, 510/2/8-20/34/9/61/91/2.
South Yorkshire: 17, 113-5/46/7, 456-4/9, 504-8/63/98, 613/7, 952/3.
Yorkshire Woollen: 5/6, 46-8/50, 118/20-45/53/6, 265/7/8/70-5/7/9-81/4/5/7/8/91/5/6, 303-5/15-28/50-7/9-81
                    384/5/7/8/91/5/6, 410-8/51/65/6/9/71/2/4, 522-7/47/8/60/2-5/8-71/85-9, 600-4/8, 771-8, 801-18
West Riding: Remainder.

Previous Registrations:
544WRA   EWX544Y

Liveries:
Cream and green (West Riding); cream and red (Yorkshire Woollen); cream and green (Selby & District); two tone blue and white (South Yorkshire).
National Express: 5/6, 46/7

WHITE ROSE

T Pickett & S Hullah, Carrwood Industrial Estate, Glass Houghton, Castleford,
West Yorkshire, WF10 4SB

OYM582A	AEC Routemaster R2RH	Park Royal	H36/28R	1959	Ex London Buses, 1994
SVS615	AEC Routemaster R2RH	Park Royal	H36/28R	1960	Ex London Buses, 1994
VYJ892	AEC Routemaster R2RH	Park Royal	H36/28R	1960	Ex London Buses, 1994
SVS618	AEC Routemaster R2RH	Park Royal	H36/28R	1960	Ex London Buses, 1994
MFF510	AEC Routemaster R2RH	Park Royal	H36/28R	1960	Ex London Buses, 1994
NOC727R	Leyland Fleetline FE30AGR	East Lancashire	H43/33F	1977	Ex West Midlands Travel, 1990
HIL4056	DAF MB200DKTL600	Plaxton Paramount 3200	C51F	1983	Ex Thomas, West Ewell, 1991
PTT1M	DAF SB2305DHS585	Caetano Algarve II	C53F	1989	Ex Collison, Stonehouse, 1993

Previous Registrations:

HIL4056	ANA438Y	OYM582A	VLT53	VYJ892	WLT395
JWG194P	JWG194P, 2444MN	PTT1M	G906WAY	SVS618	WLT548
MFF510	WLT598	SVS615	WLT346		

Named vehicles:HIL4056 *Lady Anna*; PTT1M *Lady Sheila*

Livery: White and red

White Rose operate AEC Routemasters on service in Leeds. Painted in a red and white livery they feature black-lining with their former London Buses numbers applied to the bonnet. Photographed at the Corn Exchange in Leeds is OYM582A, previously VLT53 and London's RM53. *Tony Wilson*

WILFREDA-BEEHIVE

Wilfreda Luxury Coaches Ltd, Apex Garage, Church Lane, Adwick-le-Street, Doncaster, South Yorkshire, DN6 7AY

E A Hart Ltd, Apex Garage, Church Lane, Adwick-le-Street, Doncaster, South Yorkshire.

Roeville Tours Ltd, Apex Garage, Church Lane, Adwick-le-Street, Doncaster South Yorkshire, DN6 7AY

18	URN215R	Leyland Leopard PSU5C/4R	Duple Dominant I	DP51F	1977	Ex Ribble, 1992
20	WCK136V	Leyland Leopard PSU3E/4R	Duple Dominant II Express	C49F	1980	Ex Cumberland, 1988
25	F89CWG	Scania K92CRB	Duple 320	C55F	1988	
26	JIL3715	Bova FHD12.290	Bova Futura	C49FT	1989	
27	F90CWG	Scania K92CRB	Duple 320	C55F	1989	
31	F371CHE	Scania K92CRB	Duple 320	C55F	1988	Ex BTS, Borehamwood, 1989
32	F372CHE	Scania K92CRB	Duple 320	C55F	1988	Ex BTS, Borehamwood, 1989
33	F603GET	Scania K93CRB	Duple 320	C59F	1989	
34	JIL3716	Scania K113CRB	Plaxton Paramount 3500 III	C49FT	1989	
35w	304VHN	Daimler CCG5	Roe	H33/28R	1964	Ex A1, Beighton, 19??
37	G21HKY	Scania K93CRB	Duple 320	C56F	1989	
38	G22HKY	Scania K93CRB	Duple 320	C56F	1989	
39	JIL3717	Bova FHD12.290	Bova Futura	C53F	1988	Ex Sharon, Addlestone, 1993
40	UAE259N	Leyland National 11351/2R		B44D	1974	Ex CityLine, 1989
42	JHU870L	Leyland National 1151/2R/0403		B44D	1973	Ex CityLine, 1989
43	JHU871L	Leyland National 1151/2R/0403		B44D	1973	Ex CityLine, 1989
44	JHU872L	Leyland National 1151/2R/0403		B25DL	1973	Ex CityLine, 1989
45	JHU865L	Leyland National 1151/2R/0403		B44D	1973	Ex CityLine, 1989
46	JHU869L	Leyland National 1151/2R/0403		B25DL	1973	Ex CityLine, 1989
47	JHU853L	Leyland National 1151/2R/0403		B44D	1973	Ex CityLine, 1989
60	JHU846L	Leyland National 1151/2R/0403		B44D	1973	Ex CityLine, 1990
64	HEU391N	Leyland National 11351/2R		B44D	1974	Ex CityLine, 1990
65	GAE373N	Leyland National 11351/2R		B44D	1974	Ex CityLine, 1990
66	PIJ5017	Leyland National 11351/2R	East Lancs Greenway (1992)	B44DL	1975	Ex CityLine, 1990

Wilfreda Beehive have built up a fleet of seven Scania K93s with Duple 320 bodywork out of a total of thirty built. The combination is seen in this picture of 27, F90CWG, taken in Leyburn. *Tony Wilson*

Recent arrivals with Wilfreda Beehive have been a number of Dennis Dart service buses, all with Plaxton Pointer bodywork. The north bus station in Doncaster is the location for this picture of 95, **L971NET**. *Tony Wilson*

68	UAE994N	Leyland National 11351/2R		B44D	1974	Ex CityLine, 1990
74	H511SWE	Mercedes-Benz 609D	Whittaker	B19F	1990	
75	SFJ137R	Leyland National 11351A/1R		B49F	1977	Ex Tees & District, 1992
76	CUP664S	Leyland National 11351A/1R		B49F	1978	Ex Tees & District, 1992
77	SGR124R	Leyland National 11351A/1R		B49F	1976	Ex Tees & District, 1992
78	JJG901P	Leyland National 11351A/1R		B52F	1976	Ex Ladyline, Rawmarsh, 1992
79	SGR121R	Leyland National 11351A/1R		B49F	1976	Ex Tees & District, 1992
81	ONV746	Leyland Tiger TRCTL11/3R	Plaxton Paramount 3500	C48FT	1983	Ex Funston, Chrishall, 1989
82	JIL3711	Leyland Tiger TRCTL11/3R	Plaxton Paramount 3200	C53F	1983	Ex Mashford, Doncaster, 1991
83	F647CDT	Mercedes-Benz 609D	Reeve Burgess Beaver	C19F	1988	
84	G922LTH	Leyland-DAF 400	Mellor	M16	1990	Ex Pullman, Penclawdd, 1992
85	KFU868P	Ford R1014	Plaxton Supreme III Express	C45F	1976	Ex Hornsby, Ashby, 1984
86	MED384P	Ford R1114	Plaxton Elite III	C53F	1976	Ex Smith, Wigan, 1980
88	OHL893X	Mercedes-Benz 207D	Whittaker	M12	1982	Ex Nicholson, Farnsfield, 1992
90	M875JVK	Mercedes-Benz 711D	Autobus Classique	C25F	1994	
91	K948JWE	Dennis Dart 9.8SDL3035	Plaxton Pointer	B36F	1993	
92	K945JWE	Dennis Dart 9.8SDL3035	Plaxton Pointer	B36F	1993	
93	K946JWE	Dennis Dart 9.8SDL3035	Plaxton Pointer	B36F	1993	
94	K947JWE	Dennis Dart 9.8SDL3035	Plaxton Pointer	B36F	1993	
95	L971NET	Dennis Dart 9.8SDL3035	Plaxton Pointer	B36F	1993	
96	L970NET	Dennis Dart 9.8SDL3035	Plaxton Pointer	B36F	1993	
97	L129OWF	Dennis Dart 9.8SDL3035	Plaxton Pointer	B36F	1994	
98	L130OWF	Dennis Dart 9.8SDL3035	Plaxton Pointer	B36F	1994	
	L335PWX	Bova SLD12.270	Bova Futura Club	C53F	1994	Ex Bova demonstrator, 1995
	M601WWF	Bova FHD12.370	Bova Futura	C57F	1995	

Named Vehicles: ONV746 *Angela Maria*; KFU868P *Jeanne Therese*; MED384P *Jacqueline Anne*; WLF5 *Royale 1*.

Previous Registrations:

304VHN	From new	JIL3715	F648EET	ONV746	BRN3Y
F371CHE	F372CHE	JIL3716	F601GET	PIJ5017	GEU361N
F372CHE	F371CHE	JIL3717	E668JNR	WLF5	G700LKW
JIL3711	RNY310Y				

Livery: two-tone blue

WRAY'S OF HARROGATE

A Wray & Son Ltd, 33 Montpelier Parade, Harrogate, North Yorkshire, HG1 2TG

Depots: Main Street, Dacre Banks and Ashville College, Harrogate

YHG4N	Leyland Leopard PSU3B/4R	Duple Dominant	C49F	1974	Ex Wheatley, Hetton-le-Hole, 1993
PWK12W	Leyland Leopard PSU5D/5R	Plaxton Supreme IV	C57F	1981	Ex Sweyne Coaches, Swinefleet, 1991
HSV126	Volvo B10M-61	Plaxton Paramount 3500 II	C50F	1986	Ex Wallace Arnold, 1992
A20MCW	Volvo B10M-61	Plaxton Paramount 3500 III	C53F	1988	
YMW149	Volvo B10M-60	Plaxton Paramount 3500 III	C50F	1989	Ex Wallace Arnold, 1993
G965SFT	Toyota Coaster HB31R	Caetano Optimo	C21F	1989	Ex Walker, Hampsthwaite, 1994
G503LWU	Volvo B10M-60	Plaxton Paramount 3500 III	C48FT	1990	Ex Wallace Arnold, 1993
H823AHS	Volvo B10M-60	Plaxton Paramount 3500 III	C53F	1991	Ex Park's, 1993
H824AHS	Volvo B10M-60	Plaxton Paramount 3500 III	C53F	1991	Ex Park's, 1993
H854AHS	Volvo B10M-60	Plaxton Paramount 3500 III	C53F	1991	Ex Park's, 1993
H609UWR	Volvo B10M-60	Plaxton Paramount 3500 III	C48FT	1991	Ex Wallace Arnold, 1993
H172EJF	MAN 10.180	Caetano Algarve II	C35F	1991	Ex Britannia Travel, Otley, 1994
FBZ4780	Volvo B10M-60	Plaxton Excalibur	C49FT	1992	Ex Park's, 1993
MIW5839	Volvo B10M-60	Plaxton Première 350	C48FT	1992	Ex Wallace Arnold, 1994
L532XUT	Volvo B10M-60	Plaxton Première 350	C49FT	1994	
M580JBC	Volvo B6-9M	Caetano Algarve II	C34F	1994	

Livery: Grey and red

Previous Registrations:

A20MCW	E607VNW		HSV126	C119DWR
FBZ4780	J449HDS		MIW5839	J712CWT

Wray's of Harrogate have been a major force in coaching in the Harrogate area for many years. H609UWR is a former Wallace Arnold Volvo B10M fitted with the mark III version of the Plaxton Paramount body. It shows the latest version of the Wray's grey and red livery. *Phillip Stephenson*

YORK PULLMAN

York Pullman Ltd, Byron House Seaham Grange Industrial Estate, Seaham, County Durham, SR7 0PW

Depot and outstation: Halifax Way, Airfield Industrial Estate, Elvington and Harrogate.

102	H202CRH	Volvo B10M-60	Plaxton Expressliner	C46FT	1991	Ex York Pullman Coach, 1993
103	H203CRH	Volvo B10M-60	Plaxton Expressliner	C46FT	1991	Ex York Pullman Coach, 1993
104	CAZ5104	Dennis Javelin 12SDA1907	Plaxton Paramount 3200 III	C50FT	1989	Ex York Pullman Coach, 1993
105	B40UAG	Dennis Dorchester SDA805	Plaxton Paramount 3200	C50FT	1984	Ex York Pullman Coach, 1993
106	BUT23Y	Dennis Dorchester SDA801	Plaxton Paramount 3200	C44FT	1983	Ex York Pullman Coach, 1993
107	IIL1317	Volvo B10M-61	Plaxton Paramount 3500 II	C50F	1986	Ex York Pullman Coach, 1993
108	IIL1318	Volvo B10M-61	Plaxton Paramount 3500 II	C50F	1986	Ex York Pullman Coach, 1993
141	A922LTM	Bedford YNT	Duple Laser	C53F	1983	Ex York Pullman Coach, 1993
143	A875THS	Bedford YNT	Plaxton Paramount 3200	C53F	1984	Ex York Pullman Coach, 1993
144	A839AWA	Bedford YNT	Plaxton Paramount 3200	C53F	1984	Ex York Pullman Coach, 1993
148	A659MWR	Bedford YNT	Plaxton Paramount 3200	C53F	1983	Ex York Pullman Coach, 1993
153	C738TJF	Bedford YNT	Plaxton Paramount 3200 II	C53F	1986	Ex York Pullman Coach, 1993
158	D129HML	Bedford YNV Venturer	Plaxton Paramount 3200 II	C54F	1987	Ex York Pullman Coach, 1993
172	D562RKW	Bedford YNV Venturer	Plaxton Paramount 3200 II	C54F	1987	Ex York Pullman Coach, 1993
173	AWE53T	Bedford YMT	Plaxton Supreme IV	C53F	1979	Ex York Pullman Coach, 1993
175	PKU78X	Bedford YNT	Plaxton Supreme V	C53F	1982	Ex York Pullman Coach, 1993
190	TKH259H	Leyland Atlantean PDR1A/1	Roe	H43/28D	1969	Ex Kingston-upon-Hull, 1993
191	WRH281J	Leyland Atlantean PDR1A/1	Roe	H43/28D	1970	Ex Kingston-upon-Hull, 1993
192	WRH297J	Leyland Atlantean PDR1A/1	Roe	H43/28D	1970	Ex Kingston-upon-Hull, 1993

The ownership of York Pullman has changed a number of times in recent years with Durham Travel Services being the latest owner having purchased the business from Kingston-upon-Hull in 1993. Acquired at that time was GAT203N a former Kingston-upon-Hull Leyland Atlantean fitted with a Roe body. It carries the latest York Pullman livery of cream with two-tone red stripes. *Phillip Stephenson*

193	DRH319L	Leyland Atlantean AN68/1R	Roe		O43/29F	1972	Ex Kingston-upon-Hull, 1993
194	DRH321L	Leyland Atlantean AN68/1R	Roe		O43/29F	1972	Ex York Pullman Coach, 1993
195	NAT341M	Leyland Atlantean AN68/1R	Roe		O43/29F	1973	Ex York Pullman Coach, 1993
196	NAT350M	Leyland Atlantean AN68/1R	Roe		O43/29F	1974	Ex York Pullman Coach, 1993
197	GAT203N	Leyland Atlantean AN68/1R	Roe		H43/29F	1975	Ex York Pullman Coach, 1993
	NAT345M	Leyland Atlantean AN68/1R	Roe		H43/29F	1973	Ex Kingston-upon-Hull, 1994
	GAT201N	Leyland Atlantean AN68/1R	Roe		H43/29F	1975	Ex Kingston-upon-Hull, 1993
	GAT204N	Leyland Atlantean AN68/1R	Roe		H43/29F	1975	Ex Kingston-upon-Hull, 1993
	GAT206N	Leyland Atlantean AN68/1R	Roe		H43/29F	1975	Ex Kingston-upon-Hull, 1994
	LJA649P	Leyland Atlantean AN68A/1R	Northern Counties		H43/32F	1976	Ex Elliott, Moorends, 1993
	FHE810L	Bristol VRT/SL2/6G	Eastern Coach Works		O43/34F	1973	Ex RoadCar, 1993

Previous Registrations:

CAZ5104	F54EAT		IIL1317	C107DWR		IIL1318	C117DWR

Named Vehicles:
107 - *Neville Shute*; 141 - *Alcuin*; 142 - *John Goodricke*; 143 - *James Fairfax*; 144 - *Dick Turpin*; 148 - *Joseph Terry*; 151 - *Constantine*; 153 - *Mary Clitherow*; 159 - *Joseph Rowntree*; 160 - *William Etty*; 172 - *John Carr*; 175 - *Guy Fawkes*; 195 - *Archbishop Holgate*.

Livery: Cream and red.

York, as with many of the towns and cities attracting tourists have open-top bus services from which to view their historic sights. Guide Friday also operate in York, but being based in Warwickshire are covered in the South Midlands edition of this series. Locally based, however, is York Pullman, whose Bristol VR FHE810L is seen in front of Clifford's Tower. *David Longbottom*

YORKSHIRE COASTLINER

Yorkshire Coastliner Ltd, Barleycorn Yard, Walmgate, York,
North Yorkshire, YO1 2TX

Depot: Railway Street, Malton

A subsudiary of Blazefield Holdings Ltd

401	F401XWR	Mercedes-Benz 811D	Optare StarRider	DP33F	1988	Ex Rover, Bromsgrove, 1994
403	K3YCL	Leyland Olympian ON2R50C13Z4	Northern Counties Palatine	DPH43/27F	1992	
404	K4YCL	Leyland Olympian ON2R50C13Z4	Northern Counties Palatine	DPH43/27F	1992	
405	K5YCL	Leyland Olympian ON2R50C13Z4	Northern Counties Palatine	DPH43/27F	1992	
408	L8YCL	Volvo Olympian YN2RV18Z4	Alexander Royale	DPH45/29F	1993	
409	L9YCL	Volvo Olympian YN2RV18Z4	Alexander Royale	DPH45/27F	1994	
411	G112VMM	Leyland Swift LBM6T/2RA	Wadham Stringer Vanguard II	B37F	1989	Ex Harrogate & District, 1994
412	A212SAE	Leyland Tiger TRCTL11/3R	Plaxton Paramount 3200 E	DP53F	1983	Ex Cheltenham & Gloucester, 1993
413	A213SAE	Leyland Tiger TRCTL11/3R	Plaxton Paramount 3200 E	DP53F	1983	Ex Cheltenham & Gloucester, 1993
420	G920WGS	Mercedes-Benz 709D	Reeve Burgess Beaver	B23F	1990	Ex Welwyn-Hatfield Line, 1993
421	G921WGS	Mercedes-Benz 709D	Reeve Burgess Beaver	B23F	1990	Ex Welwyn-Hatfield Line, 1993
422	M922UYG	Volvo Olympian YN2RV18Z4	Alexander Royale	DPH45/29F	1995	
423	M923UYG	Volvo Olympian YN2RV18Z4	Alexander Royale	DPH45/29F	1995	
424	M924UYG	Volvo Olympian YN2RV18Z4	Alexander Royale	DPH45/29F	1995	
425	M925UYG	Volvo Olympian YN2RV18Z4	Alexander Royale	DPH45/29F	1995	
431	G431MWU	Leyland Tiger TRCL10/3ARZA	Plaxton Paramount 3200 III	C55F	1990	Ex York City & District, 1990
432	G432MWU	Leyland Tiger TRCL10/3ARZA	Plaxton Paramount 3200 III	C55F	1990	Ex York City & District, 1990
433	G433MWU	Leyland Tiger TRCL10/3ARZA	Plaxton Paramount 3200 III	C55F	1990	Ex York City & District, 1990
434	G434MWU	Leyland Tiger TRCL10/3ARZA	Plaxton Paramount 3200 III	C55F	1990	Ex York City & District, 1990
483	E283TWW	Mercedes-Benz 811D	Optare StarRider	DP33F	1988	Ex Rover, Bromsgrove, 1994

Livery: Blue and cream

Parked on lay-over in Leeds bus station is Yorkshire Coastliner 408, L8YCL, an all-Scottish product with its Volvo Olympian chassis built near Irvine and Alexander Royal bodywork constructed in Falkirk.
Tony Wilson

A further four Volvo Olympians joined Yorkshire Coastliner during 1995, displacing three of the earlier Northern-Counties examples which are now with Keighley & District. In March 1995 all four were lined up for a team photograph together with 408 on the right. Note the differences between these two deliveries of Alexander Royale bodies. *Andrew Jarosz*

In addition to the double-deck coaches, Yorkshire Coastliner operate minibuses in the Whitby area. Photographed at Goathland while heading home is 420, G920WGS. *Tony Wilson*

YORKSHIRE RIDER

Yorkshire Rider Ltd, Windsor House, 1 Sovereign Quay, Leeds, West Yorkshire, LS1 4DQ
Rider York Ltd, PO Box 258, 36-38 Walmgate, York, North Yorkshire, YO1 2GR
Quickstep Travel Ltd, Windsor House, 1 Sovereign Quay, Leeds, West Yorkshire, LS1 4DQ

Part of the Badgerline group, and to become a subsidiary of FirstBus plc in June 1995.

Depots: Hall Ings, Bradford; Skircoat Road, Halifax; Leeds Road, Huddersfield; Low Road, Hunslet; Fitzwilliam Street, Kinsley; Henconner Lane, Bramley; Kirkstall Road, Kirkstall; Torre Road, Leeds; Millwood, Todmorden and Barbican Road, York.

3	WUM443S	Leyland National 11351A/1R		B52F	1978	Ex West Yorkshire, 1989
4	RYG764R	Leyland National 11351A/1R		B52F	1977	Ex West Yorkshire, 1989
5	RYG765R	Leyland National 11351A/1R		B52F	1977	Ex West Yorkshire, 1989
6	PEV706R	Leyland National 11351A/1R		B49F	1976	Ex Wilts & Dorset, 1992
9	RYG769R	Leyland National 11351A/1R		B52F	1977	Ex West Yorkshire, 1989
10	YWW810S	Leyland National 11351A/1R		B52F	1978	Ex West Yorkshire, 1989
16	L516EHD	DAF SB220LC550	Ikarus CitiBus	B48F	1993	
17	L517EHD	DAF SB220LC550	Ikarus CitiBus	B48F	1994	
18	L518EHD	DAF SB220LC550	Ikarus CitiBus	B48F	1994	
21	RYG771R	Leyland National 11351A/1R		B52F	1977	Ex West Yorkshire, 1989
22	RYG772R	Leyland National 11351A/1R		B52F	1977	Ex West Yorkshire, 1989
23	UOI4323	Volvo B10M-61	East Lancashire (1993)	B51F	1982	Ex Rhodeservices, 1994
26	K506RJX	DAF SB220LC550	Ikarus CitiBus	B48F	1993	Ex Yorkshire Travel, 1994
27	K507RJX	DAF SB220LC550	Ikarus CitiBus	B48F	1993	Ex Yorkshire Travel, 1994
29	F229FSU	Leyland Tiger TRBTL11/2RP	Plaxton Derwent	B54F	1988	Ex Rhodeservices, 1994
30	F300GNS	Leyland Tiger TRBTL11/2RP	Plaxton Derwent	B54F	1988	Ex Rhodeservices, 1994
42	TYG742R	Leyland National 11351A/1R		B52F	1977	Ex West Yorkshire, 1989
43	JUB643V	Leyland National 11351A/1R		B52F	1979	Ex West Yorkshire, 1989
44	JUB644V	Leyland National 11351A/1R		B52F	1979	Ex West Yorkshire, 1989
45	E345SWY	Iveco Daily 49-10	Robin Hood City Nippy	B25F	1988	Ex West Yorkshire, 1989
51	MEL551P	Leyland National 11351/1R		B49F	1976	Ex Wilts & Dorset, 1993
52	MEL552P	Leyland National 11351/1R		B49F	1975	Ex Wilts & Dorset, 1993

The Quickstep name continues for some Yorkshire Rider operations. Photographed in Leeds is 51, MEL551P, a standard Leyland National new to Hants & Dorset. *Tony Wilson*

59-65 — Iveco Daily 49-10 — Robin Hood City Nippy — B21F — 1988 — Ex West Yorkshire, 1989

59	E459TYG	61	E461TYG	63	E463TYG	64	E464TYG	65	E465TYG
60	E460TYG	62	E462TYG						

66	FPR66V	Leyland National 11351A/1R		B49F	1979	Ex Wilts & Dorset, 1992
71	E471TYG	Iveco Daily 49-10	Robin Hood City Nippy	B21F	1989	Ex West Yorkshire, 1989
72	E472TYG	Iveco Daily 49-10	Robin Hood City Nippy	B21F	1989	Ex West Yorkshire, 1989

228-236 — Renault-Dodge S56 — Reeve Burgess Beaver — B23F — 1989 — Ex York City & District, 1990

228	G251LWF	230	G253LWF	232	G255LWF	234	G257LWF	236	G259LWF
229	G252LWF	231	G254LWF	233	G256LWF	235	G258LWF		

238	G447LKW	Renault-Dodge S56	Reeve Burgess Beaver	B23F	1990	Ex York City & District, 1990
290	E166CNC	Renault-Dodge S56	Northern Counties	B23F	1988	Ex Reynard Buses, 1990
291	E385CNE	Renault-Dodge S56	Northern Counties	B23F	1988	Ex Reynard Buses, 1990

332	MNW132V	Leyland National 2 NL116L11/1R	B52F	1980	Ex York City & District, 1990
333	SWX533W	Leyland National 2 NL116AL11/1R	B52F	1981	Ex York City & District, 1990
335	SWX535W	Leyland National 2 NL116AL11/1R	B52F	1981	Ex York City & District, 1990
338	SWX538W	Leyland National 2 NL116AL11/1R	B52F	1981	Ex York City & District, 1990
340	SWX540W	Leyland National 2 NL116AL11/1R	B52F	1981	Ex York City & District, 1990
363	PNW603W	Leyland National 2 NL116L11/1R	B52F	1980	Ex York City & District, 1990
368	UWY68X	Leyland National 2 NL116AL11/1R	B52F	1982	Ex York City & District, 1990
371	UWY71X	Leyland National 2 NL116AL11/1R	B52F	1982	Ex York City & District, 1990

713-765 — Bristol VRT/SL3/6LXB — Eastern Coach Works — H43/31F — 1978-81 — Ex West Yorkshire, 1989

713	DWU296T	729	JWT762V	744	LWU472V	748	NUM339V	756	PWY42W
717	EWR165T	734	LUA717V	745	PUM148W	752	PWY38W	758	PWY44W
725	JWT758V	735	LUA718V	746	PUM149W	755	PWY41W	765	SUB789W
727	JWT760V	736	LUA719V						

With the acquisition of the West Yorkshire Road Car Company, operations in the metropolitan areas of West Yorkshire the Yorkshire Rider fleet now obtained a number of Eastern Coachworks-bodied Bristol VRTs. 765, SUB789W, carries Yorkshire Rider Wakefield fleetnames indicating that it will normally be operating from the former United Services depot at Kinsley. *David Cole*

977-994

Bristol VRT/SL3/6LXB — Eastern Coach Works — H43/31F — 1977-78 — Ex West Yorkshire, 1989

977	SWW302R	988	WWY118S	992	WWY122S	993	WWY123S	994	WWY127S
980	SWW305R								

1001-1030

Volvo B10B-58 — Alexander Strider — B51F — 1993-94

1001	K101HUM	1007	K107HUM	1013	K113HUM	1019	K119HUM	1025	L125PWR
1002	K102HUM	1008	K108HUM	1014	K114HUM	1020	K120HUM	1026	L126PWR
1003	K103HUM	1009	K109HUM	1015	K115HUM	1021	L121PWR	1027	L127PWR
1004	K104HUM	1010	K110HUM	1016	K116HUM	1022	L122PWR	1028	L128PWR
1005	K105HUM	1011	K211HUM	1017	K117HUM	1023	L123PWR	1029	L129PWR
1006	K106HUM	1012	K112HUM	1018	K118HUM	1024	L124PWR	1030	L130PWR

1171	B124PEL	Bedford YNT	Plaxton Paramount 3200 E	C53F	1984	Ex Reynard Buses, 1990

1201-1208

DAF SB220LC550 — Ikarus CitiBus — B48F — 1992

1201	J421NCP	1203	J423NCP	1205	J425NCP	1207	K527RJX	1208	K528RJX
1202	J422NCP	1204	J424NCP	1206	J426NCP				

1251-1255

DAF SB220LC550 — Optare Delta — B47F — 1989

1251	G251JYG	1252	G252JYG	1253	G253JYG	1254	G254JYG	1255	G255JYG

1256	J994GCP	DAF SB220LC550	Optare Delta	B49F	1991	Ex Yorkshire Travel, 1994

1314-1330

Leyland National 2 NL106L11/1R — B41F — 1980 — Ex WYPTE, 1986

1314	LUA314V	1318	LUA318V	1320	LUA320V	1322	LUA322V	1329	LUA329V
1317	LUA317V	1319	LUA319V	1321	LUA321V	1323	LUA323V	1330	LUA330V

1331	VWU331X	Leyland National 2 NL116AL11/1R	B49F	1981	Ex WYPTE, 1986
1332	VWU332X	Leyland National 2 NL116AL11/1R	B49F	1981	Ex WYPTE, 1986
1333	YWX333X	Leyland National 2 NL116AL11/1R	B49F	1982	Ex WYPTE, 1986
1339	JUB645V	Leyland National 11351A/1R	B52F	1979	Ex West Yorkshire, 1989
1340	JUB646V	Leyland National 11351A/1R(Volvo)	B49F	1979	Ex West Yorkshire, 1989
1341	JUB647V	Leyland National 11351A/1R(Volvo)	B49F	1979	Ex West Yorkshire, 1989
1342	JUB649V	Leyland National 11351A/1R	B52F	1979	Ex West Yorkshire, 1989

1343-1348

Leyland National 2 NL116L11/1R — B52F — 1980 — Ex West Yorkshire, 1989

1343	MNW130V	1345	PNW598W	1346	PNW599W	1347	PNW600W	1348	PNW601W
1344	MNW133V								

1349-1354

Leyland National 2 NL116AL11/1R — B52F — 1981-82 — Ex West Yorkshire, 1989

1349	SWX537W	1351	UWY72X	1352	UWY74X	1353	UWY75X	1354	UWY90X
1350	UWY69X								

1355	PWY587W	Leyland National 2 NL106AL11/1R	B44F	1981	Ex West Yorkshire, 1989
1356	PWY588W	Leyland National 2 NL106AL11/1R	B44F	1981	Ex West Yorkshire, 1989
1357	FWA473V	Leyland National 2 NL106AL11/1R	B41F	1980	Ex Pride of the Road, 1993
1366	RKA869T	Leyland National 11351A/1R(Volvo)	B49F	1978	Ex Pride of the Road, 1993
1367	MHJ723V	Leyland National 2 NL116AL11/1R	B49F	1980	Ex Eastern National, 1994
1368	MHJ726V	Leyland National 2 NL116AL11/1R	B49F	1980	Ex Eastern National, 1994
1369	MHJ728V	Leyland National 2 NL116AL11/1R	B49F	1980	Ex Eastern National, 1994
1370	STW19W	Leyland National 2 NL116AL11/1R	B49F	1980	Ex Eastern National, 1994
1400	YR3939	Volvo B10M-61	Jonckheere Jubilee P599	C32FT	1988	
1402	NIB4906	Volvo B10M-61	Jonckheere Jubilee P50	C53F	1986	Ex WYPTE, 1986
1403	NIB4905	Volvo B10M-61	Jonckheere Jubilee P50	C48FT	1987	
1404	NIB4908	Volvo B10M-61	Jonckheere Jubilee P50	C48FT	1987	
1405	GSU388	Volvo B10M-61	Jonckheere Jubilee P599	C51FT	1987	
1406	E406RWR	Volvo B10M-61	Duple 340	C57F	1988	
1407	GSU390	Volvo B10M-61	Duple 340	C57F	1988	
1416	D783SGB	Volvo B10M-61	Plaxton Paramount 3500 III	C53FT	1987	Ex Park's, 1988
1418	23PTA	Volvo B10M-60	Jonckheere Deauville P599	C48FT	1989	
1419	8995WY	Volvo B10M-60	Plaxton Paramount 3500 III	C49FT	1990	Ex Park's, 1992
1420	G76RGG	Volvo B10M-60	Plaxton Paramount 3500 III	C49FT	1990	Ex Park's, 1992
1421	H841HAS	Volvo B10M-60	Plaxton Paramount 3500 III	C53F	1991	Ex Park's, 1993
1422	L22YRL	Volvo B10M-60	Jonckheere Deauville P599	C51F	1993	
1423	L511NYG	Volvo B10M-60	Plaxton Premiére 350	C49FT	1993	
1424	L541XUT	Volvo B10M-60	Plaxton Premiére 350	C49FT	1994	

Yorkshire Rider's 1005, K105HUM, is one of thirty Volvo B10Bs with Alexander Strider bodwork purchased for the fleet in 1993. It is seen in Leeds returning to its home base in Huddersfield on limited stop service X6. *David Cole*

As part of a programme to upgrade vehicles in the Rider York fleet, a number of Ikarus-bodied DAF single-decks from dealer stock have been placed in service. One such example is 1206, J426NCP, obtained through Hughes DAF who aresole importers of Ikarus products to the UK. *Mike Fowler*

Halifax bus station is the location of this view of Yorkshire Rider 1532, JUM532V. The Leyland Leopards, fitted with Plaxton's Supreme IV Express coachwork have been used on the longer services from Halifax as typified in this picture. *Phillip Stephenson*

1425	L542XUT	Volvo B10M-60	Plaxton Premiére 350	C49FT	1994		
1426	L546XUT	Volvo B10M-62	Plaxton Premiére 350	C49FT	1994		

1451-1460

Volvo B10M-55 — Plaxton Derwent II — B51F — 1990

1451	G451JYG	1453	G453JYG	1455	G455JYG	1457	G457JYG	1459	G459JYG
1452	G452JYG	1454	G454JYG	1456	G456JYG	1458	G458JYG	1460	G460JYG

1461	JSJ429W	Volvo B58-56	Duple Dominant	B53F	1980	Ex Rhodeservice, 1994
1528	GWU528T	Leyland Leopard PSU3E/4R	Plaxton Supreme IV Express	C53F	1979	Ex WYPTE, 1986
1529	GWU529T	Leyland Leopard PSU3E/4R	Plaxton Supreme IV Express	C53F	1979	Ex WYPTE, 1986
1531	JUM531V	Leyland Leopard PSU3E/4R	Plaxton Supreme IV Express	C53F	1979	Ex WYPTE, 1986
1532	JUM532V	Leyland Leopard PSU3E/4R	Plaxton Supreme IV Express	C53F	1979	Ex WYPTE, 1986
1544	KUB548V	Leyland Leopard PSU3C/4R	Plaxton Supreme IV Express	C49F	1980	Ex West Yorkshire, 1989
1545	KUB552V	Leyland Leopard PSU3C/4R	Plaxton Supreme IV Express	C49F	1980	Ex West Yorkshire, 1989
1546	KUB671V	Leyland Leopard PSU3C/4R	Plaxton Supreme IV Express	C49F	1980	Ex West Yorkshire, 1989

1547-1553

Leyland Leopard PSU3F/4R — Duple Dominant IV Express — C49F — 1981 — Ex West Yorkshire, 1989

1547	UWY63X	1548	UWY79X	1549	UWY80X	1550	UWY81X	1553	UWY86X

1581	NPA226W	Leyland Leopard PSU3E/4R	Plaxton Supreme IV Express	C53F	1981	Ex Reynard Buses, 1990
1582	NPA227W	Leyland Leopard PSU3E/4R	Plaxton Supreme IV Express	C53F	1981	Ex Reynard Buses, 1990
1583	NPA232W	Leyland Leopard PSU3E/4R	Plaxton Supreme IV Express	C53F	1981	Ex Reynard Buses, 1990
1587	CSU244	Leyland Leopard PSU3D/4R	Plaxton Bustler (1987)	B55F	1977	Ex Reynard Buses, 1990
1592	LOI6690	Leyland Leopard PSU3D/4R	Plaxton Derwent (1987)	B55F	1977	Ex Reynard Buses, 1990
1593	VDH244S	Leyland Leopard PSU3E/4R	Duple Dominant (1985)	B55F	1977	Ex Reynard Buses, 1990
1594	ABR868S	Leyland Leopard PSU3E/4R	Plaxton Derwent II (1990)	B55F	1977	Ex Reynard Buses, 1990
1595	JKW215W	Leyland Leopard PSU3G/4R	Plaxton Derwent II (1990)	B55F	1981	Ex Reynard Buses, 1990
1596	JKW216W	Leyland Leopard PSU3G/4R	Plaxton Derwent II (1990)	B55F	1981	Ex Reynard Buses, 1990
1597	ABR869S	Leyland Leopard PSU3E/4R	Plaxton Derwent II (1990)	B55F	1977	Ex Reynard Buses, 1990
1604	WSV408	Leyland Tiger TRCTL11/3R	Plaxton Paramount 3200	C53F	1983	Ex WYPTE, 1986
1605	WSV409	Leyland Tiger TRCTL11/3R	Plaxton Paramount 3200	C53F	1983	Ex WYPTE, 1986
1606	HUA606Y	Leyland Tiger TRCTL11/2R	Plaxton Paramount 3200 E	C49F	1983	Ex WYPTE, 1986
1607	HUA607Y	Leyland Tiger TRCTL11/2R	Plaxton Paramount 3200 E	C49F	1983	Ex WYPTE, 1986
1608	WSV410	Leyland Tiger TRCTL11/2RH	Plaxton Paramount 3200	C49F	1984	Ex WYPTE, 1986
1610	B610VWU	Leyland Tiger TRCTL11/3RH	Plaxton Paramount 3200 IIE	C53F	1985	Ex WYPTE, 1986

Rider York 1657, EWR657Y, has migrated from its original home in Leeds to York. This Leyland Tiger has a Duple Dominant bus body fitted with high back seats. The city walls of York can clearly be seen behind as 1657 waits to depart for Bishopthorpe. *Mike Fowler*

1615-1622

Leyland Tiger TRCTL11/3ARZA Plaxton Paramount 3200 IIIE C53F · 1988 · *1619/20/2 are Paramount 3200 III

1615	F615XWY	1617	F617XWY	1619	F619XWY	1621	F621XWY	1622	F622XWY
1616	F616XWY	1618	F618XWY	1620	F620XWY				

1623	EWW945Y	Leyland Tiger TRCTL11/3R	Plaxton Paramount 3200 E C53F	1983	Ex West Yorkshire, 1989
1625	EWW947Y	Leyland Tiger TRCTL11/3R	Plaxton Paramount 3200 E C53F	1983	Ex West Yorkshire, 1989

1651-1672

Leyland Tiger TRBTL11/2R · Duple Dominant · DP47F · 1983-84 Ex WYPTE, 1986

1651	EWR651Y	1656	EWR656Y	1661	A661KUM	1665	A665KUM	1669	A669KUM
1652	EWR652Y	1657	EWR657Y	1662	A662KUM	1666	A666KUM	1670	A670KUM
1653	EWR653Y	1658	A658KUM	1663	A663KUM	1667	A667KUM	1671	A671KUM
1654	EWR654Y	1659	A659KUM	1664	A664KUM	1668	A668KUM	1672	A672KUM
1655	EWR655Y	1660	A660KUM						

1793	D793KWR	Freight Rover Sherpa	Dormobile	B20F	1987
1796	D796KWR	Freight Rover Sherpa	Dormobile	B20F	1987

1862-1879

Freight Rover Sherpa · Dormobile · B20F · 1987

1862	D862LWR	1865	D865LWR	1868	D868LWR	1870	D870LWR	1874	D874LWR
1863	D863LWR	1867	D867LWR	1869	D869LWR	1871	D871LWR	1879	D879LWR

2001	E201PWY	Mercedes-Benz 811D	Optare StarRider	DP33F	1987	
2002	E202PWY	Mercedes-Benz 811D	Optare StarRider	DP33F	1987	
2003	E203PWY	Mercedes-Benz 811D	Optare StarRider	DP29F	1987	
2004	E204PWY	Mercedes-Benz 811D	Optare StarRider	DP29F	1987	
2005	F546EJA	Mercedes-Benz 709D	PMT	DP25F	1988	Ex Rhodeservice, 1994

2006-2011

Mercedes-Benz L608D · Dormobile · B20F · 1986 Ex City Line, 1994

2006	D535FAE	2008	D537FAE	2009	D541FAE	2010	D539FAE	2011	D540FAE
2007	D536FAE								

2012	C222HJN	Mercedes-Benz L608D	Reeve Burgess	B20F	1985	Ex Eastern National, 1994
2013	D529FAE	Mercedes-Benz L608D	Dormobile	B20F	1986	Ex City Line, 1994
2014	D530FAE	Mercedes-Benz L608D	Dormobile	B20F	1986	Ex City Line, 1994
2015	D531FAE	Mercedes-Benz L608D	Dormobile	B20F	1986	Ex City Line, 1994
2016	D532FAE	Mercedes-Benz L608D	Dormobile	B20F	1986	Ex City Line, 1994
2021	E221PWY	MCW MetroRider MF150/34	MCW	B23F	1987	
2025	E225PWY	MCW MetroRider MF150/41	MCW	B23F	1987	
2031	E231PWY	MCW MetroRider MF150/41	MCW	B23F	1987	
2034	E234PWY	MCW MetroRider MF150/41	MCW	B23F	1987	

2035-2059

MCW MetroRider MF150/80 — MCW — B23F — 1988

2035	E235UWR	2045	E245UWR	2054	E254UWR	2056	E256UWR	2058	E258UWR
2036	E236UWR	2049	E249UWR	2055	E255UWR	2057	E257UWR	2059	E259UWR
2038	E238UWR	2053	E253UWR						

2067-2082

Iveco Daily 49-10 — Robin Hood City Nippy — B23F — 1988 — Ex West Yorkshire, 1989

2067	E326SWY	2071	E331SWY	2074	E335SWY	2077	E338SWY	2080w	E341SWY
2068	E327SWY	2072	E332SWY	2075	E336SWY	2078	E339SWY	2081	E342SWY
2069	E328SWY	2073	E334SWY	2076	E337SWY	2079	E340SWY	2082	E344SWY
2070	E330SWY								

2093	E467TYG	Iveco Daily 49-10	Robin Hood City Nippy	B21F	1988	Ex West Yorkshire, 1989
2094	E468TYG	Iveco Daily 49-10	Robin Hood City Nippy	B21F	1988	Ex West Yorkshire, 1989
2096	E470TYG	Iveco Daily 49-10	Robin Hood City Nippy	B21F	1988	Ex West Yorkshire, 1989

2100-2107

Iveco Daily 49-10 — Phoenix — B19F — 1989 — Ex York City & District, 1990

2100	G210KUA	2102	G212KUA	2104	G214KUA	2106	G216KUA
2101	G211KUA	2103	G213KUA	2105	G215KUA	2107	G217KUA

2201-2263

Mercedes-Benz 709D — Plaxton Beaver — B25F — 1994-95

2201	M201VWU	2214	M214VWU	2227	M227VWU	2240	M240VWU	2252	M252VWU
2202	M202VWU	2215	M215VWU	2228	M228VWU	2241	M241VWU	2253	M253VWU
2203	M203VWU	2216	M216VWU	2229	M229VWU	2242	M242VWU	2254	M254VWU
2204	M204VWU	2217	M217VWU	2230	M230VWU	2243	M243VWU	2255	M255VWU
2205	M205VWU	2218	M218VWU	2231	M231VWU	2244	M244VWU	2256	M256VWU
2206	M206VWU	2219	M219VWU	2232	M232VWU	2245	M245VWU	2257	M257VWU
2207	M207VWU	2220	M449VWW	2233	M233VWU	2246	M246VWU	2258	M258VWU
2208	M208VWU	2221	M221VWU	2234	M234VWU	2247	M247VWU	2259	M259VWU
2209	M209VWU	2222	M222VWU	2235	M235VWU	2248	M248VWU	2260	M260VWU
2210	M210VWU	2223	M223VWU	2236	M236VWU	2249	M249VWU	2261	M261VWU
2211	M211VWU	2224	M224VWU	2237	M237VWU	2250	M250VWU	2262	M262VWU
2212	M212VWU	2225	M225VWU	2238	M238VWU	2251	M251VWU	2263	M263VWU
2213	M213VWU	2226	M226VWU	2239	M239VWU				

The Rider Group became part of Badgerline Group in 1994. Since then a substantial investment is being made in new vehicles. A large number of Plaxton-bodied Mercedes-Benz 709D vehicles are expected in 1995 one of the first to enter service is 2204 M204VWU.
Lee Whitehead

The latest frontal treatment of Alexander's Dash product is seen on Rider Leeds' 3231, M231VWW Dennis products are being supplied to most Badgerline fleets to meet the single-deck bus requirement, and examples bodied by Plaxton and Alexander are being delivered. *Paul Wigan*

3001-3006
Volvo B6-9.8m   Alexander Dash   B40F   1994

3001	L101PWR	3003	L103PWR	3004	L104PWR	3005	L105PWR	3006	L106PWR
3002	L102PWR								

3201-3218
Dennis Dart 9.8SDL3054   Plaxton Pointer   B40F   1995

3201	M201VWW	3205	M205VWW	3209	M209VWW	3213	M213VWW	3216	M216VWW
3202	M202VWW	3206	M206VWW	3210	M210VWW	3214	M214VWW	3217	M217VWW
3203	M203VWW	3207	M207VWW	3211	M211VWW	3215	M215VWW	3218	M218VWW
3204	M204VWW	3208	M208VWW	3212	M212VWW				

3219-3268
Dennis Dart 9.8SDL3054   Alexander Dash   B40F   1995

3219	M219VWW	3229	M229VWW	3239	M239VWW	3249	M249VWW	3259	M259VWW
3220	M220VWW	3230	M230VWW	3240	M240VWW	3250	M250VWW	3260	M260VWW
3221	M221VWW	3231	M231VWW	3241	M241VWW	3251	M251VWW	3261	M261VWW
3222	M450VWW	3232	M232VWW	3242	M242VWW	3252	M252VWW	3262	M262VWW
3223	M223VWW	3233	M233VWW	3243	M243VWW	3253	M253VWW	3263	M263VWW
3224	M224VWW	3234	M234VWW	3244	M244VWW	3254	M254VWW	3264	M264VWW
3225	M225VWW	3235	M235VWW	3245	M245VWW	3255	M255VWW	3265	M265VWW
3226	M226VWW	3236	M236VWW	3246	M246VWW	3256	M256VWW	3266	M266VWW
3227	M227VWW	3237	M237VWW	3247	M247VWW	3257	M257VWW	3267	M267VWW
3228	M228VWW	3238	M238VWW	3248	M248VWW	3258	M258VWW	3268	M268VWW

4001-4048
Dennis Lance 11SDL3113   Plaxton Verde   B49F   1995

4001	M401VWW	4011	M411VWW	4021	M421VWW	4031	M431VWW	4040	M440VWW
4002	M402VWW	4012	M412VWW	4022	M422VWW	4032	M432VWW	4041	M441VWW
4003	M403VWW	4013	M413VWW	4023	M423VWW	4033	M433VWW	4042	M442VWW
4004	M404VWW	4014	M414VWW	4024	M424VWW	4034	M434VWW	4043	M443VWW
4005	M405VWW	4015	M415VWW	4025	M425VWW	4035	M435VWW	4044	M842VWT
4006	M406VWW	4016	M416VWW	4026	M426VWW	4036	M436VWW	4045	M445VWW
4007	M407VWW	4017	M417VWW	4027	M427VWW	4037	M437VWW	4046	M446VWW
4008	M408VWW	4018	M418VWW	4028	M428VWW	4038	M438VWW	4047	M447VWW
4009	M409VWW	4019	M419VWW	4029	M429VWW	4039	M439VWW	4048	M448VWW
4010	M410VWW	4020	M420VWW	4030	M430VWW				

Flagship livery is appearing on vehicles for certain Yorkshire Rider routes. Seen in Huddersfield is 5082, A82KUM. Flagship routes are developed selectively to upgrade the standard of service provided, in a similar fashion to Trent's Rainbow routes *Paul Wigan*

5018-5081

Leyland Olympian ONLXB/1R Roe H47/29F 1982-83 Ex WYPTE, 1986

• 5018	UWW18X	5026	CUB26Y	5034	CUB34Y	5042	CUB42Y	5052	CUB52Y
5019	UWW19X	5027	CUB27Y	5035	CUB35Y	5043	CUB43Y	5053	CUB53Y
5020	UWW20X	5028	CUB28Y	5036	CUB36Y	5044	CUB44Y	5054	CUB54Y
5021	CUB21Y	5029	CUB29Y	5037	CUB37Y	5045	CUB45Y	5055	CUB55Y
5022	CUB22Y	5030	CUB30Y	5038	CUB38Y	5046	CUB46Y	5065	CUB65Y
5023	CUB23Y	5031	CUB31Y	5039	CUB39Y	5047	CUB47Y	5077	EWY77Y
5024	CUB24Y	5032	CUB32Y	5040	CUB40Y	5048	CUB48Y	5081	EWY81Y
5025	CUB25Y	5033	CUB33Y	5041	CUB41Y	5051	CUB51Y		

5082-5121

Leyland Olympian ONLXB/1R Roe H47/29F 1983 Ex WYPTE, 1986

5082	A82KUM	5090	A90KUM	5098	A98KUM	5106	A106KUM	• 5114	A114KUM
5083	A83KUM	5091	A91KUM	5099	A99KUM	5107	A107KUM	5115	A115KUM
5084	A84KUM	5092	A92KUM	5100	A100KUM	5108	A108KUM	5116	A116KUM
5085	A85KUM	5093	A93KUM	5101	A101KUM	5109	A109KUM	• 5117	A117KUM
5086	A86KUM	5094	A94KUM	5102	A102KUM	5110	A110KUM	5118	A118KUM
5087	A87KUM	5095	A95KUM	5103	A103KUM	5111	A111KUM	5119	A119KUM
5088	A88KUM	5096	A96KUM	5104	A104KUM	5112	A112KUM	5120	A120KUM
5089	A89KUM	5097	A97KUM	5105	A105KUM	5113	A113KUM	5121	A121KUM

5122-5145

Leyland Olympian ONLXB/1R Roe H47/29F 1984 Ex WYPTE, 1986

5122	B122RWY	5127	B127RWY	5132	B132RWY	5137	B137RWY	5142	B503RWY
5123	B123RWY	5128	B128RWY	5133	B133RWY	5138	B138RWY	5143	B504RWY
5124	B124RWY	5129	B129RWY	5134	B134RWY	5139	B139RWY	5144	B505RWY
5125	B125RWY	5130	B130RWY	5135	B135RWY	5140	B501RWY	5145	B140RWY
5126	B126RWY	5131	B131RWY	5136	B136RWY	5141	B502RWY		

5146-5150

Leyland Olympian ONLXB/1R Optare H47/29F* 1985 *5146/7 are CO47/29F
Ex WYPTE, 1986

5146	C146KBT	5147	C147KBT	5148	C148KBT	5149	C149KBT	5150	C150KBT

Yorkshire Rider 5301, L301PWR, is a Northern Counties Palatine-bodied Volvo Olympian which was delivered in 1994. This view in Halifax shows the flagship livery into which a number of Rider vehicles are being painted as part of this programme. The livery is predominantly white with a red, yellow and blue flag. *Lee Whitehead*

5151-5175

Leyland Olympian ONCL10/1RZ   Northern Counties   H45/29F   1988

5151	F151XYG	5156	F156XYG	5161	F161XYG	5166	F166XYG	5171	F171XYG
5152	F152XYG	5157	F157XYG	5162	F162XYG	5167	F167XYG	5172	F172XYG
5153	F153XYG	5158	F158XYG	5163	F163XYG	5168	F168XYG	5173	F173XYG
5154	F154XYG	5159	F159XYG	5164	F164XYG	5169	F169XYG	5174	F174XYG
5155	F155XYG	5160	F160XYG	5165	F165XYG	5170	F170XYG	5175	F175XYG

5176-5185

Leyland Olympian ONCL10/1RZ   Northern Counties   H47/29F   1990

5176	G176JYG	5178	G178JYG	5180	G180JYG	5182	G182JYG	5184	G184JYG
5177	G177JYG	5179	G179JYG	5181	G181JYG	5183	G183JYG	5185	G185JYG

5186-5199

Leyland Olympian ONLXB/1R   Eastern Coach Works   H45/32F   1983-85 Ex West Yorkshire, 1989

5186	FUM486Y	5189	FUM492Y	5192	FUM498Y	5195	A599NYG	5198	C483YWY
5187	FUM487Y	5190	FUM494Y	5193	FUM499Y	5196	A600NYG	5199	C485YWY
5188	FUM491Y	5191	FUM495Y	5194	A686MWX	5197	A601NYG		

5200-5222

Leyland Olympian ONCL10/1RZ   Alexander RL   H47/32F*   1990   *5207-13 are H47/30F

5200	G623OWR	5205	G605OWR	5210	G610OWR	5215	G615OWR	5219	G619OWR
5201	G601OWR	5206	G606OWR	5211	G611OWR	5216	G616OWR	5220	G620OWR
5202	G602OWR	5207	G607OWR	5212	G612OWR	5217	G617OWR	5221	G621OWR
5203	G603OWR	5208	G608OWR	5213	G613OWR	5218	G618OWR	5222	G622OWR
5204	G604OWR	5209	G609OWR	5214	G614OWR				

5301-5315

Volvo Olympian YN2RV18Z4   Northern Counties Palatine   H47/29F   1994

5301	L301PWR	5304	L304PWR	5307	L307PWR	5310	L310PWR	5313	L313PWR
5302	L302PWR	5305	L305PWR	5308	L308PWR	5311	L311PWR	5314	L314PWR
5303	L303PWR	5306	L306PWR	5309	L309PWR	5312	L312PWR	5315	L315PWR

5401-5405

| | | | | Volvo Olympian YN2RC16Z4 | | Northern Counties Palatine | H47/29F | 1994 | | | |

5401	L401PWR	5402	L402PWR	5403	L403PWR	5404	L404PWR	5405	L405PWR

5501-5506

Leyland Olympian ONLXB/1R — Roe — DPH43/27F* 1984 — Ex WYPTE, *5503-6 are H47/32F

5501	B141RWY	5503	B143RWY	5504	B144RWY	5505	B145RWY	5506	B506RWY
5502	B142RWY								

5507-5511

Leyland Olympian ONTL11/1R — Optare — H47/27F — 1985 — Ex WYPTE, 1986

5507	C507KBT	5508	C508KBT	5509	C509KBT	5510	C510KBT	5511	C511KBT

5512-5516

Leyland Olympian ONTL11/1R — Optare — DPH43/27F* 1987 — *5512/4 are H47/27F

5512	D512HUB	5513	D513HUB	5514	D514HUB	5515	D515HUB	5516	D516HUB

5517	FUM489Y	Leyland Olympian ONLXB/1R	Eastern Coach Works	H42/29F	1983	Ex West Yorkshire, 1989
5518	B518UWW	Leyland Olympian ONLXB/1R	Eastern Coach Works	DPH42/29F	1985	Ex West Yorkshire, 1989
5519	B519UWW	Leyland Olympian ONLXB/1R	Eastern Coach Works	DPH42/29F	1985	Ex West Yorkshire, 1989
5520	B520UWW	Leyland Olympian ONLXB/1R	Eastern Coach Works	DPH42/29F	1985	Ex West Yorkshire, 1989
5521	B521UWW	Leyland Olympian ONLXB/1R	Eastern Coach Works	DPH42/29F	1985	Ex West Yorkshire, 1989

5601-5605

Volvo Olympian YN2RV18Z4 — Northern Counties Palatine — DPH47/29F 1994

5601	L601PWR	5602	L602PWR	5603	L603PWR	5604	L604PWR	5605	L605PWR

6001-6078

Leyland Atlantean AN68/1R — Roe — H43/33F — 1974-75 Ex WYPTE, 1986

6001	GUG533N	6030	GUG557N	6039	GUG566N	6050	HWT36N	6068	HWT54N
6005	GUG535N	6032	GUG559N	6040	GUG567N	6058	HWT44N	6073	HWT59N
6015	GUG542N	6033	GUG560N	6043	HWT29N	6059	HWT45N	6074	HWT60N
6017	GUG544N	6034w	GUG561N	6044	HWT30N	6061	HWT47N	6076	HWT62N
6024	GUG551N	6037	GUG564N	6045	HWT31N	6064	HWT50N	6078	HWT64N
6027	GUG554N	6038	GUG565N	6047	HWT33N				

6094-6175

Leyland Atlantean AN68/1R — Roe — H43/33F — 1975-77 Ex WYPTE, 1986

6094	LUG94P	6130	SUA130R	6142	SUA142R	6156	WNW156S	6165	WNW165S
6102	LUG102P	6132	SUA132R	6144	SUA144R	6157	WNW157S	6167	WNW167S
6113	LUG113P	6133	SUA133R	6147	SUA147R	6158	WNW158S	6168	WNW168S
6116	LUG116P	6134	SUA134R	6149	SUA149R	6159	WNW159S	6169	WNW169S
6117	LUG117P	6137	SUA137R	6150	SUA150R	6161	WNW161S	6171	WNW171S
6118	LUG118P	6138w	SUA138R	6152	WNW152S	6162	WNW162S	6172	WNW172S
6120	LUG120P	6139	SUA139R	6154	WNW154S	6163	WNW163S	6173	WNW173S
6127	SUA127R	6140	SUA140R	6155	WNW155S	6164w	WNW164S	6174	WNW174S
6128	SUA128R								

6176-6191

Leyland Atlantean AN68/1R — Roe — H43/33F — 1979 Ex WYPTE, 1986

6176	GWR176T	6180	GWR180T	6183	GWR183T	6186	GWR186T	6189	GWR189T
6177	GWR177T	6181	GWR181T	6184	GWR184T	6187	GWR187T	6190	GWR190T
6178	GWR178T	6182	GWR182T	6185	GWR185T	6188	GWR188T	6191	GWR191T

6192-6266

Leyland Atlantean AN68A/1R — Roe — H43/32F — 1979-80 Ex WYPTE, 1986

6192	JUM192V	6207	JUM207V	6222	KWY222V	6238	KWY238V	6253	PUA253W
6193	JUM193V	6208	JUM208V	6223	KWY223V	6239	KWY239V	6254	PUA254W
6194	JUM194V	6209	JUM209V	6224	KWY224V	6241	KWY241V	6255	PUA255W
6195	JUM195V	6210	JUM210V	6225	KWY225V	6242	KWY242V	6256	PUA256W
6196	JUM196V	6211	JUM211V	6226	KWY226V	6243	KWY243V	6257	PUA257W
6197	JUM197V	6212	JUM212V	6227	KWY227V	6244	KWY244V	6258	PUA258W
6198	JUM198V	6213	JUM213V	6228	KWY228V	6245	KWY245V	6259	PUA259W
6199	JUM199V	6214	JUM214V	6229	KWY229V	6246	KWY246V	6260	PUA260W
6200	JUM200V	6215	JUM215V	6230	KWY230V	6247	KWY247V	6261	PUA261W
6201	JUM201V	6216	KWY216V	6231	KWY231V	6248	KWY248V	6262	PUA262W
6202	JUM202V	6217	KWY217V	6232	KWY232V	6249	KWY249V	6263	PUA263W
6203	JUM203V	6218	KWY218V	6233	KWY233V	6250	KWY250V	6264	PUA264W
6204	JUM204V	6219	KWY219V	6234	KWY234V	6251	KWY251V	6265	PUA265W
6205	JUM205V	6220	KWY220V	6236	KWY236V	6252	PUA252W	6266	PUA266W
6206	JUM206V	6221	KWY221V	6237	KWY237V				

Yorkshire Rider keeps alive the memory of the many operators which have been combined to form the current company by painting a small number of vehicles in the traditional liveries of the constituent operators. Leyland Olympian 5509, C509KBT, bears the red and cream livery of the West Yorkshire Road Car Co. *Phillip Stephenson*

The large number of double decks within the Yorkshire Rider fleet is expected to deminish rapidly as the Badgerline Group philosophy is to invest heavily in single decks. The Roe-bodied Leyland Atlantean therefore would appear to have only a short time left to serve. No.6164, WNW164S, is one of these vehicles which were the standard purchase for the WYPTE Metro fleet in the 1970s. *Phillip Stephenson*

6267-6326

Leyland Atlantean AN68C/1R Roe H43/32F 1980-81 Ex WYPTE, 1986

6267	PUA267W	6279	PUA279W	6292	PUA292W	6304	PUA304W	6316	PUA316W
6268	PUA268W	6280	PUA280W	6293	PUA293W	6305	PUA305W	6317	PUA317W
6269	PUA269W	6282	PUA282W	6294	PUA294W	6306	PUA306W	6318	PUA318W
6270	PUA270W	6283	PUA283W	6295	PUA295W	6307	PUA307W	6319	PUA319W
6271	PUA271W	6284	PUA284W	6296	PUA296W	6308	PUA308W	6320	PUA320W
6272	PUA272W	6285	PUA285W	6297	PUA297W	6309	PUA309W	6321	PUA321W
6273	PUA273W	6286	PUA286W	6298	PUA298W	6310	PUA310W	6322	PUA322W
6274	PUA274W	6287	PUA287W	6299	PUA299W	6311	PUA311W	6323	PUA323W
6275	PUA275W	6288	PUA288W	6300	PUA300W	6312	PUA312W	6324	PUA324W
6276	PUA276W	6289	PUA289W	6301	PUA301W	6313	PUA313W	6325	PUA325W
6277	PUA277W	6290	PUA290W	6302	PUA302W	6314	PUA314W	6326	PUA326W
6278	PUA278W	6291	PUA291W	6303	PUA303W	6315	PUA315W		

6327-6361

Leyland Atlantean AN68C/1R Roe H43/32F 1981 Ex WYPTE, 1986

6327	VWW327X	6334	VWW334X	6341	VWW341X	6348	VWW348X	6355	VWW355X
6328	VWW328X	6335	VWW335X	6342	VWW342X	6349	VWW349X	6356	VWW356X
6329	VWW329X	6336	VWW336X	6343	VWW343X	6350	VWW350X	6357	VWW357X
6330	VWW330X	6337	VWW337X	6344	VWW344X	6351	VWW351X	6358	VWW358X
6331	VWW331X	6338	VWW338X	6345	VWW345X	6352	VWW352X	6359	VWW359X
6332	VWW332X	6339	VWW339X	6346	VWW346X	6353	VWW353X	6360	VWW360X
6333	VWW333X	6340	VWW340X	6347	VWW347X	6354	VWW354X	6361	VWW361X

6423	UNA800S	Leyland Atlantean AN68/1R	Northern Counties	H43/32F	1978	Ex G M Buses, 1988

6425-6435

Leyland Atlantean AN68B/1R Roe H43/30F 1980-81 Ex Sovereign, 1989

6425	EPH227V	6429	KPJ260W	6431	KPJ263W	6433	KPJ291W	6435	KPJ293W
6426	KPJ253W	6428	KPJ257W	6430	KPJ261W	6432	KPJ290W	6434	MPG292W
6427	KPJ255W								

7030	MNW30P	Leyland Fleetline FE30GR	Roe	H43/33F	1976	Ex WYPTE, 1986
7033	MNW33P	Leyland Fleetline FE30GR	Roe	H43/33F	1976	Ex WYPTE, 1986
7038	MNW38P	Leyland Fleetline FE30GR	Roe	H43/33F	1976	Ex WYPTE, 1986
7043	RWU43R	Leyland Fleetline FE30AGR	Roe	H43/33F	1976	Ex WYPTE, 1986
7046	RWU46R	Leyland Fleetline FE30AGR	Roe	H43/33F	1976	Ex WYPTE, 1986
7054	RWU54R	Leyland Fleetline FE30AGR	Roe	H43/33F	1976	Ex WYPTE, 1986

7073-7088

Leyland Fleetline FE30AGR Northern Counties H43/31F 1979-80 Ex WYPTE, 1986

7073	JNW73V	7079	JUM79V	7082	JUM82V	7086	JUM86V	7088	JUM88V
7078	JUM78V								

7092-7156

Leyland Fleetline FE30AGR Roe H43/33F 1977-78 Ex WYPTE, 1986

7092	WUM92S	7115	WUM115S	7131	WUM131S	7139	CWU139T	7148	CWU148T
7093	WUM93S	7119	WUM119S	7132	WUM132S	7140	CWU140T	7149	CWU149T
7095	WUM95S	7120	WUM120S	7133	WUM133S	7142	CWU142T	7150	CWU150T
7097	WUM97S	7121	WUM121S	7134	WUM134S	7143	CWU143T	7151	CWU151T
7100	WUM100S	7124	WUM124S	7135	WUM135S	7144	CWU144T	7152	CWU152T
7101	WUM101S	7125	WUM125S	7136	CWU136T	7145	CWU145T	7153	CWU153T
7109	WUM109S	7126	WUM126S	7137	CWU137T	7146	CWU146T	7155	CWU155T
7111w	WUM111S	7127	WUM127S	7138	CWU138T	7147	CWU147T	7156	CWU156T
7112	WUM112S								

7203-7211

Leyland Fleetline FE30AGR Northern Counties H43/32F 1977-78 Ex Greater Manchester, 1987

7203	PTD640S	7205	PTD646S	7207	PTD649S	7209	PTD651S	7211	PTD658S

Opposite, top: **Scania deliveries to Leeds during May 1994 featured the metallic blue and silver 'Superbus' livery in readiness for the opening of the Scott Hall Road guided busway. Seen on normal service on route 71 is 8638, L638PWR.** *Tony Wilson*
Opposite, bottom: **The latest deliveries to Huddersfield are Dennis Lances with Plaxton Verde bodywork painted in the latest Rider livery. Similar schemes have been applied to new Dennis Darts although repaints have perpetuated the older livery.** *Tony Wilson*

7214-7234

Leyland Fleetline FE30GR — Northern Counties — H43/32F — 1978-79 — Ex Greater Manchester, 1987

7214	XBU5S	7221	XBU17S	7227	ANA33T	7230	ANA44T	7233	BVR53T
7216	XBU9S	7223	ANA25T	7228	ANA34T	7231	ANA45T	7234	BVR55T
7219	XBU15S	7226	ANA31T	7229	ANA40T	7232	ANA48T		

7235-7243

Leyland Fleetline FE30AGR — Northern Counties — H43/32F — 1978-80 — Ex Greater Manchester, 1987

7235	TWH690T	7237	TWH692T	7239	TWH695T	7241	BCB610V	7243	BCB612V
7236	TWH691T	7238	TWH693T	7240	TWH696T	7242	BCB611V		

7244-7253

Leyland Fleetline FE30GR — Northern Counties — H43/32F — 1979 — Ex GM Buses, 1988

7244	BVR52T	7246	BVR67T	7248	BVR70T	7250	BVR85T	7252	BVR92T
7245	BVR65T	7247	BVR69T	7249	BVR71T	7251	BVR87T	7253	BVR97T

7511	UWW511X	MCW Metrobus DR101/15	Alexander RH	H43/32F	1982	Ex WYPTE, 1986
7520	UWW520X	MCW Metrobus DR101/15	Alexander RH	H43/32F	1982	Ex WYPTE, 1986

7521-7538

MCW Metrobus DR102/32 — MCW — H46/30F — 1983 — Ex WYPTE, 1986

7521	CUB521Y	7525	CUB525Y	7530	CUB530Y	7533	CUB533Y	7536	CUB536Y
7522	CUB522Y	7527	CUB527Y	7531	CUB531Y	7534	CUB534Y	7537	CUB537Y
7523	CUB523Y	7528	CUB528Y	7532	CUB532Y	7535	CUB535Y	7538	CUB538Y
7524	CUB524Y	7529	CUB529Y						

7541-7580

MCW Metrobus DR102/38 — MCW — H46/30F — 1984 — Ex WYPTE, 1986

7541	A541KUM	7551	A751LWY	7560	A760LWY	7567	B567RWY	7574	B574RWY
7542	A542KUM	7552	A752LWY	7561	B561RWY	7568	B568RWY	7575	B575RWY
7544	A544KUM	7553	A753LWY	7562	B562RWY	7569	B569RWY	7576	B576RWY
7545	A545KUM	7554	A754LWY	7563	B563RWY	7570	B570RWY	7577	B577RWY
7546	A546KUM	7555	A755LWY	7564	B564RWY	7571	B571RWY	7578	B578RWY
7547	A547KUM	7556	A756LWY	7565	B565RWY	7572	B572RWY	7579	B579RWY
7549	A549KUM	7557	A757LWY	7566	B566RWY	7573	B573RWY	7580	B580RWY
7550	A750LWY	7558	A758LWY						

7581-7595

MCW Metrobus DR102/66 — MCW — H46/31F — 1988

7581	F581XWY	7584	F584XWY	7587	F587XWY	7590	F590XWY	7593	F593XWY
7582	F582XWY	7585	F585XWY	7588	F588XWY	7591	F591XWY	7594	F594XWY
7583	F583XWY	7586	F586XWY	7589	F589XWY	7592	F592XWY	7595	F595XWY

Some seventy-nine MCW Metrobuses are in service with the Yorkshire Rider fleet. A 1984 example is 7575 B575RWY which carries the traditional livery of the former Leeds City Transport.
David Cole

Scania chassis have been favoured for recent purchases of full-size vehicles by Yorkshire Rider. This Alexander RH bodied N113 is seen carrying the latest version of the Yorkshire Rider livery with more green being used. So far this is the only example on non-new vehicles. *David Cole*

7596-7600   MCW Metrobus DR102/67   MCW   H46/31F   1988

7596	F596XWY	7597	F597XWY	7598	F598XWY	7599	F599XWY	7600	F600XWY

7601-7605   MCW Metrobus DR102/69   MCW   H46/31F   1988

7601	F601XWY	7602	F602XWY	7603	F603XWY	7604	F604XWY	7605	F605XWY

8001-8005   Scania N113DRB   Alexander RH   H47/33F   1990

8001	G801JYG	8002	G802JYG	8003	G803JYG	8004	G804JYG	8005	G805JYG

8006-8010   Scania N113DRB   Northern Counties Palatine   H47/33F   1990

8006	H806TWX	8007	H807TWX	8008	H808TWX	8009	H809TWX	8010	H810TWX

8011-8042   Scania N113DRB   Alexander RH   H47/31F   1991

8011	H611VNW	8018	H618VNW	8025	H625VNW	8031	H631VNW	8037	H637VNW
8012	H612VNW	8019	H619VNW	8026	H726VNW	8032	H632VNW	8038	H638VNW
8013	H613VNW	8020	H620VNW	8027	H627VNW	8033	H633VNW	8039	H639VNW
8014	H614VNW	8021	H621VNW	8028	H628VNW	8034	H634VNW	8040	H640VNW
8015	H615VNW	8022	H622VNW	8029	H629VNW	8035	H643VNW	8041	H641VNW
8016	H616VNW	8023	H623VNW	8030	H630VNW	8036	H636VNW	8042	H642VNW
8017	H617VNW	8024	H624VNW						

8401-8405   Scania L113CRL   Alexander Strider   B48F   1994

8401	M401UUB	8402	M402UUB	8403	M403UUB	8404	M404UUB	8405	M405UUB

8534	RWT534R	Leyland Leopard PSU4D/4R	Plaxton Derwent	DP43F	1976	Ex WYPTE, 1986
8600	D727GDE	Scania K92CRB	East Lancashire	B59F	1987	Ex Rhodeservices, 1994

The Rider Group are heavily involved a guided busway project for the north of Leeds. As part of this project K1YRL numbered 8635 in the Rider fleet has been fitted with glide wheels and has been extensively tested both within the United Kingdom and in Essen, Germany. This vehicle is the prototype for the super bus fleet which will operate in guided busway and these Alexander Strider bodied Scania N113s carry a revised livery of blue, silver and red. The guided busway should come into operation during 1995. *Phillip Stephenson*

8601-8634   Scania N113CRB   Alexander Strider   B50F   1993

8601	K601HUG	8608	K608HUG	8615	K615HUG	8622	K622HUG	8629 K629HUG
8602	K602HUG	8609	K609HUG	8616	K616HUG	8623	K623HUG	8630 K630HUG
8603	K603HUG	8610	K610HUG	8617	K617HUG	8624	K624HUG	8631 K631HUG
8604	K604HUG	8611	K611HUG	8618	K618HUG	8625	K625HUG	8632 K632HUG
8605	K605HUG	8612	K612HUG	8619	K619HUG	8626	K626HUG	8633 K633HUG
8606	K606HUG	8613	K613HUG	8620	K620HUG	8627	K627HUG	8634 K634HUG
8607	K607HUG	8614	K614HUG	8621	K621HUG	8628	K628HUG	

8635	K1YRL	Scania N113CRB	Alexander Strider	DP50F	1993

8636-8655   Scania N113CRB   Alexander Strider   B48F   1994

8636	L636PWR	8640	L640PWR	8644	L644PWR	8648	L648PWR	8652 L652PWR
8637	L637PWR	8641	L641PWR	8645	L645PWR	8649	L649PWR	8653 L653PWR
8638	L638PWR	8642	L642PWR	8646	L646PWR	8650	L650PWR	8654 L654PWR
8639	L639PWR	8643	L643PWR	8647	L647PWR	8651	L651PWR	8655 L655PWR

Operating companies: Rider York: 228-36/8/90/1, 332/3/5/8/40/63/8/71, 727/34/46/55, 977/80/94, 1171, 1201-8, 1333/49-57/70, 1461, 1547/53/81-97, 1623/56-8, 5186-89/93-7, 5521, 8401-5.
Quickstep: 3-72, 1366
Yorkshire Rider: Remainder

Liveries: Cream, green and red;
White, gold and red (Gold Rider):   1402-7/18/9/22, 1604/5/13-22
White and red (Quickstep):   3-72
Traditional liveries: 363, 5196 (York); 1608, 5096 (Halifax); 5156 (Todmorden); 5504/9 (West Yorkshire RCC); 5117/34(Bradford); 6299 (Huddersfield); 7575 (Leeds); 8534 (Todmorden).
Blue, silver and red (Superbus):   8635-55
Black (Jetliner):   1400
National Express: 1415/6/20/1/3-5

Previous Registrations:

23PTA	F418EWR	HUA606Y	A608XYG, WSV410	NIB4908	D404LUA
8995WY	G73RGG	K1YRL	From new	UOI4323	BKH129X
CSU244	REL402R	LOI6690	REL400R	WSV408	HUA604Y
GSU388	E405RWR	NIB4905	D403LUA	WSV409	HUA605Y
GSU390	E407UWR	NIB4906	C402EWU	YR3939	From new

YORKSHIRE TERRIER

Yorkshire Terrier Ltd, Rother Valley Way, Holbrook, Sheffield, South Yorkshire, S19 5RW
Kingsman Services Ltd, Rother Valley Way, Holbrook, Sheffield, South Yorkshire, S19 5RW

Part of the Yorkshire Traction group

1	TCY735M	Leyland National 11351/1R	B52F	1974	Ex Shearings, 1988
3	LMO227L	Leyland National 1151/1R/0402	B49F	1973	Ex Crosville Wales, 1988
4	HHA137L	Leyland National 1151/1R/2501	B51F	1973	Ex Shearings, 1988
6 w	NFM844M	Leyland National 1151/1R/0405	DP48F	1973	Ex Crosville, 1988
7	NEL853M	Leyland National 1151/1R/0402	B49F	1973	Ex Wilts & Dorset, 1992
8	LMO224L	Leyland National 1151/1R/0402	B49F	1973	Ex Crosville Wales, 1988
9	GUG123N	Leyland National 11351/1R	B52F	1975	Ex West Yorkshire, 1988
10	GUG128N	Leyland National 11351/1R	B52F	1975	Ex West Yorkshire, 1988
12 w	NAO362M	Leyland National 1151/1R/0401	B52F	1973	Ex Shearings, 1988
13	NFN65M	Leyland National 1151/1R/2402	B52F	1974	Ex Shearings, 1988
14	NFN75M	Leyland National 1151/1R/2402	B52F	1974	Ex Shearings, 1988
15	NPD168L	Leyland National 1151/1R/0402	B49F	1973	Ex Shearings, 1988
16	HHA119L	Leyland National 1151/1R/2501	B51F	1973	Ex Shearings, 1988
17	OAO563M	Leyland National 1151/1R/0401	B49F	1973	Ex Shearings, 1989
18	NPD138L	Leyland National 1151/1R/0402	B49F	1973	Ex Shearings, 1989
19	BCD810L	Leyland National 1151/1R/0102	B49F	1973	Ex Brighton & Hove, 1989
21	OAH554M	Leyland National 1151/1R/0401	B52F	1973	Ex Franks, Haswell Plough, 1989
22	MBO22P	Leyland National 11351A/1R	B49F	1976	Ex Fletcher, Skelmersdale, 1989
23	MBO23P	Leyland National 11351A/1R	B49F	1976	Ex Fletcher, Skelmersdale, 1989
24	BCD806L	Leyland National 1151/1R/0102	B49F	1973	Ex Thames Transit, 1991
25	JNO195N	Leyland National 11351/1R	B49F	1975	Ex East Midland, 1989
26	WNO562L	Leyland National 1151/1R/0401	B50F	1973	Ex East Midland, 1989
27	NEV677M	Leyland National 1151/1R/0402	B49F	1973	Ex Hastings & Distrist, 1989
28	NEV675M	Leyland National 1151/1R/0402	B49F	1973	Ex Hastings & Distrist, 1989
29	MOD855P	Leyland National 11351A/1R	B49F	1976	Ex Western National, 1990
30	VOD602S	Leyland National 11351A/1R (Volvo)	B52F	1978	Ex Western National, 1990

Yorkshire Terrier has recently taken delivery of Alexander-bodied Volvo B6s, including one of the former Volvo demonstrators. Photographed in the Norton district of Sheffield, just prior its entry into service, is 120, L860WVC. *Lee Whitehead*

Yorkshire Terrier 88 D88ALX is an East Lancashire-bodied Scania K112 which has been transformed in recent years. New as an air-side vehicle for British Airways at Heathrow, the body was rebuilt by Willowbrook so that it now has 51 dual purpose seats, and the extensive luggage accommodation has been removed.
Phillip Stephenson

Yorkshire Terrier was formed by a number of ex-SYT managers at deregulation. The fleet initially comprised of a large number of Leyland Nationals. One of six such vehicles which carry promotional vinyls for the 123 service between Crystal Peaks and Walkley is number 43, VRP528S.
Daniel Hill

Kingsman has its origins in the Silver Service of Darley Dale business, a company subsequently purchased by Yorkshire Terrier. All vehicles operate from Holbrook but carry a different livery from the main Yorkshire Terrier fleet. Seen in Kingsman yellow and white livery is 61, HPF311N recently sold to Pennine.
Keith Grimes

31	HHA155L	Leyland National 1151/1R/2501		B48F	1973	Ex Rotherham & District, 1990
32	NWT712M	Leyland National 1151/1R/0401		B52F	1973	Ex Halton, 1990
33	TUG813R	Leyland National 11351A/1R		B49F	1977	Ex Rotherham & District, 1991
34	AWT702S	Leyland National 11351A/1R (Volvo)		B49F	1978	Ex Rotherham & District, 1991
35	NWT715M	Leyland National 1151/1R/0401		B52F	1973	Ex Halton, 1990
37	YFY4M	Leyland National 1151/2R		B49F	1974	Ex Merseybus, 1991
38	MTJ769S	Leyland National 11351A/1R		B49F	1977	Ex Merseybus, 1991
39	RKA879T	Leyland National 11351A/1R (Volvo)		B49F	1978	Ex Merseybus, 1991
40	RKA881T	Leyland National 11351A/1R		B49F	1978	Ex Merseybus, 1991
41	RKA883T	Leyland National 11351A/1R		B49F	1978	Ex Merseybus, 1991
42	RKA885T	Leyland National 11351A/1R		B49F	1978	Ex Merseybus, 1991
43	VRP528S	Leyland National 11351A/1R		B49F	1977	Ex United Counties, 1991
44	VRP529S	Leyland National 11351A/1R		B49F	1977	Ex United Counties, 1991
45	VRP530S	Leyland National 11351A/1R		B49F	1977	Ex United Counties, 1991
46	XVV534S	Leyland National 11351A/1R		B49F	1978	Ex United Counties, 1991
47	CBV777S	Leyland National 11351A/1R(Volvo)		B49F	1977	Ex Thames Transit, 1991
48	CBV778S	Leyland National 11351A/1R		B49F	1977	Ex Thames Transit, 1991
49	CBV789S	Leyland National 11351A/1R		B49F	1977	Ex Thames Transit, 1991
50	CBV770S	Leyland National 11351A/1R(Volvo)		B49F	1977	Ex Thames Transit, 1991
51	CBV771S	Leyland National 11351A/1R(Volvo)		B49F	1977	Ex Thames Transit, 1991
52	OKJ507M	Leyland National 1151/1R/0102		B49F	1973	Ex Brighton, 1991
53	OKJ511M	Leyland National 1151/1R/0102		B49F	1973	Ex Brighton, 1991
54	CBV788S	Leyland National 11351A/1R		B49F	1977	Ex Thames Transit, 1991
55	BCD816L	Leyland National 1151/1R/0102		B49F	1973	Ex Brighton, 1991
56	YCD86T	Leyland National 11351A/2R		B49F	1978	Ex Thames Transit, 1991
57	MLJ918P	Leyland National 11351/1R		B49F	1976	Ex Wilts & Dorset, 1992
58	MLJ921P	Leyland National 11351/1R		B49F	1976	Ex Wilts & Dorset, 1992
59	PTF759L	Leyland National 1151/2R/0402		B50F	1973	Ex Victoria Travel, Earlestown, 1992
85	D85ALX	Scania K112CRB	East Lancashire	DP51F	1987	Ex British Airways Heathrow, 1992
87	D87ALX	Scania K112CRB	East Lancashire	DP51F	1987	Ex British Airways Heathrow, 1992
88	D88ALX	Scania K112CRB	East Lancashire	DP51F	1987	Ex British Airways Heathrow, 1992
91	D91ALX	Scania K112CRB	East Lancashire	DP51F	1987	Ex British Airways Heathrow, 1992
92	D92ALX	Scania K112CRB	East Lancashire	DP51F	1987	Ex British Airways Heathrow, 1992
93	D93ALX	Scania K112CRB	East Lancashire	DP51F	1987	Ex British Airways Heathrow, 1992
101	K1YTB	Dennis Dart 9.8SDL3017	Plaxton Pointer	B40F	1993	
102	K2YTB	Dennis Dart 9.8SDL3017	Plaxton Pointer	B40F	1993	
103	K3YTB	Dennis Dart 9.8SDL3017	Plaxton Pointer	B40F	1993	
104	L4YTB	Dennis Dart 9.8SDL3025	Plaxton Pointer	B40F	1993	
109	K9YTB	Dennis Dart 9.8SDL3017	Plaxton Pointer	B40F	1993	
120	L860WVC	Volvo B6-9.9M	Alexander Dash	B40F	1994	
121	M121UET	Volvo B6-9.9M	Alexander Dash	B40F	1994	
122	M122UET	Volvo B6-9.9M	Alexander Dash	B40F	1994	
123	M123UET	Volvo B6-9.9M	Alexander Dash	B40F	1994	
124	M124VAK	Volvo B6-9.9M	Alexander Dash	B40F	1995	
125	M125VAK	Volvo B6-9.9M	Alexander Dash	B40F	1995	
201	E412EPE	Renault-Dodge S56	Northern Counties	B20F	1987	Ex Stagecoach South, 1993

Kingsman

3	THL290Y	Leyland Tiger TRCTL11/3R	Plaxton Paramount 3500	C47FT	1983	Ex Kingsman, Matlock, 1992
4	128NNU	Leyland Tiger TRCTL11/3R	Plaxton Paramount 3500	C49FT	1983	Ex Kingsman, Matlock, 1992
5	DBZ918	Leyland Tiger TRCTL11/3R	Plaxton Paramount 3500	C49FT	1983	Ex Kingsman, Matlock, 1992
6	A159EPA	Leyland Tiger TRCTL11/2RH	Plaxton Paramount 3200 E	C53F	1984	Ex Kingsman, Matlock, 1992
12	BCD822L	Leyland National 1151/1R/0102		B49F	1973	Ex Kingsman, Matlock, 1992
60	MDL882R	Leyland National 11351A/1R (Volvo)		B52F	1978	Ex Beeston, Hadleigh, 1992
64	KPA371P	Leyland National 11351/1R		B49F	1975	Ex Stagecoach South, 1993
65	PJT263R	Leyland National 11351A/1R		B49F	1976	Ex Stagecoach South, 1993

Previous Registrations:

128NNU	LFE777Y	354TRT	MNM44V	M121UET	L860WVC
DBZ918	BAJ637Y,2090VT,DFP492Y,MIA2192,YOI139				

Livery: Green yellow and white (Yorkshire Terrier); yellow and white (Kingsman).

YORKSHIRE TRACTION

The Yorkshire Traction Co Ltd, Upper Sheffield Road, Barnsley,
South Yorkshire, S70 4PP

Depots: Upper Sheffield Road, Barnsley; Milethorn Lane, Doncaster; Penistone Road, Huddersfield; Dale Road, Rawmarsh;
Weetshaw Lane, Shafton and Brampton Road, Wombwell.

1	6078HE	Scania K93CRB	Plaxton Paramount 3500 III	C46FT	1992	
2	5562HE	Scania K93CRB	Plaxton Paramount 3500 III	C46FT	1992	
3	3030HE	Scania K93CRB	Plaxton Paramount 3500 III	C46FT	1992	
4	J19ARK	Scania K93CRB	Van Hool Alizée	C46FT	1992	Ex Barnsley & District, 1995
14	1737HE	Leyland Tiger TRCL10/3ARZM	Plaxton Paramount 3500 III	C49FT	1989	Ex Richardson, South Anston, 1994
15	RHE353	Leyland Tiger TRCTL11/3ARZ	Plaxton Paramount 3500 III	C46FT	1988	Ex Hills, Tredegar, 1992
16	6341HE	Leyland Tiger TRCTL11/3ARZ	Plaxton Paramount 3500 III	C46FT	1988	Ex Hills, Tredegar, 1992
17	6087HE	Leyland Tiger TRCTL11/3ARZ	Plaxton Paramount 3500 III	C46FT	1988	Ex Hills, Tredegar, 1992
31	HE8054	Scania K92CRB	Plaxton Paramount 3200 III	C55F	1988	
41	374YTC	Hestair Duple 425	Duple 425	C57F	1992	
48	PHE692	DAF SB3000DKV601	Van Hool Alizée	C46FT	1989	Ex Barnsley & District, 1995
49	HSV389	DAF SB3000DKV601	Van Hool Alizée	C51FT	1988	Ex Barnsley & District, 1995
50	YCT49	Volvo B10M-60	Plaxton Paramount 3500 III	C47FT	1990	Ex Ambassador Travel, 1994
51	RHE194	Volvo B10M-61	Plaxton Paramount 3500 III	C46FT	1988	Ex Shearings, 1992
52	NHE340	Volvo B10M-61	Plaxton Paramount 3500 III	C46FT	1988	Ex Shearings, 1992
53	L53NWJ	Volvo B10M-60	Plaxton Premiére 350	C46FT	1993	
54	L54NWJ	Volvo B10M-60	Plaxton Premiére 350	C46FT	1993	
55	M655VWE	Volvo B10M-62	Plaxton Premiére 350	C47FT	1995	
56	M656VWE	Volvo B10M-62	Plaxton Premiére 350	C47FT	1995	
57	M957VKY	Volvo B10M-62	Plaxton Premiére 350	C47FT	1995	
61	A249BHL	Leyland Tiger TRCTL11/3R	Plaxton Paramount 3500	C53F	1984	
62	A248BHL	Leyland Tiger TRCTL11/3R	Plaxton Paramount 3500	C53F	1984	
71	2542HE	Scania K93CRB	Plaxton Paramount 3500 III	C46FT	1991	
75	OHE50	Scania K93CRB	Plaxton Paramount 3500 III	C46FT	1991	
76	YTC856	Scania K113CRB	Plaxton Paramount 3500 III	C46FT	1990	
77	2408HE	Scania K113CRB	Plaxton Paramount 3500 III	C46FT	1990	
78	1619HE	Scania K113CRB	Plaxton Paramount 3500 III	C46FT	1990	
79	YHE91	Scania K112CRB	Plaxton Paramount 3500 III	C48FT	1988	
80	FHE428	Scania K113CRB	Plaxton Paramount 3500 III	C46FT	1990	Ex Shearings, 1993

91-95		Auwaerter Neoplan N722/3	Plaxton Paramount 4000	CH53/18DT	1986	

91	YTC838	**92**	HE5362	**93**	3880HE	**94**	2316HE	**95**	4195HE

96	3141HE	Auwaerter Neoplan N722/3	Plaxton Paramount 4000	CH53/18DT	1986	Ex Yorkshire Voyager, 1991
99	HE8899	MCW Metroliner DR140/3	MCW 400GT	CH53/18DT	1988	

Yorkshire Traction operate six Plaxton Paramount 4000 all based on Neoplan chassis. These vehicles have spent a considerable period of time on National Express services but now perform more general coaching duties. 92, HE5362, is seen with the Coach Link Ridings Travel fleetnames carried by Yorkshire Traction coaches.
Phillip Stephenson

In recent years the Scania chassis has been favoured by Yorkshire Traction for coach duties and single deck purchases. Of the ten Wright Endurance-bodied K93 vehicles five are allocated to Huddersfield and regularly perform on the Huddersfield to Leeds service. Leeds bus station is the location of this view of 266 L266LHE, one of 5 vehicles delivered in 1993. *David Cole*

101	UET1S	Leyland Leopard PSU3E/4R	Plaxton Supreme III Express	C49F	1978	DAF engine fitted
108	1901HE	Leyland Leopard PSU5D/4R	Plaxton Supreme IV	DP32DL	1981	TL11 engine fitted
109	1975HE	Leyland Leopard PSU5D/4R	Plaxton Supreme IV	DP32DL	1981	DAF engine fitted
111	1533HE	Leyland Tiger TRCTL11/2R	Plaxton Paramount 3200	C53F	1983	Ex RoadCar, 1989

207-226

Leyland National 2 NL116L11/1R*   B52F   1980   *224 fitted with a Volvo engine

207	EDT207V	211	EDT211V	216	EDT216V	220	EDT220V	224	EDT224V
208	EDT208V	212	EDT212V	217	EDT217V	221	EDT221V	225	EDT225V
209	EDT209V	213	EDT213V	218	EDT218V	222	EDT222V	226	EDT226V
210	EDT210V	215	EDT215V	219	EDT219V	223	EDT223V		

227-264

Leyland National 2 NL116AL11/1R   B52F   1981-82

227	LWE227W	235	LWE235W	243	NKU243X	251	OHL251X	258	OHL258X
228	LWE228W	236	LWE236W	244	NKU244X	252	OHL252X	259	TWE259Y
229	LWE229W	237	LWE237W	245	NKU245X	253	OHL253X	260	TWE260Y
230	LWE230W	238	LWE238W	246	NKU246X	254	OHL254X	261	TWE261Y
231	LWE231W	239	MWE239W	247	NKU247X	255	OHL255X	262	TWE262Y
232	LWE232W	240	MWE240W	248	OHL248X	256	OHL256X	263	TWE263Y
233	LWE233W	241	MWE241W	249	OHL249X	257	OHL257X	264	TWE264Y
234	LWE234W	242	NKU242X	250	OHL250X				

265-269

Scania K93CRB   Wright Endurance   B53F   1993

265	L265LHE	266	L266LHE	267	L267LHE	268	L268LHE	269	L269LHE

270-274

Scania N113CRB   Alexander PS   B51F   1991

270	H270THL	271	H271THL	272	H272THL	273	H273THL	274	H274THL

Following de-regulation, Shearings commenced commercial operations in Greater Manchester and Shropshire with Leyland Lynx and Tigers. The Lynx were sold in 1991, eight now operating with Yorkshire Traction in the Barnsley area. Photographed with a modified front is 283, E23UNE.
Cliff Beeton

275-279 — Scania K93CR60 — Wright Endurance — B53F — 1992

275	K275EWA	276	K276EWA	277	K277EWA	278	K278EWA	279	K279EWA

281-288 — Leyland Lynx LX112L10ZR1 — Leyland — B49F — 1987-88 Ex Shearings, 1991

281	E21UNE	283	E23UNE	285	F41ENF	287	F43ENF	288	F44ENF
282	E22UNE	284	E24UNE	286	F42ENF				

290-294 — Scania L113CRL — Northern Counties Paladin — B52F — 1994

290	M290TWB	291	M291TWB	292	M292TWB	293	M293TWB	294	M294TWB

295-299 — Scania L113CRL — East Lancashire — B53F — 1995

295	M295TWB	296	M296TWB	297	M297TWB	298	M298TWB	299	M299TWB

301	F501EKY	Mercedes-Benz 811D	Optare StarRider	B33F	1989

302-306 — Mercedes-Benz 811D — Optare StarRider — B31F — 1989

302	F302FWB	303	F303FWB	304	F304FWB	305	F305FWB	306	F306FWB

307	F479FUA	Mercedes-Benz 811D	Optare StarRider	B29F	1989	Ex Optare, 1989
308	F369BUA	Mercedes-Benz 811D	Optare StarRider	B33F	1987	Ex Optare, 1989
309	G123KUB	Mercedes-Benz 811D	Optare StarRider	B29F	1990	Ex Optare, 1990
310	G841LWR	Mercedes-Benz 811D	Optare StarRider	DP33F	1990	Ex Optare, 1990
311	H202TWE	Mercedes-Benz 811D	Reeve Burgess Beaver	B33F	1990	
312	H201TWE	Mercedes-Benz 811D	Reeve Burgess Beaver	B33F	1990	
313	H313TWE	Mercedes-Benz 811D	Europa Enterprise	B31F	1990	
315	H315TWE	Mercedes-Benz 811D	Carlyle	B31F	1990	
316	H319TWE	Mercedes-Benz 811D	Carlyle	B33F	1991	
317	H317TWE	Mercedes-Benz 811D	Carlyle	B31F	1990	
318	H98UWA	Mercedes-Benz 811D	Carlyle	B31F	1991	
319	F793DWT	Mercedes-Benz 811D	Optare StarRider	B33F	1989	Ex Barnsley & District, 1991

Town Link is the name carried by Yorkshire Traction's minibus fleet. Photographed as it leaves the north bus station in Doncaster is 339, F709CWJ. One of sixty MetroRiders in the fleet, it is a 31-seat MCW model obtained from SUT in 1989.
Tony Wilson

One of three Autobus Classique minibuses in the Yorkshire Traction fleet is 391, J391AWB. Based on the Mercedes-Benz 811D chassis, the minibus fleet has been supplemented by the aquisition of the entire RB batch of Reeve Burgess-bodied Renault S75s with London Buses. These have been divided between RoadCar, Strathtay and Traction.
Tony Wilson

There are now 29 Dennis Darts in the Yorkshire Traction fleet with both Wright and Reeve Burgess/Plaxton Pointer bodies being represented. One of the Wright-bodied vehicles is 426, L426LET, seen here leaving Barnsley bus station for Mexborough on service 395.
Lee Whitehead

320	J320AWB	Mercedes-Benz 811D	Autobus Classique	B31F	1992

321-330

MCW MetroRider MF158 — MCW — B33F — 1989

321	F321FDT	323	F323FDT	325	F325FDT	327	F327FDT	329	F329FDT
322	F322FDT	324	F324FDT	326	F326FDT	328	F328FDT	330	F330FDT

331-340

MCW MetroRider MF154/17 — MCW — B33F — 1988 — Ex SUT, 1989

331	F701CWJ	333	F703CWJ	335	F705CWJ	337	F707CWJ	339	F709CWJ
332	F702CWJ	334	F704CWJ	336	F706CWJ	338	F708CWJ	340	F710CWJ

361-370

Renault S75 — Reeve Burgess Beaver — B31F — 1991

361	H361TWJ	363	H363TWJ	365	H365TWJ	367	H367TWJ	369	H369TWJ
362	H362TWJ	364	H364TWJ	366	H366TWJ	368	H368TWJ	370	H370TWJ

371-383

Renault S75 — Reeve Burgess Beaver — B31F* — 1990 — Ex London Buses, 1994
*371 is DP29F

371	G871WML	374	G874WML	377	G877WML	380	G880WML	382	H132AML
372	G872WML	375	G875WML	378	G878WML	381	H131AML	383	H133AML
373	G873WML	376	G876WML	379	G879WML				

391	J391AWB	Mercedes-Benz 811D	Autobus Classique	DP33F	1992
392	J392AWB	Mercedes-Benz 811D	Autobus Classique	DP33F	1992
393	J393AWB	Mercedes-Benz 811D	Autobus Classique	DP33F	1992

401-406

Dennis Dart 9.8SDL3012 — Reeve Burgess Pointer — B41F — 1991

401	J401XHL	403	J403XHL	404	J404XHL	405	J405XHL	406	J406XHL
402	J402XHL								

407-415

Dennis Dart 9.8SDL3017 — Wright Handy-bus — B41F — 1992

407	K407EWA	409	K409EWA	411	K411EWA	413	K413EWA	415	K415EWA
408	K408EWA	410	K410EWA	412	K412EWA	414	K414EWA		

416	J416CWF	Dennis Dart 9.8SDL3012	Wright Handy-bus	B40F	1992	Ex Wright demonstrator, 1992

417-421

Dennis Dart 9.8SDL3025 — Wright Handy-bus — B41F — 1993

417	K417HWG	418	K418HWG	419	K419HWG	420	K420HWG	421	K421HWG

422-426

Dennis Dart 9.8SDL3035 — Wright Handy-bus — B41F — 1993

422	L422LET	423	L423LET	424	L424LET	425	L425LET	426	L426LET

427	L51ONW	Dennis Dart 9.8SDL3035	Plaxton Pointer	B39F	1994	Ex South Yorkshire, 1994
428	L52ONW	Dennis Dart 9.8SDL3035	Plaxton Pointer	B39F	1994	Ex South Yorkshire, 1994
429	L53ONW	Dennis Dart 9.8SDL3035	Plaxton Pointer	B39F	1994	Ex South Yorkshire, 1994
492	HE6762	Leyland Tiger TS7	Weymann (1950)	B34F	1935	

528-536

MCW MetroRider MF150/36 — MCW — B23F — 1987

528	D528SKY	530	D530SKY	533	D533SKY	534	D534SKY	536	D536SKY
529	D529SKY	531	D531SKY						

537-546

MCW MetroRider MF150/33 — MCW — B23F — 1987

537	E537VKY	539	E539VKY	541	E541VKY	543	E543VKY	545	E545VKY
538	E538VKY	540	E540VKY	542	E542VKY	544	E544VKY	546	E546VKY

547-561

MCW MetroRider MF150/77 — MCW — B23F — 1988

547	E547XWG	550	E650XWG	553	E553YKW	556	E556YKW	559	E559AWF
548	E548XWG	551	E551XWG	554	E554YKW	557	E557AWF	560	E560AWF
549	E549XWG	552	E552YKW	555	E555YKW	558	E558AWF	561	E561AWF

| 562-568 | | MCW MetroRider MF150/77* | | MCW | | B23F | 1988 | Ex RoadCar, 1989 |
| | | | | | | | | *564/5/8 are MF150/108 |

562	E231DTV	564	F236HTO	566	E233DTV	567	E234DTV	568	F235HTO
563	E232DTV	565	F237HTO						

| 601-673 | | Leyland Olympian ONLXB/1R* | | Eastern Coach Works | | H45/32F* | 1981-85 | *668-71/3 are DPH43/29F |
| | | | | | | | | *668/71/3 are ONLXCT/1R |

601	NKU601X	616	SHE616Y	631	A631WDT	646	A646OCX	660	B660CET
602	NKU602X	617	SHE617Y	632	A632WDT	647	A647OCX	661	B661CET
603	NKU603X	618	SHE618Y	633	A633WDT	648	A648OCX	662	B662CET
604	OWG604X	619	SHE619Y	634	A634WDT	649	A649OCX	663	B663CET
605	OWG605X	620	SHE620Y	635	A635WDT	650	A650OCX	664	B664CET
606	OWG606X	621	SHE621Y	636	A636WDT	651	A651OCX	665	B665CET
607	OWG607X	622	SHE622Y	637	A637WDT	652	A652OCX	666	B666EWE
608	OWG608X	623	SHE623Y	638	A638WDT	653	A653OCX	667	B667EWE
609	SHE609Y	624	SHE624Y	639	A639WDT	654	A654OCX	668	B668EWE
610	SHE610Y	625	SHE625Y	640	A640WDT	655	A655OCX	669	C669GET
611	SHE611Y	626	SHE626Y	641	A641WDT	656	A656OCX	670	C670GET
612	SHE612Y	627	UKY627Y	642	A642WDT	657	A657OCX	671	C671GET
613	SHE613Y	628	UKY628Y	643	A643WDT	658	A658OCX	672	C672GET
614	SHE614Y	629	UKY629Y	644	A644WDT	659	B659CET	673	C673GET
615	SHE615Y	630	A630WDT	645	A645OCX				

701	D701NWG	MCW Metrobus DR102/57	MCW	DPH43/29F	1986
702	D702NWG	MCW Metrobus DR102/57	MCW	DPH43/29F	1986
703	D703NWG	MCW Metrobus DR102/57	MCW	DPH43/29F	1986
704	D704NWG	MCW Metrobus DR102/57	MCW	DPH43/29F	1986
705	D705NKY	MCW Metrobus DR102/56	MCW	H46/33F	1986
706	D706NKY	MCW Metrobus DR102/56	MCW	DPH43/29F	1986

The Yorkshire Traction Metrobuses are unusually built to a low height specification. The white roof of 707, D707NKY, contrasts with the stormy skyline over Huddersfield in this picture taken in February 1995. *Tony Wilson*

Metrobus 564, F236HTO, was originally purchased for the Gash of Newark fleet but when that operation was absorbed by RoadCar the vehicles were quickly transferred into Yorkshire Traction, the parent fleet. *Mike Fowler*

All 73 ECW-bodied Leyland Olympians purchased by Yorkshire Traction in National Bus Company days are still operated by this fleet. They now carry the revised Yorkshire Traction livery of red and white with red and blue bands. No.604, OWG604X is an early example of this type seen leaving Barnsley bus station for Brierley. *Lee Whitehead*

707-716 MCW Metrobus DR102/56 MCW H46/33F 1986

| 707 | D707NKY | 709 | D709NKY | 711 | D711NKY | 713 | D713NKY | 715 | D715NKY |
| 708 | D708NKY | 710 | D710NKY | 712 | D712NKY | 714 | D714NKY | 716 | D716NKY |

720	KJW304W	MCW Metrobus DR102/22	MCW		H43/30F	1981	Ex West Midlands Travel, 1990
721	KJW307W	MCW Metrobus DR102/22	MCW		H43/30F	1981	Ex West Midlands Travel, 1990
722	GOG154W	MCW Metrobus DR102/18	MCW		H43/30F	1980	Ex West Midlands Travel, 1990
723	GOG160W	MCW Metrobus DR102/18	MCW		H43/30F	1980	Ex West Midlands Travel, 1990
724	BOK24V	MCW Metrobus DR102/12	MCW		H43/30F	1980	Ex West Midlands Travel, 1990
901	E734HFW	Volvo B10M-55	East Lancashire		CH49/31F	1988	Ex Lincoln, 1993
902	E735HFW	Volvo B10M-55	East Lancashire		CH49/31F	1988	Ex Lincoln, 1993
903	E736HFW	Volvo B10M-55	East Lancashire		CH49/31F	1988	Ex Lincoln, 1993
904	E737HFW	Volvo B10M-55	East Lancashire		CH49/31F	1988	Ex Lincoln, 1993

Previous Registrations:

1533HE	YAL511Y, MSV926	6078HE	K801FWE	HE8899	E99AAK
1619HE	G78MWJ	6087HE	E215RDW	HSV389	E353EVH
1737HE	G115VMM, MSV922	6341HE	E214RDW	J416CWF	LDZ6040
1901HE	JHE98W	A248BHL	A713SKH, PHE692	NHE340	E665UNE
1975HE	JHE99W,UHE383	A249BHL	A712SKH, YTC858	OHE50	J964YWJ
2316HE	C94KET	E734HFW	KIB6474	RHE194	E664UNE
2408HE	G77MWJ	E735HFW	KIB6527	RHE353	E213RDW
3141HE	C752CWX	E736HFW	KIB6620	YHE91	E69WWF
374YTC	J241BWE	E737HFW	KIB6708	YTC49	G125MNG, MSV927
3880HE	C93KET	FHE428	G890VNA	YTC838	C91KET
4195HE	C95KET	HE5362	C92KET	YTC856	G76MWJ
5562HE	K802FWE	HE8054	E51WWF		

Livery: Red, white and blue; National Express 1-4, 48, 51-7, 71/5-8, 80; blue and white(Mexborough & Swindon) 208-15; white and brown (County) 636, 724.

Other Books in the series:

The North West Bus Handbook - £9.95
The North East Bus Handbook (6/95) - £9.95
The North Midlands Bus Handbook - £8.95
The South Midlands Bus Handbook - £8.95
The East Midlands Bus Handbook - £8.95
The Eastern Bus Handbook (9/95) - £9.95
The Welsh Bus Handbook - £9.95
The Scottish Bus Handbook - £9.95
Stagecoach Bus Handbook - £9.95
Badgerline Group Bus Handbook - £6.95
The Fire Brigade Handbook - £8.95
The Model Bus Handbook (6/95) - £9.95

Order your copy now (post free in Europe) from:
British Bus Publishing
**The Vyne, 16 St Margaret's Drive, Wellington,
Telford, TF1 3PH (Fax 01952 255669)**

ISBN 1 897990 01 4
Published by *British Bus Publishing*
The Vyne, 16 St Margarets Drive, Wellington,
Telford, Shropshire, TF1 3PH

Printed by Graphics & Print
Unit A13, Stafford Park 15
Telford, Shropshire, TF3 3BB